NEW
CELTIC
COOKING

NEW
CELTIC
COOKING

Kathleen Sloan-McIntosh
& Ted McIntosh

McArthur & Company

TORONTO

First published in Canada in 2003 by
McArthur & Company
322 King St. West, Suite 402
Toronto, Ontario
M5V 1J2
www.mcarthur-co.com

National Library of Canada Cataloguing in Publication

Sloan-McIntosh, Kathleen
    New Celtic cooking/ Kathleen Sloan-McIntosh, Ted McIntosh.

Includes index.
ISBN 1-55278-348-0

1. Cookery, Celtic. I. McIntosh, Ted II. Title.

TX717.2.S57 2003   641.59'2916   C2003-904015-1

Text Design and Composition: Tania Craan
Cover Design: Tania Craan
Front cover landscape photograph: Corbis
Front cover food photograph: Foodpix
Colour recipe photographs on back cover and interior pages by Chris Freeland
Food styling by Rosemarie Superville
Prop styling by Oksana Slavutych
Black and white photographs by Kathleen Sloan-McIntosh and Ted McIntosh
Page 9 — Rock of Cashel Round Tower, Co. Tipperary. Courtesy of Tourism Ireland
Printed in Canada by:Transcontinental Printing

The publisher would like to acknowledge the financial support of the Government of Canada through the Book Publishing Industry Development Program, the Canada Council, and the Ontario Arts Council for our publishing activities. We also acknowledge the Government of Ontario through the Ontario Media Development Corporation Ontario Book Initiative.

10 9 8 7 6 5 4 3 2 1

TABLE OF CONTENTS

Foreword

by John W. Maxwell

Celtia is where we come from and where we live, said my father. Pushed to the very edge of western Europe and the islands beyond, the last remnants of the Celtic people drifted even farther west to Maritime Canada, Quebec, Ontario and New England. That is our country, Father said, Brittany and Galicia, Cornwall and Wales, Ireland and Scotland and now the New World. We are like the Kurds, without a nation but endowed with a grand culture — history, tradition, language, music and, of course, food.

My Maxwell family followed the timeworn path westward from Scotland to Antrim and Galway, thence to Vermont. And my personal journey brought me to Toronto, where in 1979 I opened a restaurant, "Joe Allen," on long-forgotten John Street (but not unimportant to the Celtic diaspora — a plaque on the corner at King marks the location of the fever sheds that from 1847 housed the plague-tortured Irish fleeing the famine). He who gave his name to this enterprise, Joseph Campbell Allen, it might be noted, is a fine Scottish American.

It was soon thereafter that Kathleen Sloan came to my attention. She was one of the smartest and ablest restaurant critics of the time, someone who saw her job as the judgement of an establishment in light of its success in meeting its own, often highly particular, goals. Kathleen brought the insight and knowledge of the foodservice professional to this judgement and wrote with flair and real style. We watched her move on to *The Insider's Report*, the groundbreaking supermarket journal that did so much to stimulate a public interest in quality food and its preparation. Then her books began to roll out, at least one a year from 1998 onwards, and all informed by the keen eye, intelligence and wit that are her hallmarks. How could I, a man who serves the noble spud nine different ways on his menu, not be seduced by a cookbook entitled *Great Potatoes*.

And now comes *New Celtic Cooking*, in collaboration with Ted McIntosh, one of the top wine, beer and spirits men in Canada. Deep into our shared Celtic roots, conviction only slightly enhanced by the whisky and beer to hand, we three often discussed the existence of Celtia and the shared traditions of its people, our people, maintained despite obstacles of geography and national boundary. Kathleen and Ted have undertaken the travel, the research, the thought and the writing to bring this culture delightfully to life, with food explained by the broader tradition of which it is a part. *New Celtic Cooking* is not only, then, a compendium of fascinating recipes, but it is also a travel guide, history lesson and personal journal.

It is also Kathleen's best cookery book to date.

Slainte
August 2003

CELTIA

A State of Mind, Heart & Spirit

And every little wind that blows
Shall take my message as it goes.
A heart may travel very far
To come where its desires are . . .
– Louise Driscoll

An American-born Canadian whose father came from County Antrim, John W. Maxwell is the ebullient owner of Allen's, the warm establishment in Toronto's east end that is fashioned after a traditional New York Irish saloon, and a place synonymous in this city with all things Celtic. It was my good friend John who first told me about Celtia — the concept his father described to him — the spiritual place that is the collective diaspora of Celtic peoples.

Now, Celtia doesn't exist, physically, materially. You can't buy a ticket and fly there. But if you have Celtic roots you don't need to travel to reach it, in the conventional sense. Just like Dorothy, you're already there.

When I was a little girl growing up in Toronto, one of our yearly rituals was the Santa Claus Parade that took place each year. Flanked by my parents, I would hold their outstretched hands and wait with great anticipation for my favourite part of the parade. I waited, not for the upside-down clowns or the glittering gown of the Snow Queen. I waited for the rip-roaring pipe band and the exciting, barely containable thrill I always felt when they passed by, walking in brilliant unison, the men's kilts swinging and the pipes, the pipes, that ancient sound that filled the air with such strength, such force, such volume, the massive drums keeping time. I could squeal as loud as I was able and not be heard. It was magic.

My dad was from Belfast and he needed to hear those pipes, that music, that sound; it mattered little what tune was played. I didn't know what the intense feeling was that moved up my chest and rose in my throat, making me want to sing and dance all at once. I didn't know then it was my father's gift to me.

But I know now. I know it was Celtia. It was pride of place and I feel it every time I hear the Scottish bagpipes or *uillean* pipes, the Irish *bodhràn*, the Celtic harp, the flute, tin whistle and fiddle. I feel it strongly when I watch young Irish or Scottish dancers. It rushes through me when I listen to Canada's Leahy, John McDermott, the sweet voices of the Rankin sisters, the music of the Chieftains, the Barra MacNeils, Sinéad O'Connor, Van Morrison, Natalie MacMaster, Great Big Sea and so many other musicians who work to keep these common music traditions alive. I see it in my daughter Jenna, in her stride and her strength, and in her older sister Alysa's laugh and in the way she tosses her head. It's there in the strong spirit of my little grandson Colsen. And always I see it in my husband's warm blue eyes as I did in my father's.

Celtia is in the skirl of Highland bagpipes, in the lilt of Irish laughter and the beautiful voices of the Welsh. It's there in Cape Breton at a Saturday night *ceilidh* or a kitchen party or in a dark grotto in Brittany at the night music gatherings called *Fest Noz*. And it's in the northwest corner of Spain in Galicia where I watched in amazement as a young woman in jeans played the bagpipes on a street corner.

Celtia lives in those of us with roots in Ireland, Scotland, Wales, Brittany, Galicia, Cornish England, the Isle of Man and Cape Breton. And in every one of these places, there is an undeniable kindred spirit with each of the others. No matter where they call home, or what language they speak, the Celtic peoples of the world are inextricably linked, spiritually, emotionally, intellectually and artistically.

And, as this book shows, the commonality extends to the look of the land, the great influence of the sea and the food and drink on the table. When I first had the idea for this book devoted to the common food and drink of the Celtic communities and nations around the world, I had just met my husband. As the daughter of an Ulsterman, I am strongly aware of my inherited link to Ireland, my Celtic connection if you will. It was lovely to meet this man who felt the same way about the importance, the influence of his Scottish ancestry. Perhaps the two of us were more willing to investigate the mystery of our common Celtic link because we were in the perfect romantic frame of mind to do so. A door was open that perhaps we wouldn't have noticed or entered on our own. As so many with Celtic roots have done before us, we shared the same instinctive longing for that ancient connection to our past and dreamed about walking the Scottish Highlands and Lowlands and along rugged Irish shores. We started to gather even more books, music and reams of information about Ireland and Scotland, and to plan trips to each country. The more I read, the more I became convinced of the strong culinary link between them.

Just as exciting was the fact that some of the world's most vibrant and innovative food was emanating from these countries. As a food writer, I imagined a book project that would enable both of us to explore these places we had been daydreaming about and longing to experience. Our conversation with John Maxwell immeasurably reinforced what we were planning. It was John who put a name to what we were feeling. When he spoke of Celtia, he pointed out that it extended beyond Ireland, Scotland, Wales and Cape Breton. "You'll have to include Spain and France's bit of Celtia — Brittany and Galicia," he said.

And so we did.

The food within these pages is not exclusively old nor modern, but recipes and ideas truly inspired by both times. The truth is it would have been easy to devote an entire book to the "auld ways" focusing on traditional recipes alone, but there is so much newness to catalogue — especially in Ireland, Scotland, Spain and Wales. All this newness is reflected in these pages, and our hope is that it will inspire others — with or without that visceral Celtic link — to explore these beautiful green lands as we did.

Just before this book was completed, I watched a television documentary about a group of Cape Breton musicians who made a musical pilgrimage to the beautiful Scottish island of Uist. Towards the end of the documentary, Glaswegian folksinger and songwriter Archie Fisher, a glass of single malt (I don't *think* it was a blended whisky) in hand, spoke about the connection between these two harmonious groups of visiting musicians. Listening to him, I thought how perfectly he was describing what we felt. These are his fitting words to lead you into this book, our tribute to Celtia. We do hope you enjoy it.

Both of our music traditions are in their own way quite fragile, but if you take two strong cultures and — if I may use a liquid analogy — blend them together like two good whiskies, they don't dilute each other, they actually fortify each other. . . .

We might have a different blend and distillation of culture but we're brewed from the same yeast, and we're stronger together than we would be apart.

Kathleen Sloan-McIntosh
Ted McIntosh
Niagara, April 2003

CHAPTER 1

BROTHS, SOUPS & SAVOURIES

Beautiful soup, so rich and green,

Waiting in a hot tureen,

Who for such dainties would not stoop?

Soup of the evening, beautiful Soup.

Soup of the evening, beautiful Soup!

– Lewis Carroll

Soups and broths that emanate from the Celtic nations have traditionally been unfailingly substantial and sustaining in nature; just as you would expect from a rustic people used to living in proximity to the wildness of the sea but with a close association to the land. Cabbage, kale, leeks, onions, potatoes, seafood and pork have all figured largely in traditional nourishing soups. Contemporary chefs from these countries base their modern renditions on the same ingredients, offering their own spin on the well-loved classics. As well, small savoury dishes, often made with pastry, are hallmarks of Celtic cooking — such as the famous meal-sized empanadas or, in smaller version, *empanadillas*, the little pastry turnovers from Galicia that can contain any number of meat fillings. You'll find these again in Ireland in the form of Dingle pies, minced lamb pastries and pies, or in Cornwall's well-known Cornish pasties. Scotland has Forfar bridies, rich pastry enclosing beef and onions, while the Welsh name for these sorts of meat pies is ciste, derived from the word for coffin.

Pratie Soup with Chives & Smoked Salmon

Caldo Gallego

Ballymaloe Cabbage Soup with Gujarati Spices

Celery & Cashel Blue Soup

Carrot & Tarragon Soup

Chilled Buttermilk Soup with Shrimp & Parsley

Cullen Skink

Allen's Burns Night Cock-a-Leekie

Cream of Leek, Potato & Porcini Soup

Mussel Soup with Cream & Garlic

Dublin Castle Bacon & Egg Pie

Beech Hill's Goat Cheese Tart with Figs & Balsamic Beetroot Drizzle

Stirling Bridies

Galician *Empanadillas*

Honest Welsh Rabbit with Onion Jam

Pratie Soup with Chives & Smoked Salmon

Ted's Choice Try Jameson Triple Distilled Irish Whiskey.

Makes 4–6 servings

Revered in Ireland and beloved in Galicia — where Spain's best potatoes are grown — each and every Celtic people, from the Welsh and Manx to the folks in Cape Breton, strongly favour potatoes. Here is a substantial potato soup that is at once satisfying and elegant.

2 tbsp. (30 mL) butter

1 tbsp. (15 mL) olive oil

3 large leeks, trimmed, washed, thinly sliced

1 clove garlic, minced

1 large onion, finely chopped

3 large floury potatoes, peeled, diced

4 cups (1 L) chicken broth

1 cup (250 mL) whipping cream

1/4 cup (60 mL) chopped chives

1/2 lb. (225 g) smoked salmon, chopped

Melt the butter and oil in a large saucepan over medium heat. Add the leeks, garlic and onion and sauté, stirring occasionally, until the vegetables are softened, about 5 minutes. Do not allow vegetables to brown. Add the potatoes and broth, bring to a boil, reduce the heat, cover and let simmer for about 25 minutes, stirring now and then. When the potatoes are quite soft, use a hand-held blender to purée the soup (or purée it in small batches in a food processor or blender) until relatively smooth. Wipe the saucepan clean, return the soup to the pan and add the cream and salt and pepper. If the soup is thicker than you would like, add a little milk and simmer until heated through. Serve hot, garnished with the chives and the smoked salmon.

CALDO GALLEGO

Ted's Choice Torrontés, a white grape variety originally grown in Galicia. Known as the "ex-pat" grape, it is now also grown in Argentina and Chile.

Makes 4–6 servings

Galician meat and vegetable soup is based on the most fundamental ingredients: beans, pork, potatoes and greens. Although this soup is classic Galician, this preparation is very popular throughout the country. It is traditional to use the first young tops of turnips in this soup, but any substantial leafy green may be used. With good, crusty bread and a selection of some of Spain's fantastic cheeses — *manchego, tetilla, roncal* — this will make a wonderfully substantial supper. Start preparations for this dish the night before.

Soak the beans overnight in cold water to cover. Drain and transfer to a large soup pot. Cover them with 8 cups (2 L) of cold water. Add the ham hock, the salt, pepper and paprika and bring to a boil over high heat. Reduce heat to allow the pot to simmer for about an hour. Remove the ham hock and add the potatoes, greens and chorizo and cook for another 20 minutes or so before serving. Remove the skin and fat from the ham hock. Pull off the meat, chop roughly and return to the pot. If the broth is not as thick as you would like, use a slotted spoon to remove a chunk or two of cooked potatoes and beans to a bowl. Mash with a fork and return to the pot to thicken the broth.

1 1/2 cups (375 mL) dried white beans

1 fresh ham hock

2 tsp. (10 mL) salt

2 tsp. (10 mL) freshly ground black pepper

2 tsp. (10 mL) Spanish paprika

3 large floury potatoes, peeled, diced

1 bunch collard greens or kale, rinsed, trimmed, roughly chopped

2 3-inch (7.5-cm) chorizos, cut into pieces

Ballymaloe Cabbage Soup with Gujarati Spices

Ted's Choice Fino sherry, well chilled.

Makes 4–6 servings

This is my version of the amazingly good soup that I first enjoyed at Ballymaloe House, Ireland's first and foremost country house hotel in Cork, home to one of the finest kitchens in Ireland. Food maven Myrtle Allen and her chef Rory O'Connell create splendid dishes for their menu that always includes seasonal, local specialties. Seeing this dish on the menu, I anticipated a hearty, rustic preparation chock full of cabbage and spuds, but what I received was a beautiful pale green soup, gently infused with spice — the very definition of genteel, contemporary Irish cuisine. This is also very nice with cauliflower in place of the cabbage. Gujarat is an Indian province famous for inventive ways with vegetables and spices.

3 tbsp. (45 mL) olive oil

2 medium onions, peeled, chopped

3 cloves garlic, peeled, chopped

1 tsp. (5 mL) ground cumin

2 tsp. (10 mL) ground coriander

1/4 tsp (1 mL) turmeric

1/4 tsp (1 mL) cayenne

2 medium-sized floury potatoes, peeled, diced

1/2 head cabbage, outer leaves removed, cored, shredded

7 cups (1.75 L) chicken broth

salt and freshly ground white pepper to taste

1 cup (250 mL) whipping cream

Heat the oil over fairly high heat in a large soup pot. Add the onions and garlic and sauté quickly for a few minutes, until the onions are just slightly brown. Add the cumin, coriander, turmeric, cayenne; stir together for less than a minute, then add the potatoes, cabbage and chicken broth. Bring to a boil, cover, reduce heat to low and simmer gently for 15 minutes or until potatoes and cabbage are tender. Add salt and pepper. Working in batches if necessary, transfer the mixture to a blender or food processor and blend thoroughly. Wipe the pot clean. Pass the mixture through a sieve placed over the pot, pressing down on the solids to get as much of the purée as possible. Add the cream, gently reheat the soup until hot and serve.

Ballymaloe House

Ballymaloe House in County Cork is renowned throughout Ireland and the world. Food lovers agree this establishment is one of the best reasons to visit the country and the region. Ballymaloe is still considered the country's foremost country house hotel and it remains the home of Ireland's beloved culinary maven Myrtle Allen. She runs it, as she has since opening her doors in 1964, with warmth and in an Irish-country style. Set in the middle of a 400-acre farm that is owned and run by the Allen family, the estate is just outside the town of Cloyne on the road to the diminutive seaside village of Ballycotton. As splendid and well run as the hotel is, perhaps the reason that guests return is because of the quality of the food. Myrtle Allen has long been a propagandist for the goodness of regional Irish food products, and the menu at Ballymaloe reflects this philosophy. Many of the ingredients are grown on the grounds or in the surrounding area. The quality of everything from baked goods to condiments, from soups to seafood, is outstanding, with the menu often drawn up at the last minute to include whatever the fishing boats have brought in that day. Not far from here is the Ballymaloe Cookery School, founded in 1983 by Darina Allen, Myrtle's daughter-in-law, and her husband Tim. The school works to promote the "country house hotel" cooking style that is the trademark of Myrtle Allen, culling the best from local producers while keeping contemporary international trends and influences at the forefront. Set in the lushness of the East Cork countryside, the busy school grows much of its own food — including wheat for bread-making — and is home to a fabulous herb and ornamental fruit garden, all of which help to inspire and instruct students in the art of good Irish food, from the earth to the table.

CELERY & CASHEL BLUE SOUP

Ted's Choice A medium-sweet white wine from a small appellation in Loire, such as Menetou-Salon.
Makes 4–6 servings

Cashel in County Tipperary is known for two things: the great Rock of Cashel, the medieval walled stronghold that is especially impressive viewed at night when it is floodlit, and world-famous Cashel Blue, the semi-soft blue-veined cheese. Here it is used to great effect to lift the flavours of this subtle soup.

2 tbsp. (30 mL) butter

1 tbsp. (15 mL) olive oil

2 tbsp. (30 mL) all-purpose flour

1 large head of celery, washed, trimmed, finely chopped

2 cloves garlic, finely chopped

1 small onion, finely chopped

4 cups (1 L) hot chicken broth

2/3 cup (150 mL) whipping cream

salt and freshly ground white pepper to taste

4 oz. (125 g) Cashel Blue cheese, crumbled

1/4 cup (60 mL) finely chopped chives

Combine the butter and oil in a large saucepan set over moderate heat. Sauté the celery and onion for about 10 minutes or so, until softened. Blend in the flour, stirring it well into the vegetables. Gradually add the hot broth, using a whisk to blend and avoid lumps. Continue to cook for about 10 minutes or so until vegetables are quite soft. Working in batches if necessary, add the mixture to a blender or food processor and process until relatively smooth. At this point, if you want the final soup to be quite smooth, pass it through a sieve. Alternatively, wipe the saucepan clean and return the blended mixture to it. Add the cream and a little salt and pepper, gently stir the mixture and bring to a gentle boil. Reduce the heat and add the cheese and chives. Serve at once.

Cashel

Home of Cashel Blue cheese, Cashel is Gaelic for "stone fort" and, indeed, this lovely old town is dominated by the impressive medieval stronghold called the Rock of Cashel. Dating from the fifth century, this was the seat of the Kings of Munster who eventually placed the complex in the hands of the Church, where it remained for hundreds of years until Cromwell and his army laid siege to it. Floodlit at night, the romantic image is even more dramatic. Just near here are the ruins of Hore Abbey, a thirteenth-century Cistercian abbey. And, as for the cheese itself, Louis and Jane Grubb make the famous Cashel Blue (and also a white) cow's milk cheese in County Tipperary. Firm and tangy when young, the blue softens and can become a little runny as it ripens to a wonderfully smooth and creamy spiciness.

CARROT & TARRAGON SOUP

Ted's Choice Sauvignon Blanc from the Loire Valley, such as Quincy.

Makes 4–6 servings

On our first night at Ballymaloe House in County Cork, Ireland, a hesitant young server with an undeniably Southern Irish lilt rhymed off his memorized list of specials, among them a "cart 'n' TAR-gon" soup. After he blushed and repeated it for about the third time, I finally understood — carrot and tarragon! It was wonderful, due no doubt to the quality of locally grown carrots, another supremely produced Irish vegetable. Here is my version of that splendid soup. No one ever leaves a drop behind.

2 tbsp. (30 mL) butter

1 tbsp. (15 mL) olive oil

1 large onion, finely chopped

2 cloves garlic, finely chopped

2 lbs. (1 kg) carrots, scraped, sliced

4 lengths fresh tarragon

salt and freshly ground white pepper to taste

4 cups (1 L) vegetable or chicken broth

1/4 cup (60 mL) whipping cream

2 tbsp. (30 mL) chopped fresh tarragon

Melt the butter in a large saucepan over moderate meat. Add the olive oil, onion and garlic and sauté for a few minutes. Add the carrot to the pan and toss together until well coated. Add the lengths of fresh tarragon and toss together. Add a little salt and pepper, lower the heat and cover the vegetables with a piece of buttered wax or parchment paper. Press it down on top of the vegetables. Cover and let the vegetables cook over low heat for about 10 minutes. Remove the lid and the paper, add the broth and bring to a boil. Cook vegetables until soft. Remove and discard the tarragon stems. Using a hand-held blender or regular blender or food processor, blend the vegetables to a purée. When smooth, add the cream and reheat until quite hot, then serve with a little fresh tarragon for a garnish.

Nairns

Nairns restaurant in Glasgow's west end is a fine-dining restaurant featuring the best of local, seasonal food in a clever, modern Scottish style. Residents, visitors and big names like Prime Minister Tony Blair book tables on a regular basis. Owner Chef Nick Nairn, a former merchant navy seaman, teamed up with his brother to open Nairns in 1997, after earning his first Michelin star in 1996. Now, after much success that has included a BBC-TV series and a cookbook, there is an affiliated cooking school – Nairns Cook School in Stirling. Not only that, the chef partnered with famed Scottish food producer Baxter's to offer food lovers a line of sauces. (One of them, Creamy Peppercorn and Whisky Sauce, is inspiring with a seared strip loin of beef.) The next time you visit Glasgow, book a table at Nairns, but don't overlook the chef's other favourite city spots: the restaurant known as Rogano and another dubbed Mother India ("Order their spiced smoked haddock . . . true fusion," says Chef Nairn). For good beer, good chat and great service, he heads to a pub known as Stravaigin in Gibson Street.

Chef John Higgins

One of Canada's culinary stars, Scottish-born John Higgins has cooked for everyone from the Queen of England to many heads of state. After working as executive chef at Toronto's King Edward Hotel for 13 years, he is now realizing a long-time dream to teach young culinary hopefuls at the George Brown chef's school in Toronto. Higgins' passion for good food began when, as a 10-year-old boy, he visited the famed Gleneagles Hotel near his home in Scotland. After graduating from Motherwell College in Scotland, he worked for a time at the famed hotel and then at Buckingham Palace before coming to Canada. John Higgins was the first Chef Artist in the popular Absolut Vodka Culinary Arts Awards.

CHILLED BUTTERMILK SOUP WITH SHRIMP & PARSLEY

Ted's Choice Cava Segura Viudas or other dry sparkling wine.

Makes 4 servings

My Belfast-born dad loved his glass of icy cold buttermilk whether it was partnered with food or just on its own. In Brittany, fresh buttermilk is served with that region's famous buckwheat crepes, and in Wales with similar flat cakes based on oatmeal. Buttermilk is used extensively in Celtic cuisine, in leavened and unleavened breads and griddle cakes, and in soups such as this one that is so refreshing — and so effortless — on a hot summer's day.

5 cups (1.2 L) buttermilk

1/2 seedless cucumber, peeled, diced

1 1/2 tsp. (7 mL) sugar

1 tsp. (5 mL) dry mustard

1 tsp. (5 mL) salt

1/2 tsp. (2 mL) white pepper

3 tbsp. (45 mL) chopped fresh parsley

1/2 lb. (225 g) small cooked shrimp

Pour the buttermilk into a large bowl. Add the cucumber, sugar, mustard, salt, pepper, parsley and shrimp and blend gently. Cover with plastic wrap and chill for 2–3 hours. When ready to serve, ladle the soup into chilled bowls and serve.

Peadar O'Donnell's Pub in Derry

This busy pub sits next door to the Gweedore Bar in Derry's Waterloo Street and is one of the very best places to enjoy great Irish session music that happens here on a nightly basis. The pub was named for a Donegal man who gained fame and respect as the organizer of the Irish Transport and General Workers' Union and who fought in the Civil War of the 1920s, escaped from prison and went on to take part in the Spanish Civil War.

CVLLEN SKINK

Ted's Choice A "white" beer, such as Blanc de Chambly from Quebec-based Unibroue.

Makes 4 servings

I love the name of this very traditional fish soup based on good smoked haddock and potato — two foods beloved by Celts then and now. *Skink* derives from the Gaelic meaning "essence." But I've also read that skink describes a thin, oatmeal gruel. Today it refers to a stew-like soup. Absolutely perfect on a cold wintry night.

Place the haddock in a large, wide saucepan along with the onion and milk. Place over medium-high heat and bring to a gentle boil; reduce the heat and simmer for 5–10 minutes, until the fish is tender. Use a slotted spoon to remove the fish from the liquid and transfer it to a plate. Skin and bone the fish, breaking the meat into small chunks as you work. Set the fish to one side. Return the skin and bones to the liquid in the saucepan and simmer for about 20 minutes. Strain the liquid through a sieve set over a bowl. Wipe the saucepan clean and return the cooking liquid to it. Add the chunks of fish and enough mashed potato to achieve the desired creamy consistency. Stir in the cream and heat through for a minute or two. Add the pieces of butter and season to taste. Sprinkle with parsley and serve immediately.

2 lbs. (1 kg) smoked haddock fillets

1 medium-sized onion, thinly sliced

4 cups (1 L) whole milk

2 cups (approx.) freshly made mashed potato

1/2 cup (125 mL) whipping cream

3 tbsp. (45 mL) chilled butter, cut into small pieces

salt and freshly ground white pepper to taste

1/4 cup (60 mL) chopped fresh flat-leaf parsley

Glassdrumman Lodge, Co. Down

We spent one memorable night at this beautiful lodge owned by Graeme and Joan Hall. It sits at the heart of the ancient Kingdom of Mourne on the County Down coast, so no surprise then to find wonderful local fish and seafood on the extensive menu. Palm-sized oysters are a specialty. The family-run restaurant is well recommended, many of the staff having trained at Ballymaloe Cookery School in Cork. It's peaceful, relaxed and very comfortable.

Allen's Burns Night Cock-a-Leekie

Ted's Choice A Scottish Lowland single malt whisky, such as the triple-distilled Auchentoshan.

Makes 4–6 servings

In Toronto, there is no better place to celebrate Burns Night than Allen's on the Danforth in the city's east end. Celebrants are always served a tradition-inspired menu, heralded by a soup very like this one and ending with a complement of haggis. Ancient Scottish cooking at its best. While the soup apparently improves immeasurably if the bird in question was the loser in a cockfight, this simple, contemporary version relies on ready-made broth and boneless chicken breasts — ingredients that are a wee bit more accessible.

8 cups (2 L) chicken broth

2 boneless, skinless chicken breasts

3 leeks, rinsed, trimmed, thinly sliced

2 carrots, peeled, thinly sliced

1/4 cup (60 mL) long-grain rice

6–8 pitted prunes, halved

salt and freshly ground pepper to taste

1/4 cup (60 mL) chopped fresh flat-leaf parsley

Heat the chicken broth in a large saucepan. When the broth has come to a boil, reduce heat to a simmer and add the chicken breasts. Cover and cook gently for 10 minutes or so. Remove chicken with a slotted spoon and set to one side to cool. When cool enough to handle, slice the chicken into thin strips. Add the leeks, carrots and rice to the saucepan and cook over medium heat until rice is tender, about 12–15 minutes. Return chicken to the saucepan along with the prunes and cook gently for another 5 minutes. Add salt and pepper, ladle into soup bowls and garnish with parsley.

Allen's

The owner of Allen's, Toronto's New York–style Irish bar and restaurant, is John Maxwell, as unique as the place itself. A native New Yorker, Maxwell came to Toronto in 1979 from London, England, where he had lived for more than 10 years. He taught English before working as the manager of the Joe Allen bar in London. He then owned Toronto's Joe Allen bar and restaurant and the critically acclaimed and much-missed Italian restaurant called Orso. Maxwell opened Allen's in 1987 on the Danforth, in an east-end neighbourhood, and has

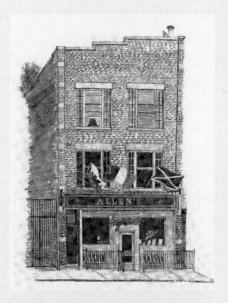

enjoyed a loyal following ever since. With his Irish roots — Maxwell's father came from Ireland's County Antrim — it is no surprise to learn that he has a wide-ranging interest in the subject of fine ales and whiskies, the latter including ryes from Canada, malts from Scotland and Ireland and American bourbons. Allen's is, without question, Toronto's best all-round whisky bar. Each time I ask John about his favourite whisky, I have to say I receive a different answer and that's just as it should be. Clearly, the choice depends on the day and the taster. He loves Ireland's Jameson for solid everyday drinking and unbeatable value. Lagavulin for the same reason. But Irish Connemara, Tyrconnell and the 12-year-old Redbreast also figure prominently. For a special treat, he says he has a few "heralded choices" — Longmorn 15-year-old and, for desert island forays, he'd opt for a case of his favourite Islay malt, Caol Ila 1974, 22-year-old. "It's not an unrelenting blast of the sea and is beautifully moderated by other flavours and notes; subtle and sophisticated," he says, which is a perfectly fair comment on Allen's itself.

Cream of Leek, Potato & Porcini Soup

Ted's Choice A dry cider like Scrumpy Supreme Cider.

Makes 4–6 servings

The Walnut Tree Inn is something of a culinary icon in Wales. Situated on a country road outside of Abergavenny that is the gateway to Wales, for 37 years it was owned and run by Ann and Franco Taruschio, who skillfully treated the best of local Welsh food to an Italian culinary sensibility. This soup is a good example. Today the Walnut Tree continues to be a thriving dining room with a menu that still shows the influence of the original owners.

1 oz. (28 g) dried porcini

3 tbsp. (45 mL) olive oil

3 large leeks, rinsed, white and
　pale green parts only

3 large floury potatoes, peeled,
　diced

4 cups (1 L) rich chicken or
　vegetable broth

1 1/3 cups (325 mL) whole milk

2/3 cup (150 mL) table cream

3 1/2 oz. (100 g) Italian Fontina
　cheese, grated

6 slices baguette, toasted

extra virgin olive oil to garnish

Rehydrate the porcini with enough hot water to cover. Set to one side. Warm the olive oil in a skillet over medium-high heat. Add the leeks and sauté for a few minutes until softened. Add the potato and continue to cook for another few minutes. Add the broth and milk, season with salt and pepper and gently simmer for 30 minutes, at which time the potatoes should be quite soft. Preheat oven broiler. Transfer the mixture to a blender or food processor, add the cream and blend until quite smooth. Wipe the saucepan clean, return the blended mixture to it and bring to a gentle boil. Set a sieve over a small bowl and pour the porcini and liquid into it. (Reserve the liquid for another use in sauces, stews or soups.) Roughly chop the porcini. Set 6 soup bowls on a baking tray and divide the soup between the bowls. Place a toast on each one and cover with a portion of cheese and a little porcini. Slip the tray holding the soups beneath the hot broiler just to melt the cheese. Serve with a drizzle of excellent extra virgin olive oil.

Mussel Soup with Cream & Garlic

Ted's Choice A dry cider from a small producer, such as Brittany's Cidrerie des Vergers.

Makes 4 servings

This lustrous soup could be from any one of the Celtic nations, but I had one of the best versions ever in a decidedly Celtic pub in the lovely little town of Quimper in Brittany. As any French-food lover will tell you, the finest fish and seafood in France emanates from Brittany. And I would add cider, cream and butter to that list.

After cleaning the mussels, check to see if any remain open after being tapped firmly. If so, discard them. Warm the cider or wine in a large saucepan. Add the mussels, cover and let cook over a high heat, shaking the pan vigorously now and then. After a few minutes, when the mussels are open, remove from the heat. Discard any unopened mussels. Pour the contents of the pan into a sieve or colander placed over a bowl to catch the liquid. Working over the bowl to catch any liquid in the shells, remove the mussels from their shells. Set the mussels to one side briefly. Return the liquid to the saucepan, place over moderate heat. Add the garlic, leek, celeriac, cream and salt and pepper. Reduce heat to a simmer and cook for a couple of minutes to soften vegetables. Add the mussels and saffron threads and continue to simmer until hot. Serve immediately with chopped parsley scattered over the surface of each serving.

2 1/2 lbs. (1.1 kg) mussels, cleaned, debearded

2 cups (500 mL) dry cider or dry white wine

2 cloves garlic, very thinly sliced

1 leek, trimmed, rinsed well, very thinly sliced (use all the white part and a portion of the green)

1 small piece of celeriac, peeled, very thinly sliced

2 cups (500 mL) whipping cream

salt and freshly ground white pepper to taste

12 saffron threads

1/4 cup (60 mL) chopped fresh flat-leaf parsley

Dublin Castle Bacon & Egg Pie

Ted's Choice Fuller's London Pride Premium Ale.

Makes 6–8 servings

Many years ago, living and working in London, I used to frequent a sweet little pub in Camden Town called the Dublin Castle. Owned and run by an Irish couple, the "Dub" was famous for very good, reasonably priced lunches. It was here, at the urging of Seamus who worked the bar, that I had my first Guinness. And, as I recall, my second and third. Can't remember if I had a fourth . . . however, I was able to return to work, just across the road, and perform my tasks relatively unimpeded thanks to a portion of the pub's renowned bacon and egg pie. Huge, oversized trays of this pie would sit on the counter until the lunch crowd would descend on the pub and order great whacks of it to eat right out of hand. You will need a fairly deep 10-inch (25-cm) pie dish for this recipe.

2 cups (500 mL) all-purpose
   flour
1 cup (250 mL) chilled butter,
   chopped (or a combination of
   butter and vegetable
   shortening)
1 egg yolk
2–3 tbsp. (30–45 mL) ice water
1 egg, lightly beaten with a little
   milk

For the filling:
1 tbsp. (15 mL) olive oil
1 onion, chopped
10 slices naturally smoked
   bacon, roughly chopped
10 eggs

Combine the flour and butter in the bowl of a food processor and pulse until crumbs form. Add the egg yolk and ice water and pulse again a few times, just until mixture comes together. Transfer mixture to a lightly floured surface and knead slightly. Divide into two pieces, one a little larger than the other. Wrap each in plastic wrap and refrigerate for at least 1 hour.

Preheat oven to 400F (200C). Roll out the larger piece of pastry and line a deep, 10-inch (25-cm) pie dish with it. Lay a sheet of foil or parchment paper on the surface of the pastry, fill with pie weights or dried beans and bake for 15 minutes. Remove the weights and continue to bake for another 5 minutes or until pastry is just beginning to colour.

Warm the oil over medium-high heat and add the onion and bacon. Cook for about 10 minutes until onion is soft and bacon is cooked. (If there is a great deal of fat, pour off most, but not all. Save for another use or discard.) Set to one side to cool.

Crack an egg into a small bowl or cup and slide into the cooled pastry shell, being careful not to break the yolk. Repeat with remaining eggs. Distribute the cooled bacon and onion mixture over the eggs and follow with the cheese, parsley, chives and pepper. Brush the edge of the pie with some of the egg and milk mixture. Roll out the remaining pastry and carefully place over top of the pie, pressing edges together to seal. Brush the surface with more of the egg and milk mixture. Bake at 375F (190C) for 40–45 minutes or until pastry is golden and filling is set.

2 cups (500 mL) grated Irish Cheddar (or other good-quality white Cheddar)
2 tbsp. (30 mL) chopped flat-leaf parsley
2 tbsp. (30 mL) chopped chives
freshly ground pepper to taste

The Clarence Hotel

Fans of U2 will want to head to Dublin's Clarence Hotel co-owned by Bono and "The Edge." Order a Black Velvet (Guinness and Champagne) and a plate of Irish smoked salmon with soda scones in the Octagon Bar. Or head to the Tea Room (the hotel dining room) for pan-fried foie gras with onion *tarte tatin* licked with a sauce based on Dublin Brewing Co.'s Wicked Organic Apple Cider.

Beech Hill's Goat Cheese Tart with Figs & Balsamic Beetroot Drizzle

Ted's Choice Hunters Sauvignon Blanc, from Marlborough, New Zealand.

Makes 4 servings

Just outside the historic walled city of Derry (or Londonderry, as it is also known), is the grand Irish country house hotel called Beech Hill. Set in beautiful landscaped grounds, the hotel offers quiet comfort and excellent cuisine thanks to the work of head chef Philippe Petrani. Originally from Nice, Chef Petrani acquired fine training at a three-star Michelin restaurant in his native France before working in Ireland. This recipe is inspired by one I enjoyed at Beech Hill. Make the balsamic beetroot drizzle first and proceed with the tarts. Serve these tarts warm over a bed of dressed salad greens. A very pretty presentation with splendid flavour combinations.

For the balsamic beetroot dressing:

4 small, whole cooked beets, roughly chopped (canned may be used)

1/2 cup (125 mL) balsamic vinegar

1 cup (250 mL) extra virgin olive oil

Combine the beets with the balsamic vinegar in a food processor. Process until smooth. With the motor running gradually add the olive oil in a stream until completely incorporated. Transfer to a plastic squeeze bottle (or a measuring cup with a spout) and set to one side.

Preheat oven to 400F (200C). Roll out the puff pastry to about 1 1/2 times its original size. Using a 6-inch (15-cm) pastry cutter cut out four rounds. Spray a baking sheet with a little cooking spray (or lightly butter) and transfer the rounds of pastry to it. Use a fork to prick the pastry in a few places, then bake for about 15–20 minutes or until golden brown. While the pastry is baking, combine the butter and oil in a sauté pan set over medium-high heat. Cook onion until softened, about 10 minutes. Season with salt and pepper. Remove from heat and set to one side. Remove pastry from the oven. Divide onion mixture between the pastry rounds. Slice open each fig, keeping them connected, and place one in the centre of each pastry round (use two pieces of each of the remaining figs to garnish). Add a slice of goat's cheese to each of the split figs. Preheat oven broiler to high and slip the tarts beneath it just to brown the cheese slightly. Have plates ready with dressed greens. Remove tarts from the oven and place one on each of the four plates. Drizzle the balsamic beetroot dressing around the tart and serve immediately.

For the tarts:

1 pkg. frozen puff pastry, thawed (397 g)

1 tbsp. (15 mL) olive oil

2 tbsp. (30 mL) butter

1 medium red onion, chopped

salt and freshly ground pepper to taste

8 oz. (225 g) goat's cheese log

6 fresh figs (preferably black)

dressed salad greens, as needed

Hunters Wines

There may be no wineries of distinction within Northern Ireland itself, but we tasted a Sauvignon Blanc with a Celtic connection in Derry, at the Beech Hill Country House Hotel. The wine list described Hunters Sauvignon Blanc out of Marlborough, New Zealand, as "a classic with intense tropical/gooseberry flavours dominating the palate and with a lingering finish," and we concurred. The late Ernie Hunter, originally from Belfast, established this New World winery in Marlborough. Today, the business is carried on by his wife, Jane, a highly qualified viticulturist with a family background in the subject. Jane was awarded an OBE for her achievements and contribution to the New Zealand wine industry, and Hunters continues to enjoy a reputation as one of the most successful wineries in the country.

Stirling Bridies

Ted's Choice Caledonian 80 Shilling — no question.

Makes 4 servings

Cornish pasties, *empanadillas*, and, when made in individual portions, the Irish savouries known as Dingle pies are all very similar meat-filled pastries. And that's exactly what Scottish bridies are. This invention stemmed from Jollys, a bakery in Forfar, the small county capital of Angus. Originally Forfar bridies held a mixture of quality chopped beef and onion cooked in a bit of stock for flavouring. I shared my first bridie with Ted outside a bakery in Stirling that featured endless variations on the theme, some based on chicken, lamb, beef and even a vegetarian and cheese version. We went the classic route and scarfed down a warm, flaky, golden pastry holding a richly seasoned beef filling. One between two was definitely not enough.

For the pastry:

2 cups (500 mL) all-purpose flour

1/2 cup (125 mL) chilled butter

1/2 cup (125 mL) chilled lard or
   vegetable shortening

pinch of salt

1 egg yolk

1/3–1/2 cup (75–125 mL) ice
   water

Combine the flour, butter, shortening and salt in the bowl of a food processor and pulse until crumbs form. Add the egg yolk and ice water and pulse again a few times, just until mixture comes together. Transfer mixture to a lightly floured surface and knead slightly. Divide into four pieces and wrap each in plastic wrap and refrigerate for at least 1 hour while you prepare the filling.

Using a sharp chef's knife, or a food processor, cut the slices of meat into small dice. Transfer to a mixing bowl and add the suet, onion, mustard, Worcestershire sauce, salt and pepper. Stir together until all the ingredients are well blended.

Preheat oven to 400F (200C). Roll out each piece of dough into an 8-inch (20-cm) round. Place about a cup (250 mL) of the beef filling on half of the dough round.

Moisten the edges of the pastry with a little milk and carefully fold the other half of the pastry over the filling, pinching edges of pastry together to seal. Repeat with remaining pastry and filling. Transfer to a baking sheet and prick each bridie with a fork or skewer to allow steam to escape while baking. Brush the top of each bridie with a little beaten egg. Bake for about 20 minutes. Reduce oven temperature to 350F (180C) and continue to bake for another 20–30 minutes until pastry is golden brown and the filling is cooked through. Cool for about 5 minutes before serving warm.

For the filling:
1 1/2 lbs. (750 g) lean round steak, thinly sliced
1/4 cup (60 mL) finely chopped beef suet (or vegetable shortening)
1 medium onion, minced
1 tsp. (5 mL) dry mustard
1 tbsp. (15 mL) Worcestershire sauce
salt and freshly ground pepper
1 egg, beaten

The Caledonian Brewery

This relatively small Edinburgh-based brewery dates back to 1869 and produces some of Scotland's maltiest beers. That may be due to the influence of Russell Sharp, who worked in the whisky trade for Chivas Regal before running the Caledonian. Hardly surprising then that the ales from this brewery have outstanding malt aroma and flavour. Scotland obviously cultivates barley for malting, but its climate is too cool for the growing of hops. This is why Scottish ales emphasize the malt aspect – the best possessing a smooth, round maltiness rather than a sharp hoppiness. Interestingly, this is one of the few UK breweries to boil its kettles by direct flame rather than steam. As Sharp says, "We are boiling not stewing the brew," and this obviously influences the flavours of the beer.

Good-beer lovers in North America will be familiar with Caledonian 80 Shilling, one of the brewery's most popular products. The shilling was a unit of currency in the UK before decimalization. Sixty, 70, 80 or 90 shilling is a reference to the early price of a particular barrel of beer, sort of a good, better, best concept. Today the rank is used more to indicate the ascending strength and body of a particular ale. There is no link between the number and the alcohol content, as many believe. Ask for a pint of "wee heavy" in Scotland and you'll probably receive a pint of 90 shilling. The brewery also makes several organic ales and a ruby ale called the Flying Scotsman, named after the famous train that travels between London and Edinburgh.

Galician Empanadillas

Ted's Choice Cava from Vallformosa Winery in Penedés.

Makes about 20 tapas portions

Empanadillas translates as "wrapped in dough." The dough in question may be either puff or basic pastry, or a more substantial bread dough, and the filling for these little pies may include pork, lamb or fish. This recipe combines good canned tuna, olives and tomatoes — beats your average tuna sandwich hands down. Great as an appetizer with a glass of Spain's renowned Cava. For a larger, feed-a-crowd empanada made using a yeast dough, see the recipe for Galician Empanada with Berberecho Clams on page 222.

For the filling:

1 tbsp. (15 mL) olive oil

1 clove garlic, minced

1 green onion, minced

2 cups (500 mL) chopped plum tomatoes, peeled

2 tbsp. (30 mL) chopped green olives

1 tsp. (5 mL) chopped fresh thyme

1 cup (250 mL) flaked tuna, well drained

salt and freshly ground pepper

Warm the oil in a skillet over medium heat and sauté the garlic and onion gently for a few minutes until the onion is golden, being careful not to brown the garlic. Add the tomatoes, olives and thyme and gently blend the ingredients together as they cook, pressing down on the tomatoes to release their juice. Cook until mixture thickens to a sauce, about 10–12 minutes. (If the mixture is too wet, the resulting *empanadillas* will be soggy.) Blend in the tuna and let mixture simmer for a minute. Season with salt and pepper and set to one side to cool while you make the pastry.

Combine the flour and salt in a sieve set over a small bowl. Sift the dry ingredients together into the bowl. Combine the oil, wine and water in a small saucepan and heat gently until warm (your finger should be able to tolerate it). Pour this warm liquid into the flour mixture and stir until it comes together into a ball. Transfer to a lightly floured surface and knead until it is soft and elastic. Roll it with your hands into a long, thin sausage-like shape and cut into 20 pieces. Roll each piece into a little ball, then roll out each ball of dough (use a little more flour if needed) into a thin disc about 5 inches (12 cm) across. Preheat oven to 400F (200C). Lightly oil a baking sheet.

Add a spoonful of the filling onto one side of the disc, moisten the edges with a little water and then fold over to enclose the filling. Use a fork to seal the edges. Continue with remaining pastry and filling, transferring the pastries to the baking sheet as you work. Bake for about 15 minutes, until puffed golden brown and crisp.

For the pastry:

1 1/4 cups (310 mL) self-rising flour

1/2 tsp. (2 mL) salt

4 tbsp. (60 mL) olive oil

2 tbsp. (30 mL) white wine

3/4 cup (150 mL) water

Cornish Pasties

For centuries, the Cornish pasty was workingman's fare, especially where tin miners were concerned. Since there was no way within the confines of a mine to wash their hands clean of the toxic tin, miners would take these large hand-held pastries for lunch and hold them by the thick ropelike bit of pastry that formed the seal for the meat turnover. After eating the pasty, that bit of pastry handle was discarded. Traditionally, the miner's pasty filling consisted of a mixture of chopped potato and turnip at one end, chopped beef or lamb with onions in the centre and a bit of jam at the other. A miner's wife would make sure to bake the meat pie with a pastry initial at one end so that if the meal were interrupted, the owner would always know his pasty.

Honest Welsh Rabbit with Onion Jam

Ted's Choice A strong ale like the Welsh Brains S.A.

Makes 6–8 servings

In the midst of the ancient hills of the beautiful Brecon Beacons, one of the most modern of new food movements is alive and well. It's not surprising that this is the first area of Wales to become part of the international Slow Food organization — since it's also home to some of the best places to eat. One of the simplest is the Bull's Head at Craswall, a lovely old pub also renowned for its music evenings. If you visit, order a "huffer," a mammoth, homemade bread roll packed with Welsh Cheddar flavoured with hops. Or try this honest-to-goodness rendition of a deliciously comforting and classic Welsh savoury.

For the onion jam:

2 tbsp. (30 mL) butter

2 tbsp. (30 mL) olive oil

1/2 cup (125 mL) dark brown
  sugar

1/4 cup (60 mL) granulated sugar

1 1/2 lb. (750 g) medium red
  onions, thinly sliced

3/4 cup (175 mL) red wine

1/3 cup +1 tbsp. (90 mL) sherry
  vinegar

salt and freshly ground pepper to
  taste

Start by making the onion jam: in a large saucepan, melt the butter with the oil over low heat. Add the sugar and stir to dissolve completely. Add the onions all at once and stir to coat with the butter and sugar mixture. Cover loosely and cook for about 30 minutes, stirring occasionally.

Stir in the wine and vinegar and increase the heat. When it has come to a boil, reduce the heat and simmer gently, uncovered, for another 30 minutes or until the liquid has evaporated and the onions are tender. Season with salt and pepper. The mixture should be thick and jamlike. Remove from the heat and cool. Transfer to a bowl, cover with plastic wrap and refrigerate until ready to use.

Combine the grated Cheddar with the ale in a large, heavy saucepan. Stir over low heat until the cheese is melted. Do not allow to boil or the cheese will separate. One by one, add the flour, breadcrumbs and mustard powder, using a whisk to incorporate each ingredient well before adding the next. Continue to stir and cook until the mixture starts to pull away from the sides of the pan and forms a ball. Remove the pan from the heat and whisk in the Worcestershire sauce and seasoning. Set to one side to cool.

When it has cooled slightly, use a whisk to blend in the eggs and then the egg yolks. Use immediately, or transfer the mixture to a bowl, cover with plastic wrap and refrigerate.

Preheat the broiler and grill the slices of bread on both sides. (Or toast the bread if you prefer.) Keep the broiler on.

Gently reheat the onion jam and pile a good bit on each of the toasts. Spoon out a generous portion of the cheese mixture on top of the onion, place on a non-stick baking sheet and slip beneath the preheated broiler. When the rabbit is bubbling and beginning to brown in places, remove from the oven.

For the rabbit:

1 lb. (500 g) old Welsh Cheddar cheese, grated (or other extra old Cheddar)

2/3 cup (150 mL) ale

2 tbsp. (30 mL) all-purpose flour

4 tbsp. (60 mL) fresh, fine white breadcrumbs

1 tbsp. (15 mL) dry mustard

2 tsp. (10 mL) Worcestershire sauce

salt and freshly ground pepper to taste

2 eggs

2 egg yolks

1 loaf country-style bread, thickly sliced

S.A. Brain

Established in 1882, this is the best-known brewery in Wales. Samuel Arthur Brain and his uncle Joseph Benjamin Brain started the company, which is still family-owned. Among their brews is an amber ale dubbed S.A. Export, the initials standing for Special Ale. However, locals have nicknamed it Skull Attack, owing to its higher alcohol content (5.2% abv), making it, apparently, not for the faint of heart. The company owns over two hundred pubs specializing in cask-conditioned ale. Also popular, their Celtic Dark Ale is full-bodied and lighter in taste than a traditional stout — this was their flagship ale that was originally developed to "slake the thirsts of miners, steelworkers and dockers." Timothy Cooper, who runs the well-known Cooper & Sons Brewery in Adelaide, Australia, had been a medical student in Cardiff and loved this dark ale so much that when he returned to Oz, he developed the now popular Coopers Dark in remembrance of that Welsh ale. Interesting for a country of lager lovers. Other products include Dylan's Smooth Ale, a golden Welsh-style ale, complete with a picture of Wales' most famous son on the label.

CHAPTER 2

THE BAKESTOПE & GRĬDDLE

Rye bread will do you no good

Barley bread will do you no harm

Wheaten bread will sweeten your blood

Oaten bread will strengthen your arm

– Old Irish rhyme

If there is but one defining characteristic of the cuisine of the Celtic nations it is in the rich culinary tradition of breads and baking common to each. Breads and scones, flatbreads and buns, griddle cakes, tortillas, crepes, biscuits, butteries and baps, the list of traditional items based on flour is almost endless. Leavened with sourdough, barm (made from beer), the fermented juice of oat husks called sowans, fermented potato juice, buttermilk, soda or yeast – or not leavened at all – hefty and grainy or thin and fine, many stemmed from the need to feed and sustain families. Crepes, which originated in Brittany, rarely held fillings but were used as replacements for bread. Based on buckwheat, these *krampouez krass* were wrapped around sausages. Crepes that hold savoury fillings are always based on buckwheat, whereas delicate dessert crepes are made from white flour.

Many other items were made in celebration of special days, such as the bannock made in Scotland in honour of Beltane, the Celtic spring fire festival that occurs on the first of May. Barmbrack — brack, for short — is Ireland's (and Scotland's) cross between a cake and bread and is studded with raisins, lemon peel, nuts and other dried fruit. It's beloved by children at Samhuinn (Halloween) on October 31, the eve of the Celtic New Year, when charms would be added for them to find.

Rough, wholemeal breads based on wonderful flours that hold the whole grain are torn and spread thick with cool, rich butter — this is an experience that can be had often in every one of the Celtic nations. In Brittany, for example, there was great respect and reverence for this staff of life as illustrated by writer Pierre-Jakez Hélias in his book *The Horse of Pride: Life in a Breton Village*:

Those who made their own bread were well aware of the price involved. Sweat and anxiety. And a kind of religion as well. They would always make the sign of the cross on the bottom of each round loaf. Some of the old people would still cross themselves before cutting into it. And you'd have had to watch them eat it to realize that they were observing a rite. They would sniff it, chew it slowly, and then savour it, deep in thought. The crumbs that fell on the table were carefully gathered up into their palms and every last one of them was gobbled up. To them bread was their body.
(New Haven: Yale University Press, 1979)

Brittany Cider Bread

Ballymaloe Brown Bread

Kathleen's Irish Soda Bread

Gaelic Soda Bread

Brittany's Savoury Buckwheat Crepes

Manx Potato Griddle Cakes

Ulster Fadge

Gail's Aberdeen Butteries

Oaten Thyme Farls

Cape Breton Bannocks

Guinness & Treacle Bread

McCann's Oat Brown Bread

Fresh Herb Oatmeal Pancakes

Scotland's Breakfast Baps

Gaelic Pratie Oaten

Carrickfergus Wheaten Bread

Brittany Cider Bread

Makes 1 large round loaf

As I walked through a market in Quimper in Brittany, I noticed an elderly woman selling huge, round loves of dark, crusty bread. She spoke only Bretagne and from our conversation and the printed tissue paper she used for wrapping, I gathered this was organic bread made with natural leavening derived from the spontaneous activity of wild, airborne yeast. Made with stone-ground flour, spring water and grey salt from Brittany, these beautiful loaves were baked in a wood-fired oven "with wood pruned from hedges," as the label read. How I wish I could buy her bread all the time. Instead, I make this very good loaf. Brittany's love of cider is evident throughout the province; indeed, it is the universal drink in Brittany. In this traditional bread, good cider takes the place of beer or other liquids, resulting in a rustic, crusty loaf. The more authentic the cider, the better the bread. Use your electric mixer fitted with a dough paddle to make this bread or beat the dough by hand.

1 1/4 cups (310 mL) lukewarm water

1 1/2 tbsp. (15 mL) active dry yeast

pinch of granulated sugar

1 1/4 cups (310 mL) lukewarm cider

2 tbsp. (30 mL) olive oil

1 tbsp. (15 mL) sea salt

1/4 cup (60 mL) bran

3/4 cup (175 mL) rye flour

3/4 cup (175 mL) whole wheat bread or all-purpose flour

4–5 cups (1–1.25 L) unbleached bread or all-purpose flour

Pour the water into a small, warmed measuring cup. Sprinkle the yeast and sugar into the water; stir to dissolve. Leave at room temperature for about 10 minutes.

Combine the cider, oil, salt, bran, rye flour and whole wheat flour in the mixing bowl. Beat until the mixture is well blended and creamy, about a minute or so. Stir in the proofed yeast mixture along with 1 cup (250 mL) of the unbleached flour. Beat until well blended and then add the remaining flour, about 1 cup (250 mL) at a time, until the dough comes away from the sides of the bowl and forms a rough mass. Lightly flour a work surface and turn the dough out onto it. Lightly flour your hands and begin to knead the dough until it becomes smooth, using a little extra flour if necessary, until no stickiness remains.

Lightly oil or butter a warm mixing bowl. Transfer the dough to it, turning it over once or twice to coat it. Cover with plastic wrap and a clean tea towel and set in a warm place to rise until double in bulk, about 1 1/2 hours. When it has doubled in size, punch it down and turn it out onto the lightly floured work surface. Knead it a couple of times and reform it into a round shape. Lightly oil or butter a baking sheet and sprinkle some whole wheat flour over the surface. Roll the loaf in flour to coat. Then place, seam-side down, on the baking sheet. Cover with the plastic wrap and tea towel and leave again in a warm place for about an hour until doubled in bulk once again.

Preheat oven to 400F (200C). Use a sharp knife to slash the knife in a couple of places across the centre. Place in the centre of the oven and bake for 45–50 minutes, at which time the loaf should be golden brown and sound hollow when tapped on the bottom. Transfer to a rack to cool.

BALLYMALOE BROWN BREAD

Makes 1 large loaf or 2 small loaves

Ballymaloe House is a lovely old Georgian manor house and the home of Myrtle Allen, Ireland's internationally renowned chef and enthusiastic propagandist for traditional Irish food. It is also a country house hotel, situated in County Cork in southwest Ireland, whose kitchen and dining room are well known to food lovers around the world. We were lucky enough to spend a few days at Ballymaloe and enjoyed many memorable meals there. Breakfasts at the hotel unfailingly provide a host of wonderful house-baked breads, including white and brown soda breads, lovely little rolls and this nutty, flavourful whole wheat bread that absolutely anyone can make — it's dead easy and very quick to produce because no kneading is involved. It doesn't result in a sky-high loaf of bread, but rather a dense, ultramoist and deeply good-tasting one. I have experimented with different flours to try and duplicate the whole wheat flour used in Ireland. I am convinced the coarser texture of the Irish flour (lots of bran left intact) is the reason it tastes so good. This bread will disappear not long after it is made.

1 1/2 cups (325 mL) stone-ground soft whole wheat flour

1 1/2 cups (325 mL) stone-ground whole wheat bread or all-purpose flour

1/2 cup (125 mL) unbleached bread or all-purpose flour

1/2 cup (125 mL) bran

2 tsp. (10 mL) sea salt

2 cups (500 mL) lukewarm water

1 1/2 tbsp. (15 mL) active dry yeast

2 tbsp. (30 mL) molasses

Combine the flours, bran and salt together in the bowl of an electric mixer and stir until well blended. Add 1/2 cup of the warm water to a warmed measuring cup. Sprinkle the yeast over the surface, add the molasses and stir together well. Leave to stand for about 10 minutes. Butter a 9x5x3 (2 L) loaf pan or two smaller ones. Preheat oven to 450F (230C).

With the mixer running, add the remaining water and the proofed yeast mixture to the flour and blend until you have a thick, sticky dough. The dough should be too wet to knead. Pour this dough into the prepared loaf pan and cover loosely with a piece of buttered parchment paper. Cover with a clean tea towel and place in a warm place for about 20–30 minutes or until the dough just reaches the top of the loaf pan. Place in the centre of the oven and bake for 10 minutes. Reduce temperature to 425F (220C) and continue to bake until the top is deep brown and it sounds hollow when tapped on the bottom. Transfer to a rack to cool before slicing with a serrated knife.

James Neill Ltd.

In Northern Ireland I purchased a bag of James Neill's wonderful coarse wholemeal flour and was thrilled to be able to make the same terrific bread we had so enjoyed in Ireland at home. When I ran out of it, I contacted the company by email about how I could approximate their product in Canada. Here is the response I received from Bill Cleland of Allied Mills:

> Good to hear from you, Kathleen and Ted. I have many relatives around the Toronto area and like yourself they take back Neill's wholemeal and soda bread flour! We buy Canadian wheat for bread-making flour. It is very hard and good quality but tends to mill much finer, so we always use soft wheat varieties for our wholemeals and soft flours for home baking. I'm sure there are soft Canadian wheat varieties available. Have a look at our website, www.neillsflour.co.uk; there are recipes which may be of use to you.

I managed to approximate the lovely flour of this Northern Ireland company by using a combination of soft whole wheat flour, hard (bread or all-purpose) whole wheat flour and adding a bit of bran. The resulting loaf is not quite as rough-crusty or texturally satisfying as those memorable Irish loaves, but it's still very good bread and loaded with nutrition.

An interesting note from Ted is that of the longstanding co-relation between the brewing industry and bread-making. In times past, whenever a new town developed, the first thing that was sown was barley or wheat to make bread. Brewing quickly followed to make use of the surplus grain grown for the bread-making (a tradition that formed the basis for the highly successful rye whisky business in Canada). Also, it was a lot safer in those days to drink the beer than the suspect water, a tradition and belief to which Ted steadfastly clings — you just can't be too careful.

Kathleen's Irish Soda Bread

Makes 1 loaf

Although my dear mum was from Nottingham, she had an Irish name. She passed it on to me, doubtless making my dad very happy, especially because he could sing *"I'll take you home again, Kathleen"* to the two of us. This is her recipe for traditional Irish soda bread, and the sight of these just pulled from the oven made us all happy. Make sure to serve warm with lots of good butter.

1 tsp. (5 mL) butter

4 cups (1 L) unbleached bread or all-purpose flour

1 tsp. (5 mL) baking soda

1 tsp. (5 mL) sea salt

1/2–1 cup (125-250 mL) butter-milk

Preheat oven to 425F (220C). Sift the flour, soda and salt into a large bowl. Use a wooden spoon to gradually beat in 1/2 cup (125 mL) of buttermilk. You want to achieve a dough that is smooth and relatively firm. If necessary, add more buttermilk. Transfer the dough to a lightly floured surface and shape it into a flat, round loaf. Lightly butter a baking sheet and lightly flour the surface. Place the loaf in the centre and, using a sharp knife, cut a deep cross on the surface. Bake for 30–35 minutes or until the top is golden brown and it sounds hollow when tapped on the bottom. Transfer to a rack to cool slightly before slicing.

Chef Gordon Ramsay — The Michelin Man

The Glaswegian "chef for all seasons," superstar chef Gordon Ramsay didn't start out in the kitchen. A professional soccer player for the Glasgow Rangers in an earlier life, Ramsay still looks the part of the rough and tumble footballer with a fiery temperament and aggressive manner to match. And while his strong personality and take-no-prisoners attitude precedes him, none can argue with his remarkable talent and the incredible success he has achieved. He is the chef and owner of the restaurant Gordon Ramsay in London's Chelsea area. The dining room was awarded its third Michelin star in 2001 — its the only three-starred restaurant in London and one of only two in Britain. There are two other Ramsay restaurants in London: Petrus and Gordon Ramsay at Claridge's. In his hometown of Glasgow, there is the renowned Amaryllis placed in the luxury hotel in Glasgow known as One Devonshire Gardens — the restaurant was awarded a Michelin star in its first year of business. And Gordon is reputed to have plans to open a New York–style café in Edinburgh. He has written a number of beautiful cookbooks and has been involved in a television series. He is married with four children and is a relentless perfectionist. He hates the term "celebrity chef," yet he is the only Scottish chef to be awarded the coveted trio of Michelin stars.

GAELIC SODA BREAD

Makes 4 servings

I have enjoyed these triangular-shaped soda breads in Scotland, Ireland, Toronto, Wales and Cape Breton. These soda bread quarters (or farls, as they are also known) resemble large scones and are cooked on a flat griddle, not baked in the oven. If you don't have a griddle, a heavy, cast iron pan will work perfectly. Vary this recipe by using half whole wheat flour in place of all white flour. Self-rising flour is widely available in supermarkets right alongside all the other flours, but if you can't find it or want to make your own, use this equation: 1 cup (250 mL) all-purpose flour, 1 1/4 tsp. (7 mL) baking powder and a pinch of salt for every 1 cup (250 mL) of self-rising flour.

3 1/4 cups (810 mL) self-rising flour

1 tsp. (5 mL) granulated sugar

1/2 tsp. (2 mL) sea salt

2 tbps. (30 mL) chilled butter, diced

1 1/2 cups (250-375 mL) buttermilk

a little vegetable oil for the griddle or pan

Sift the dry ingredients into a large mixing bowl. Rub in the diced butter with your fingers until the mixture resembles fine breadcrumbs. Work lightly, rubbing the butter into the flour and lifting it up from the bowl to fall through your hands, in an effort to incorporate some air into the mixture. Add the buttermilk gradually, stirring it in with a wooden spoon, using just enough to moisten the dough and create a soft dough; don't overmix. Heat a griddle or place the cast iron pan on medium-low heat for a few minutes. Turn the dough out onto a lightly floured surface and knead gently until it comes together into a ball. Pat the ball until it becomes a disk shape, about 8 inches (20 cm) across and about 1 inch (2.5 cm) thick. Using a sharp knife cut the dough into quarters.

Lightly brush the heated griddle or pan with a bit of vegetable oil. Using a metal spatula, transfer the quarters to the heated griddle and cook over medium-low heat for 15 minutes or so, covered, turning the quarters two or three times to encourage even cooking. When the quarters are golden brown and nicely risen, remove from the pan to a rack to cool slightly before serving warm.

The Celtic Griddle

Used in Scotland, Ireland, Wales, Brittany and Spain for an assortment of flat breads, oatcakes, crumpets (or pikelets from the Welsh *pyglyd*), scones, pancakes, farls, crepes and empanadas, the large round flat griddle (originally known as a girdle) or bakestone may have been made of iron, slate or stone. Along with the cauldron or bastible, it formed the two fundamental components of the Celtic kitchen. This early cookware, and what could be done with it, strongly influenced the daily diet. Before the advent of conventional ovens, the bakestone, also called a *planc*, was easily adapted to mimic an oven by inverting an iron pot over whatever foods were cooking on the hot stone. The small, sweet sconelike items known as Welsh cakes and *pice ar y maen* in Welsh, literally translate as "cakes on the stone." Besides soups, grains, stews and the like, breads were baked, too, inside the cast iron cauldron that was hung suspended over the red hot embers of an open fire. The dough would be placed within the iron pot and covered with a lid upon which were heaped hot ashes from the fire to encourage the round loaf to cook evenly.

The Celtic Cross Bun

Hot cross buns have long been associated with Easter, one of the most important dates on the Christian calendar. Yet the fragrant, currant-studded sweet buns with their distinctive cross are of pagan Celtic origin. Long before they were used to herald the Christian holiday, these little round buns were baked by Celts. The round shape was of great significance because it represented the sun, and the cross divided the circle into four sections, each one representative of the four seasons of the Celtic year.

Brittany's Savoury Buckwheat Crepes

Makes 16 crepes

Our first true crepe experience took place in Creperie La Forge, a lovely old place near St. Nicolas du Pelem in the tranquil Côte d'Armor area of Brittany. Crepes are all they make here and people come from all over the area to enjoy them. Our host and cook was a typical Bretonne woman who urged us to have a couple glasses of *chouchenn*, which Ted decided was a sort of cider *eau de vie*. "Drink it and you'll walk backwards," she told us smiling.

With her husband as her assistant, she quickly poured a modicum of batter onto a weathered, smooth black griddle. Using a wooden spreader that looked to me like a short-handled window wiper, she deftly spread the batter into a circle. Once it was browned on one side, she quickly passed it to cook on the other side to the second hot griddle, which was manned by her husband-in-waiting and where the chosen fillings were added. It was then neatly and beautifully folded into a square envelope before being flipped out onto a warm plate.

By the way, when savoury fillings are used — cheese, ham, mushrooms, onions, tomato, egg or bacon — the crepe is made using buckwheat flour and is called a *galette*. Dessert crepes are made with white flour (see page 234 for a dessert crepe recipe).

2 cups (500 mL) buckwheat flour

1 cup (250 mL) unbleached
   all-purpose flour

3 eggs, well beaten

2 cups (500 mL) whole milk

1 1/2 tbsp. (15 mL) sea salt

3 cups (750 mL) water

1 tbsp. (15 mL) vegetable oil

3 tbsp. (45 mL) melted butter

1 lb. (500 g) Gruyère cheese,
   grated

In the bowl of an electric mixer (or a regular mixing bowl using a whisk) combine the flours, eggs, milk and salt. Beat the mixture until you have achieved a very smooth, lump-free batter.

Add the water gradually, about 1/2 cup (125 mL) at a time, continuing to blend well. Lastly, blend in the oil.

Place a 9-inch (23-cm) non-stick skillet (or cast iron skillet) over medium heat. After a couple of minutes, lightly brush it with some of the melted butter and add 1/4 cup (60 mL) of the batter. Immediately swirl the batter around so that it evenly coats the surface of the pan.

Cook for a minute or two until golden brown. Loosen the edges with a metal spatula and flip over onto the other side to cook. Transfer to a plate and keep warm in a low oven while making the remaining crepes. When ready, return one cooked crepe to the pan, sprinkle about 1/4 cup (60 mL) of the cheese in the centre, use a metal spatula to fold the crepe into a square envelope (up from the bottom, down from the top, in from each of the sides). Cook like this for about another 30 seconds until the cheese melts. Serve immediately, seam-side down, with a small piece of butter melting in the centre.

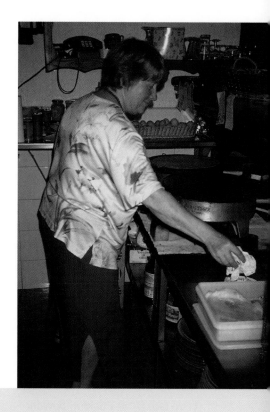

Fest Noz in Brittany

Our visit to Brittany was made all the more Celtic for us when we attended our first *Fest Noz*. This night festival, like a great Cape Breton *ceilidh*, took place in a grotto lit by huge torches. A stage was filled with musicians playing Breton pipes, Scottish pipes, Breton bombards and Scottish drums. A true and natural all-age event, the huge crowd of men, women and children joined hands and held their arms aloft and danced en masse in rounds, their almost instinctive footwork helping to shape the rhythm of the music. It was an incredible spectacle, steeped at once in ancient ritual and tradition and yet, new somehow. And very exciting. The music itself is haunting, some of it melancholic, some rousing, all of it thoroughly Celtic. For us, it stirred the same feelings aroused by Scotland's highland bagpipes or Ireland's *uillean* pipes, flutes and *bodhrán*, the traditional Irish drum. A true "phenomenon that produces a trance without artifice," as I later read it described. In between dancing, the crowd revived with glasses of ale — *brun* or *blonde* — powerful cider and plates of quickly made buckwheat crepes. We had to remind ourselves that we were in modern France — we felt we'd been transported back in time.

Manx Potato Griddle Cakes

Makes 4 servings

On the Isle of Man, potato cakes are made from the same ingredients as this recipe features
— cooked potato, flour, cheese, butter and seasonings. However, they are rolled to make thin
cakes, whereas the resulting mixture for this recipe produces a sort of thick batter that is
then dropped onto a hot cooking surface. I devoured a version of these in Scotland on the
morning of my wedding, along with fresh eggs, local sausages, fat, grilled mushrooms and
a lovely pot of tea.

2 large floury potatoes, cut into
   chunks
sea salt
1 cup (250 mL) unbleached
   all-purpose flour
1 1/2 tsp. (7 mL) baking powder
1/2 tsp. (2 mL) sea salt
1 egg, beaten
2/3 cup (150 mL) whole milk
1/2 cup (125 mL) old white
Cheddar cheese
sea salt and freshly ground
   pepper to taste
3 tbsp. (45 mL) vegetable oil

Place the potatoes in a saucepan, cover them with cold water, bring to a boil, add a little salt and cook until tender. Drain the potatoes well and place on low heat to dry them thoroughly, shaking the pan over the heat a few times. Using a potato masher, dry mash (without milk or butter) the potatoes and transfer them to a mixing bowl. Blend the flour with the baking powder and 1/2 teaspoon (2 mL) salt and add the mixture to the mashed potato along with the egg, milk and cheese. Using a wooden spoon, beat this mixture to incorporate all the ingredients well. Season with a little salt and pepper. Using a pastry brush, gloss the surface of a cast iron skillet or griddle with a little oil. Drop large spoonfuls (not too much) of the batter onto the pan, give each a slight pat with a metal spatula, and cook for 1–2 minutes. Flip the scones and cook the other side for the same length of time. Transfer them to a baking sheet as they are cooked; keep warm and repeat with remaining mixture.

Ulster Fadge

Makes 4–6 servings

In Scotland, these delicious little potato breads are called tattie scones. In the south of Ireland I've heard them referred to as potato cakes or parleys. My dad and Uncle Bob — both Ulstermen — called them potato bread, and when I visited Northern Ireland they were termed *fadge*. Whatever you decide to call them, share them only with the most deserving of eating partners. Wonderful at breakfast with good bacon, scrambled eggs and any smoked fish.

Preheat the oven to warm. Combine the mashed potatoes with half the flour and half the butter, using your hands to blend the ingredients as you would when making pastry. When the dough is still a little sticky, turn it out onto a floured surface and work in the remaining flour (use a little more as needed). Knead the dough lightly a few times, and then roll it out to about a 1/2-inch (1-cm) thickness. Cut the dough into pie-shaped wedges. Heat a griddle or cast iron pan over medium heat. Melt a bit of the remaining butter and fry the potato breads in batches, cooking them until golden speckled brown on both sides. Keep the cooked breads warm in the oven as you work. Serve them hot with a wee bit more butter and salt.

5 cups (1.25 L) warm mashed potatoes

1 cup + 1 tbsp. (250 mL + 15 mL) unbleached all-purpose flour

1/2 cup (125 mL) chilled butter (approx.)

sea salt

Gail's Aberdeen Butteries

Makes about 20

My Aberdeen-born friend Gail first told me about these gems when we were discussing favourite breads one day. "Have you ever heard of butteries?" she asked. "They're also called rowies. They're so good, rich and flaky like a croissant, but I've never seen them outside of Scotland. I used to work at a bakery in Aberdeen called Hutchison's, and when I came into work early in the morning, they'd just be taking them from the oven. What an incredible smell!" Well, I *hadn't* heard of them, but I did a bit of research and found them to be traditional square or sometimes oval-shaped butter yeast breads, and I set about making these little beauties. No wonder Scottish ex-pats such as Gail hold them in fond memory. Some recipes call for lard, some for butter and others for a mixture of the two. The first time I made butteries, I hadn't any lard at hand, so used all butter and that's what I have always used. Besides they *are* called butteries, right? Enjoy these without reservation about their levels of fat — they taste far too good to make you feel guilty.

4 3/4 cups (1150 mL) unbleached
  bread or all-purpose flour
1 tbsp. (15 mL) sea salt
2 1/2 tsp. (1 envelope) active dry
  yeast
2 cups (500 mL) lukewarm water
1 tbsp. (15 mL) granulated sugar
1 1/2 cups (375 mL) butter,
  softened
milk for brushing

Sift the flour and salt together into a large mixing bowl. Make a well in the centre of the dry ingredients. Combine the yeast with the sugar and water in a large measuring cup and let stand for 10 minutes. Pour the yeast mixture into the well of the dry ingredients and work in the flour until a soft, but not sticky, dough forms, adding a little more flour to achieve this, if necessary.

Turn out the dough onto a lightly floured work surface and knead gently for 10 minutes or until the dough is smooth. Wipe clean and dry the mixing bowl. Return the dough to the bowl, cover with a clean tea towel and leave to rise in a warm place for about 1 1/2 hours until it is doubled in size.

Divide the softened butter into three equal portions. When the dough has risen, punch it down and roll it out on a lightly floured work surface into a rectangle sized about 18x6 inches (45x15 cm) with the shorter side facing you. Spread the top two-thirds of the dough with the first portion of butter, leaving a 1/2-inch (1.2-cm) border at the edges. Fold the unbuttered part of the dough over half of the buttered dough, and then fold the remaining buttered dough into a sort of three-layered dough sandwich about 6 inches (15 cm) square with the enclosed side at the top. Seal the edges by pressing down with a rolling pin. Wrap the dough in plastic wrap and refrigerate for about half an hour. Remove from the refrigerator and repeat the rolling, spreading with butter, folding and chilling twice more. Make sure to always roll the dough out with the completely enclosed side to your left.

Preheat oven to 400F (200C). After the final chilling, remove the dough from the refrigerator and roll out once more to about a 1/2-inch (1-cm) thickness. Leave to rest for about 5 minutes, then use a lightly floured biscuit cutter to cut out about 20 squares (ovals or rounds). Lightly flour two or three baking sheets and place the butteries, upside down and well spaced, on the sheets. Lightly brush with milk. Bake for 20–25 minutes until golden brown and crisp. Transfer to racks to cool slightly and serve warm.

Edradour

One late afternoon, Canadian musician Murray McLauchlan walked into Allen's restaurant in Toronto and sat at the bar. Contemplating what to choose from the vast selection of single malts on the bar list, he bet the bartender that there was no way his favourite would be found there. The bartender said, "I'll bet it is. What's the name?" "Edradour," came the reply. Ted turned around and located the bottle and presented it to the astonished McLauchlan, happy he hadn't actually made that bet. Edradour is the product of the world's smallest whisky distillery, based in Pitlochry, Perthshire. Back in 1825, locals who were already in the business of making whisky for themselves established a co-operative distillery. Since 1986, the annual whisky production has been about 600 gallons (90,000 L), roughly the equivalent of a week's output from the average Speyside malt distillery. Edradour uses local barley and its stills are the smallest in Scotland, a factor in the malt's distinctive richness. In fact, if their stills were any smaller, they would be disallowed by the department of Customs & Excise because they could easily be hidden from the canny eye and long arm of the law.

Oaten Thyme Farls

Makes 8 farls

Walking up Shipquay, a slightly uphill thoroughfare in Derry, I found a lovely little bakery called the Baker's Oven. The window was filled with all manner of traditional Northern Irish baked goods, and inside were shelves of farls — soda farls, oat and wheaten (whole wheat) farls, treacle farls and potato farls. *Farl* stems from the ancient word *fardel*, which means fourth part or quarter. Soda and buttermilk provide the leavening in these lovely little brown farls that are best enjoyed on the day they are made. Very good with old Cheddar or a classic Irish stew. If you want to produce more, smaller farls, cut the dough into six or eight. They could also be baked in true traditional Celtic fashion on a hot griddle.

1 cup (250 mL) unbleached bread or all-purpose flour

2 tsp. (10 mL) baking soda

2 tsp. (10 mL) cream of tartar

1 tsp. (5 mL) sea salt

1 cup (250 mL) rolled oats (regular or quick-cooking)

3 tbsp. (45 mL) chopped fresh thyme

2 1/2 cups (625 mL) buttermilk

Preheat oven to 400F (200C). Sift together into a mixing bowl the flour, baking soda, cream of tartar and salt. Stir in the oatmeal and thyme. Gradually add the buttermilk and mix to form a soft dough. Lightly flour your hands and transfer the dough to a lightly floured surface. Knead the dough lightly, and then divide in two. Form each piece of dough into a round shape about 1 inch (2.5 cm) thick. Flour a baking sheet well and transfer the two dough rounds to it. Using a sharp knife, cut all the way through (but not separating) to make four farls. Dust with a little extra flour and bake for 20 minutes until they are browned and puffed.

Remove from the oven and wrap each round in a clean tea towel and allow to cool on a rack. Reheat slightly before breaking into wedges and serving.

CAPE BRETON BAΠΠOCKS

Makes 8 bannocks

When I was a girl living in the east end of Toronto, the area favoured by English, Irish and Scottish immigrants at the time, I passed a little bakery each morning on the way to school. The woman who baked all the lovely breads, tarts, buns and scones spoke with a lilt not unlike my dad's, so I always thought she too came from Ireland. I called her "the Irish baking lady" until my mum told me she was Canadian, pointing to the sconelike cakes in the window speared with a little tag that read "Cape Breton Bannocks."

Combine the flours, oats, sugar, baking powder and salt together in a mixing bowl. Add the melted butter, raisins and buttermilk and stir together to form a sticky dough. Add a little water if the dough seems too thick. Butter a 9-inch (23-cm) pie pan. Lightly flour your hands and pat the mixture evenly into the pan. Mark into wedges by cutting through the dough. Bake in the oven for 25 minutes until a tester set in the centre emerges clean. Serve warm.

1 cup (250 mL) whole wheat flour
1/2 cup (125 mL) unbleached all-purpose flour
1/2 cup (125 mL) rolled oats
2 tbsp. (30 mL) granulated sugar
2 tsp. (10 mL) baking powder
1/2 tsp. (2 mL) sea salt
3 tbsp. (45 mL) melted butter
1/3 cup (75 mL) raisins
1 cup (250 mL) buttermilk

The Spirit of Cape Breton

There is only one place in the world where single malt Scotch whisky is produced, one country that can lay claim to the ownership of this truly noble spirit, and it isn't Nova Scotia. Nor is it Japan, where canny whisky producers once attempted to name a town Scotland in an effort to circumvent the rules. Like Champagne from northeast France, only whisky from Scotland is Scotch.

Yet, on the way to Inverness on Cape Breton's beautiful Ceilidh Trail, sits the wee hamlet of Glenville, so small it doesn't even warrant a designation on the map. It's just up the road from Mabou, the home of the rollicking Rankins. Fellow musicians, fiddlers Natalie MacMaster and Ashley MacIsaac, come from even smaller communities nearby. This is Celtic Canada, where Mc's and Mac's proliferate, where Gaelic is spoken, bagpipes played, Highland games won, and the *ceilidh* defines Saturday night. But this treasured piece of Canada may soon be renowned for more than great Celtic music, fish suppers and traditional Cape Breton hospitality.

Glenville, this blink-and-you've-missed-it spot, is home to Canada's only single malt whisky distillery. Nestled in a lush Highland glen at the foot of rounded green-clad hills sits the profoundly impressive Glenora Distillery, designed by the Scottish architect David Forsyth in the classic style of Scotland's most revered malt distilleries and looking for all the world as though it means business.

The imposing whitewashed structure has distinctive distillery features like the pagoda roof and adjoining storehouse that quietly proclaim the business within. It includes a country inn, pub, dining room and shop. The entire complex is clustered round a shimmering brook of incredible clarity running through the property that sits, as most of the island does, on a granite base. The Cape Breton Highland breezes are sweet and unsullied, rippling MacLellan's Brook as it flows gently over granite stones, fed by more than 20 crystal streams. The distillery purchased the rights to the surrounding land upstream to ensure that the water remains as pure as it is.

Not so unusual, then, to find Canada's only single malt whisky distillery here — along with yeast and good Scottish malt, these are the natural features on which great malts are founded.

Built in the eighties by a Cape Breton businessman, the late Bruce Jardine, much of Glenora's first run was used to make a 5-year-old product that is still available in the distillery's gift shop. It's called Kenloch Single Malt Scotch Whisky, a serviceable spirit that is the result of a collaboration between Glenora and its Scottish mentor, Bowmore, one of Scotland's oldest and most revered distilleries. Because more than half the whisky used in the production of Kenloch was from Bowmore, the distillery was allowed to call it "single malt Scotch."

Ken Roberts, who is in charge of the distilling operation at Glenora and has been here from its inception, explains the connection. "Mr. Jardine started the place. He went to Scotland and made the first contact with Bowmore and got the equipment. In fact, these two stills are from Bowmore," says Roberts of the huge handsome copper stills that were used for Bowmore's first 40-year-old single malt whisky, now extremely rare. The massive weathered "washbacks" (the vessels where the fermentation process starts) beautifully illustrate the Canada–Scotland collaboration. "They're made of BC fir that was taken to Scotland for the production and then brought back to us here," Roberts says.

Certainly, barley is grown in Canada but the imported barley used at Glenora is malted in Scotland and is a strain developed over many years, just for whisky production, and is best suited to the chosen yeast. When asked about peat production in Canada, Roberts responds, "Well, there isn't any around here and just a little peat is grown in PEI."

Originally from Cape Breton, Halifax businessman Lauchie MacLean is Glenora's current owner. "Basically we're not out to beat our Scottish ancestors at their own game, I mean they've got hundreds of years of experience over us. We think we have a unique distillery and a unique product and aren't out to sell hundreds of thousands of cases of it, more like thousands. Hopefully this will provide the funds needed to continue the operation," he says.

In 1997, esteemed whisky writer Jim Murray — one of a privileged few to taste the original 10-year-old (of which there is little left) — described the 1990 malt as "a little feinty [which refers to a cereal odour] but no worse than many malts I have tasted from Scotland. Its strength lies in that sweetness which…has taken on a honey-tinge…One thing is certain; it has the weight to become a malt of character."

He also described that original 10-year-old in *Millionaire Magazine* as "simply gorgeous." Bob Scott, marketing manager for the distillery, says because of the small quantity left (most was "married" to Bowmore's contribution at the beginning of the

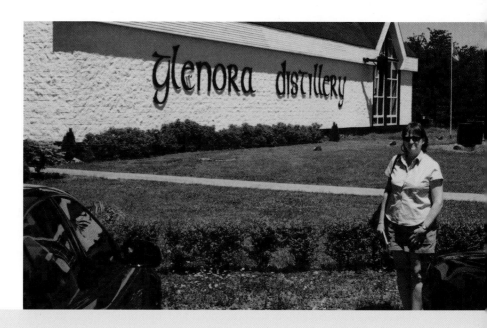

distillery's history and sold to create much-needed revenue), that particular vintage will probably be sold at a "super premium price." All of which bodes quite well for its close relation, the 8-year-old Glen Breton Rare Canadian Single Malt Whisky, the "new" product that is causing some measure of excitement at Glenora and surrounding area.

In a blind tasting involving professional whisky tasters in Scotland, the malt was likened to a Speyside. Speyside malts are Highland whiskies, noted for their elegance and floweriness with heathery honey notes and very lightly peated. They are generally sweet and are thought of as the most complex and sophisticated of malt whiskies.

Glen Breton Rare Canadian Single Malt Whisky is an 8-year-old malt that consists solely of whisky made here at Glenora. Based on imported Scottish malt, a special strain of yeast from South Africa and the magnificent MacLellan's Brook water, this is the made-in-Canada spirit that may soon have single malt–loving tongues wagging from here to Edinburgh. Have a look at www.glenoradistillery.com.

Carrot & Tarragon Soup – Page 10

Beech Hill's Goat Cheese Tart with Figs &
Balsamic Beetroot Drizzle — Page 20

Guinness & Treacle Bread

Makes 1 loaf

The very modern Halo restaurant in Dublin's stylish Morrison Hotel is home to French-born chef Jean-Michel Poulot, who has created a hybrid French-Irish cuisine featuring the best of Irish food influenced by the culinary styles of haute French cooking. We enjoyed this lovely, moist bread spread with creamy Irish butter as we perused a menu that held the likes of seared salmon raviolo with Jerusalem artichokes, a watercress and celeriac soup with smoked salmon cannelloni, loin of Co. Wicklow lamb with sun-dried tomato tapenade, sigh. Marvellous.

Preheat oven to 400F (200C). Sift together the flours, baking soda, cream of tartar and salt in a large mixing bowl. Blend together well. Add the melted butter, sugar, egg, buttermilk, Guinness and treacle or molasses and mix together thoroughly and quickly. Lightly butter an 8x4-inch (1.5-L) loaf pan. Transfer the mixture to the pan, smooth the top and bake for about 40 minutes until crusty and brown. Turn it out and tap the bottom to make sure it sounds hollow. Transfer to a rack to cool slightly before serving.

1 1/2 cups (375 mL) unbleached bread or all-purpose flour

1/2 cup (125 mL) whole wheat flour

1 tsp. (5 mL) baking soda

1/2 tsp. (2 mL) cream of tartar

1/2 tsp. (2 mL) sea salt

4 tbsp. (60 mL) melted butter

1 tbsp. (15 mL) granulated sugar

1 egg, beaten

3/4 cup (175 mL) buttermilk

1/2 cup (125 mL) Guinness

2 tbsp. (30 mL) treacle or molasses

McCann's Oat Brown Bread

Makes 2 loaves

One of the best products Ireland has to offer is the award-winning John McCann's Irish Oatmeal housed in the distinctive white, black and gold tin. These are whole grain steel-cut oats, packed with nutrition and a wonderful nuttiness that help to make this delicious bread so good. This recipe also calls for McCann's more conventional quick-cooking oatmeal, a product that I have only just recently been able to find in North America. If you can't find it, use any quick-cooking oatmeal, but make sure to use McCann's Steel-cut Oatmeal in this recipe for best results.

3 cups (750 mL) unbleached
    bread or all-purpose flour
1 1/2 cups (375 mL) whole wheat
    flour
1/2 cup (125 mL) McCann's
    Quick-Cooking Oatmeal
    (or other quick-cooking
    oatmeal)
1/3 cup (75 mL) McCann's
    Steel-cut Oatmeal
2 1/2 tsp. (12 mL) baking soda
1/4 cup (60 mL) granulated sugar
1/4 cup (60 mL) chilled butter,
    cut into 1/2-inch (1.2-cm)
    pieces
2–2 1/2 cups (500–625 mL)
    buttermilk

Preheat oven to 425F (220C). Lightly dust the surface of a baking sheet with flour. Stir together the flours, oats, sugar and baking soda in a large mixing bowl. Using your fingertips, quickly rub in the butter. Make a well in the centre and gradually stir in the buttermilk with a wooden spoon until the dough is soft and manageable (you might not use all the buttermilk).

Turn the dough out onto a lightly floured surface and knead for about 1 minute. Divide in half. Shape the dough into two balls and place in the centre of the baking sheet. Use the palm of your hand to flatten the dough into disks about 1 1/2-inches (4-cm) thick. Use a sharp knife to cut a fairly deep cross into each disk so that it will break apart easily into quarters after baking. Bake for approximately 35 minutes or until browned and the tester emerges clean and the bottom sounds hollow when tapped. Cool slightly on a rack before serving warm.

FRESH HERB OATMEAL PANCAKES

Makes about 8 small pancakes

The lovely colour of these modern Celtic griddle cakes make them perfect for St. Patrick's Day, especially when topped with a bit of crème fraîche and slices of good smoked salmon or trout. These pancakes are also very good in place of English muffins when making eggs Benedict or eggs Florentine.

Pour the oatmeal into a large mixing bowl. Bring the milk to a gentle boil in a small saucepan over medium-high heat. Pour the milk over the oatmeal and leave to soak for 10 minutes.

Stir the egg, all the chopped herbs, salt and pepper into the oatmeal mixture, blending well. Melt 2 tablespoons (30 mL) of the butter in a skillet over medium-high heat. Add the shallots and onion and cook gently, stirring frequently, until softened, but not browned, about 3–4 minutes. Cool slightly and then stir the onion mixture into the oatmeal mixture.

Preheat the oven to warm. Wipe the skillet clean, and then melt the remaining butter in it over medium-high heat. Use 2 tablespoons (30 mL) of the oatmeal mixture per pancake, dropping the batter into the skillet to form small pancakes. Cook, turning once, until the pancakes are golden brown, about 1–2 minutes altogether. Transfer to a large plate and keep warm in the oven before serving as described above.

1 1/2 cups (375 mL) old-fashioned rolled oats (not quick-cooking oatmeal)

1/2 cup (125 mL) whole milk

1 egg

1 tbsp. (15 mL) chopped fresh flat-leaf parsley

1 tbsp. (15 mL) chopped fresh cilantro

1 tbsp. (15 mL) chopped fresh chervil

1 tbsp. (15 mL) chopped fresh tarragon

1 tbsp. (15 mL) chopped fresh dill

1 tbsp. (15 mL) chopped fresh chives

sea salt and freshly ground black pepper to taste

1/4 cup (60 mL) unsalted butter

2 small shallots, minced

1 small white onion, finely chopped

Scotland's Breakfast Baps

Makes about 12 baps

Floury and flattish white baps, which are soft-crusted rolls, are popular all over Scotland. While they are traditionally served warm at breakfast, I think they are terrific at lunch filled with good ham, smoked salmon or sharp Cheddar and chutney.

2 1/2 tsp. (22 mL) active dry yeast

1/2 tsp. (2 mL) granulated sugar

1 3/4 cups (425 mL) mixture of half milk, half water, heated to lukewarm

4–4 3/4 (1 L–1175 mL) unbleached bread or all-purpose flour

1 1/2 tbsp. (20 mL) sea salt

1/4 cup (60 mL) lard or vegetable shortening

milk for brushing

unbleached white bread or all-purpose flour for dusting

Add the yeast and sugar to a measuring cup and pour in about 2 tablespoons of the lukewarm milk and water mixture. Set aside for about 10 minutes until foamy. Combine the 4 cups (1 L) of flour and salt in a large mixing bowl. Use your fingers to blend in the lard or shortening as if making pastry, until the mixture resembles fine breadcrumbs.

Make a well in the centre of the dry ingredients. Add the yeast mixture and the remaining milk and water mixture to the well and mix in with the flour to form a soft dough. Add the remaining flour a little at a time just until the dough is smooth and loses its stickiness. Turn out onto a lightly floured surface and knead for 10 minutes or until it is smooth and soft, adding a little more of the remaining flour if necessary to prevent any stickiness. Wipe clean the mixing bowl and lightly butter it. Place the ball of dough in the bowl and turn it over once or twice to cover it lightly with the butter. Cover with a clean tea towel and leave to rise in a warm place for about an hour until it is doubled in size. (If you prefer, let it rise overnight refrigerated and continue with instructions in the morning.)

Punch down the dough and turn out onto a lightly floured surface. Knead just a few times, then roll the dough into a long sausage length and divide it into 12 equal pieces. Lightly butter two baking sheets, and then lightly flour your hands. Form each piece of dough into a little oval shape. Place well spaced apart on the baking sheets (6 per sheet). Brush with a little milk and dust with flour. Set them in a warm place to rise, uncovered, for about 30 minutes, no longer. Preheat oven to 425F (220C). Dust again with white flour. Then, to prevent the dough from blistering and to help it stay flattish, use your thumb to make an indentation in the centre of each bap. Bake for 15–20 minutes until lightly golden. Transfer to a rack to cool slightly before serving warm.

Craigmill Brewery, Strathaven

This very traditional brewery is situated in an eighteenth-century water mill on the bank of the River Avon, near Glasgow. Craigmill specializes in historic Scottish ales based on ingredients indigenous to Scotland for thousands of years, such as seaweed, heather, spruce, pine and gooseberries. Their family of "historic ales of Scotland" includes:

• Grozet (the old Scottish name for gooseberries), a wheat ale that has gooseberries added during the second fermentation; another very old ingredient in this beer, one that adds a distinct dryness, is bog myrtle;

• Alba (Gaelic for Scotland), a strong ale infused with young pine sprigs and spruce shoots;

• Ebulum, an elderberry black ale;

• Kelpie, a seaweed ale; and

• Fraoch, a heather ale. Heather ale has been brewed in Scotland since 2000 BC, making it probably the oldest style of ale still produced in the world. Flowering heather tips are added during the boil that also includes malted barley and sweet gale. Then the hot ale is poured back into the hop over more fresh heather flowers to infuse before fermentation. This light amber ale with a floral-peaty aroma has a spice-herb flavour and a finish not unlike an herbaceous Sauvignon Blanc.

Gaelic Pratie Oaten

Makes 12 little "cakes"

Pratie is the Irish word for potatoes and, in this recipe they are dry mashed (without butter or milk) before being combined with rolled oats and butter. These are wonderful slathered with butter for breakfast.

2 cups (500 mL) warm,
   dry-mashed potatoes
1/4 cup (60 mL) unbleached
   bread or all-purpose flour
3/4 cup (175 mL) old-fashioned
   rolled oats
1/2 tsp. (2 mL) sea salt
1/2 cup (125 mL) melted
   unsalted butter

Combine the mashed potatoes with the flour, all but 1 tablespoon (15 mL) of the oats and the salt. Using your hands, work the mixture together to form a soft dough. Add the melted butter to the dough and blend it in. (If the dough seems too sticky or dry, add a little more flour or butter as required.)

Preheat the oven to 375F (190C). Scatter the remaining oats on a dry surface and roll out the dough about 1/4-inch (5-mm) thick (or as thin as you can).

Using a biscuit cutter cut out rounds of the dough and transfer them to a baking sheet covered with parchment paper. Bake for about 20 minutes, checking now and then to see that they are not browning too quickly. When they are crisp and lightly browned, remove from the oven and let cool on the baking sheet for a few minutes before transferring to a cooling rack with a metal spatula.

CARRICKFERGUS WHEATEN BREAD

Makes 1 loaf

I have named this simple-to-make bread after the place where my dad was born. Carrickfergus is a lovely little town not far from Belfast. We stopped there to admire the beautiful, and completely intact, castle before heading into a little tearoom where we shared a pot of tea and this good bread with Irish ham. I have added a bit of bran to replicate Irish whole wheat flour, which is not milled as finely as the whole wheat in North America. This is for all those cooks who think making bread is too time-consuming.

Preheat oven to 400F (200C). Generously butter a 9x5-inch (2-L) loaf pan. Combine all the dry ingredients in a large mixing bowl. Mix together well and stir in the buttermilk to make a thick, wettish batter. Pour this mixture into the prepared pan.

Bake for 1 to 1 1/2 hours or until well browned and crusty on the top. Turn it out and tap the bottom to make sure it sounds hollow. Then transfer to a rack to cool.

2 1/2 cups (625 mL) whole wheat flour
1 cup (250 mL) unbleached bread or all-purpose flour
1/4 cup (60 mL) bran
2 tsp. (10 mL) baking soda
1 tsp. (5 mL) cream of tartar
1 tbsp. (15 mL) dark brown sugar
1 3/4–2 cups (425–500 mL) buttermilk

CHAPTER 3

OF THE DAIRY & LARDER

Did you ever eat colcannon

when 'twas made with yellow cream,

And the kale and praties blended

like the picture in a dream?

Did you ever take a forkful

and dip it in the lake

Of clover-flavoured butter

that your mother used to make?

– From an old folk song

Flying over any one of the countries mentioned in this book will instantly tell you why the dairy products from these cultures with their collectively green and pleasant lands are so renowned. The naturally lush, green carpets common to all provide the backdrop and the fodder for cows, sheep and goats whose milk — to paraphrase a cheese-loving gastronome — goes on to achieve immortality. Many of the farmhouse and artisanal cheeses in Ireland, Wales and Spain are made by small producers with their own dairy herds. Production may be limited, but that is precisely why many of the cheeses are as unique as they are.

Northern Spain, from Galicia in the west to the Pyrenees in the Catalan Region by the Mediterranean Sea, is known as "green Spain." The climate is cool and quite rainy, conditions that help to foster the bucolic, cultivated meadows and natural pastures, whether high in the mountains or down in the valleys. Each area lends its own distinctive characteristics to its products, which gives Spain countless variations on one particular cheese theme, if you will. The common ingredient to all these northern Spanish cheeses, however, is cow's milk.

Ireland's cheese-making tradition is far more relevant to the entire world of cheese than is commonly known. Dairy products were known as *banbidh* or white meats, an indication of how importantly they featured in the Irish diet. Fresh milk, sour milk and buttermilk, cream, butter, curds and cheese all came from the rich Irish cow's milk. But sheep's milk cheese and products from goat's milk were also prized.

For centuries, the Irish were considered among the world's great cheesemakers. It is said that when they set up monasteries on the Continent, Irish monks taught the French how to make cheese. From the seventh century, the monasteries in Ireland were esteemed cultural and learning centres. The Irish monks who founded one such monastery in Germany's Münster valley in 668 are also thought to be responsible for the development of that region's famous cheese of the same name. Today, Ireland has more than 170 artisanal farmhouse cheeses with their own association — Cashel Blue, Gubbeen,

Ardrahan, Milleen, to name just a few of the many that are produced throughout the country. Wales, too, is renowned today for much more than Caerphilly.

The varied and award-winning artisanal cheeses from Ireland, Wales, Spain, Brittany and Scotland are an important part of their history, culture and diet. Whether on their own or in concert with other dairy products — sweet milk, buttermilk, butter and a rich assortment of creams — they form the basis for an eclectic range of dishes, both sweet and savoury.

Raclette Bacon & Potato Cake

Tetilla & Potato Tortilla with Chorizo

Chevre in Prosciutto-wrapped Figs with Irish Wildflower Honey Drizzle

Cashel Blue Puffy Omelet

Scots Eggs

Pear, Cashel Blue & Endive Salad with Walnuts

Poached Eggs with Mushrooms on Toasted *Pain de Campagne*

Anglesey Eggs

Glamorgan Sausages with Onion Chutney

Double-baked Dubliner Soufflé

Gower Peninsula Piperade with Cockles

Fromage Blanc with Fresh Herbs

Sticky Onion Tart with Teifi Valley Cheese

Cheddar Buck Rabbit with Back Bacon

Raclette Bacon & Potato Cake

Ted's Choice A strong ale such as Bière Bretonne Lancelot. This is a non-filtered, non-pasteurized beer with second fermentation within the bottle, resulting in a naturally carbonated, full-flavoured malty ale.

Makes 4–6 servings

Shopping for provisions in the town near our little cottage in Brittany meant visiting the one and only grocery store – the Super U. Ted would get lost in the beer, wine and cider aisle while I tried to restrain myself from buying every dairy product in the store. This rich dish is a combination of a number of things that I brought home one day that were just too good to resist: *fromage à raclette, pomme de terre primeur* and hand-sliced gently smoked bacon. Raclette is the cheese commonly used in the dish of the same name that features the cheese melted over boiled potatoes. All this needs is a well-dressed salad that contains some bitter greens and good crusty bread.

2 ¹/₂ lbs. (1.25 kg) Yukon Gold
  potatoes
1 tbsp. (15 mL) olive oil
¹/₂ lb. (225 g) good-quality
  bacon, thinly sliced
12-oz. (350-g) piece raclette,
  shredded
freshly ground black pepper

Peel the potatoes and place them in cold water for 15 minutes or so. Pat them dry and slice thinly. Place the slices in fresh cold water for another 5 minutes. Pat them thoroughly dry.

Preheat oven to 425F (220C). Use the olive oil to grease the bottom and sides of an oval or round 9-inch (23-cm) baking dish. Arrange the slices of bacon on the bottom and sides of the dish, in a spiral fashion, allowing a little more than half the length of each slice to hang over the side.

Use one-third of the potato slices to cover the bacon in the dish and sprinkle with one-third of the cheese. Repeat this procedure with remaining potatoes and cheese. Use the overhanging bacon to cover the tops of the potatoes. (Potatoes should be exposed in the centre.)

Bake the dish for about 55 minutes, until the bacon is cooked and potatoes are tender and golden. Remove from the oven and let sit for 15 minutes before seasoning with pepper and serving.

Breton Beer

Brittany lies north of France's wine belt, so well-wrought cider, its derivatives and locally made draught beer prevail and are of much more significance here than wine, perhaps the only place in France where this is true. The beer comes in two styles — *blonde* or *brun*. However, in the extreme south of Brittany, near Nantes at the head of the estuary of the Loire, the dry, fruity Muscadet (from *muscade*, meaning "nutmeg") is often paired with the local seafood. Some wine grapes are grown in the area of Brittany's Rhuys peninsula, but even the Bretons are critical of it. If you want to drink it, they say, you will need four strong men and a stone wall: one man to pour it, one to drink it, two to hold onto him and the stone wall to prevent him from backing away.

Tetilla & Potato Tortilla with Chorizo

Ted's Choice A fresh fruity red from Valdeorras D.O., the easternmost wine region of Galicia.

Makes 4 servings

Tetilla is a Galician cheese with an ultrasmooth texture and mild, buttery flavour. As the name suggests, the shape is not unlike a woman's breast, which rather makes sense because when I was in Galicia, a shopkeeper told me this cheese is traditionally made only by the women in a fishing village whose menfolk are away at sea. Tetilla makes this Spanish potato and sausage omelet spectacular. Enjoy the tortilla in small pieces, tapas-style, just warm or at room temperature. Don't be alarmed by the quantity of olive oil used in this dish; it is quite traditional and once you taste the results you'll understand why potato tortilla is so revered all over Spain. A true tortilla is flipped over once one side is cooked, to cook the other side. However, because of the cheese, I have opted to finish the cooking beneath a hot broiler.

3/4 cup (175 mL) approx. olive oil, preferably Spanish

8 oz. (225 g) chorizo sausages, thinly sliced

1 lb. (500 g) waxy potatoes, peeled, thinly sliced (1/8-inch/3-mm)

1 large onion, thinly sliced

6 eggs

pinch of saffron combined with 1 tbsp. (15 mL) boiling water

8 oz. (225 g) Tetilla, finely diced

Heat 1 tablespoon (15 mL) of the olive oil in a 9-inch (23-cm) heavy-based skillet. Add the chorizo and cook over medium heat for about 5 minutes until browned. Remove from the pan with a slotted spoon and drain on paper towels. Let cool.

Add the remaining oil to the skillet and place over medium heat. When the oil is heated (not smoking), add potato and onion slices, alternately, and cook for about 10 minutes, turning the potatoes and onions over now and then. When the potatoes are tender, pour the contents of the pan into a colander set over a bowl. Return 2 tablespoons (30 mL) of the oil to the pan (reserve the remaining oil to use for frying potatoes or other vegetables). Cool the potato and onion mixture.

Crack the eggs into a mixing bowl along with the saffron mixture. Season with salt and pepper and whisk together. Add the cooled potato mixture and chorizo slices and stir gently to make sure everything is well coated with egg. Let stand at room temperature for 5 minutes.

Preheat broiler to high. Heat the skillet containing the 2 tablespoons of oil over high heat. When the pan is hot (just before it smokes), add the egg mixture. Reduce heat to medium and cook the egg mixture until it is beginning to set around the edges, reduce heat, and then continue to cook until it is almost set and brown on the bottom. Sprinkle the diced cheese evenly over the surface of the tortilla, then slip beneath the broiler to melt the cheese and cook the surface of the tortilla, about 3 minutes.

Let the tortilla sit for about 15 minutes before transferring to a plate. Serve cut into thin wedges or squares.

Chèvre in Prosciutto-wrapped Figs with Irish Wildflower Honey Drizzle

Ted's Choice A Sauvignon Blanc from either Sancerre or Pouilly-Fumé.

Makes 4 servings

About 12 miles outside Belfast is Bangor, a little seaside commuter town offering golf, yacht clubs and the largest marina in Ireland. Blackwood Golf Centre has as its signature restaurant, Shanks, arguably the finest restaurant experience in Ireland. Robbie Millar is the chef and owner and he is scrupulous about sourcing and using the best of local food products with great integrity. Every plate shines with his creativity. The following recipe is inspired by a starter that I enjoyed immensely at the beginning of what was to be a wonderful evening at Shanks. If you like, toss some arugula with a simple vinaigrette as a foundation for the stuffed figs, once they are ready to serve.

½ cup (125 mL) warmed wildflower honey (any fragrant floral honey may be used)

8 large ripe purple-black mission figs

8 oz. (250 g) chèvre

extra virgin olive oil for brushing

8 slices prosciutto

Preheat oven to 425F (220C). Slice stems off the figs and cut each fig ¾ of the way through the centre lengthwise. Drizzle a little of the honey into the centre of each fig, and then place a piece of goat's cheese in the cavity. Brush each fig with a bit of olive oil. Using tongs, place the figs on a parchment-covered baking sheet and transfer to the oven for about 6 minutes or until the cheese is warmed through and beginning to colour. Remove from oven.

To serve: place two figs on a serving plate, loosely arrange the prosciutto around each and drizzle the figs and the plate with the warmed honey.

Crowdie & Cranachan

Crowdie is a fresh soft-curd cheese that was used primarily as a breakfast food by the Scots in years past. Made for centuries in Highland crofts by souring milk naturally, this is a traditional method that lends the cheese a light, lemony taste. Today, many chefs make their own crowdie and use it in sweet and savoury dishes. Crowdie is also the central ingredient in the dessert called cranachan, where it is combined with oatmeal, heather honey and fresh raspberries.

Cashel Blue Puffy Omelet

Ted's Choice A light, fruity red Beaujolais or Champagne.

Makes 1

You can, of course, use any good blue cheese to make this individual omelet, sort of a cross between an oven-baked soufflé and a classic omelet. However, Ireland's famed Cashel Blue cheese, the original farmhouse blue, boasts the finest combination of salty tang and creamy softness that I've ever tasted in a blue cheese. Firm and nicely sharp when young, it softens and even becomes a little runny as it ripens, developing a rich, creamy spiciness. A thoroughly great cheese.

Serve this sumptuous omelet with lots of crusty, thickly sliced hot buttered toast and greens tossed in a mustardy vinaigrette.

3 oz. (80 g) Cashel Blue cheese, crumbled

3 large eggs, at room temperature, separated

1 tbsp. (15 mL) butter

1 tbsp. (15 mL) finely chopped chives or green onion

salt and freshly ground pepper to taste

Preheat the oven broiler. Place a 7-inch (18-cm) frying pan on medium-high heat. Whisk the egg whites in a bowl until soft peaks form; set to one side. Beat the yolks in another bowl and season with salt and pepper. Melt the butter in the hot pan, ensuring it doesn't burn. As it melts, work quickly to fold in the yolks, half of the cheese and all the chives into the egg whites.

At this point the butter should be foaming in the pan. Pour the egg mixture into the hot pan, swirling it around to evenly distribute the mixture. Cook for about 1 minute and then slide a metal spatula around the edge to loosen it from the pan. Scatter the remaining cheese over the surface and then place beneath the broiler about 4 inches (10 cm) from the heat. Cook for about another minute, until it is golden brown in places and the cheese has melted. Remove from the oven and using the metal spatula, carefully loosen it around the edges again and fold one half over the other. Slide it out onto a warm plate and serve immediately.

Ireland's Best Blues

While Cashel Blue is perhaps Ireland's best-known cheese — lovely when accompanied with green or red grapes — the same producer makes Crozier Blue, a cheese derived from ewe's milk and matured for four months. It has a moist and grainy texture with a strong, distinctively rich flavour belying its sheep origins. Wonderful with a piquant chutney or fresh pears, it would also be very good crumbled into peppery greens.

Scots Eggs

Ted's Choice A full-bodied beer with malty richness, such as McEwan's Scotch Ale.
Makes 4

Yes, these are also (mistakenly) called Scotch eggs, but since they contain not a dram of Scotch — and never have — Scots eggs, their true name, it is. These substantial snacks are great with a salad or as part of a ploughman's lunch plate. Ted says they work really well as "soakage" — foods to accompany a night of happy aleing. Quite right, too. Easily doubled. Make sure to hard boil the eggs correctly so their yolks are not discoloured: place in cold water, bring to a rolling boil, let boil for just a minute, remove from the heat, cover and let stand 15–17 minutes. Run under cold water and let sit in the cold water for 5 minutes before shelling and using.

2 tbsp. (30 mL) butter

3 green onions, finely chopped

8 oz. (250 g) lean ground pork or packaged sausage meat

1 tbsp. (15 mL) oat bran or whole wheat flour

1 tbsp. (15 mL) Worcestershire sauce

pinch of nutmeg

salt and freshly ground pepper

4 large eggs, hard-boiled

vegetable oil for deep-frying

1–2 eggs, beaten

1/2 cup (125 mL) approx. dry breadcrumbs

Melt the butter in a skillet and sauté the onions for a few minutes until softened. Allow to cool completely before scraping the contents of the pan into a bowl holding the pork. Add the oat bran or flour, Worcestershire sauce, nutmeg and salt and pepper and mix well to incorporate ingredients. Dry the eggs with a clean tea towel. Lightly flour your hands and, using 1/4 of the pork mixture, shape the meat around the egg, completely enclosing it. Repeat with remaining eggs and meat mixture. Dip the sausage-covered eggs in the beaten egg mixture, and then roll in the breadcrumbs, pressing the coating well onto the eggs. Let the eggs sit at room temperature for 30 minutes to air-dry before frying. Half-fill a deep-fryer or heavy-based pot with oil and heat until a frying thermometer reads 365F (185C).

Deep-fry the eggs until golden brown all over, turning them frequently, for about 6–8 minutes. Drain on paper towels. Let cool before serving warm, at room temperature or chilled.

Feathers Brewpub

When it comes to single malt whiskies from Scotland, Toronto's Feathers Brewpub is the place to go. Boasting well over 200 single malts, Feathers is owned by Edinburgh-born Ian Innes, a man of few words but many malts. His is a real, honest-to-goodness pub with a true-to-spirit atmosphere complete with great service, a happy absence of video machines and seriously good whisky and beer selection. He decided to feature a serious single malt selection early on when his own interest in the subject was stimulated. One of the most attractive things offered by the pub is the monthly single malt tasting evenings. Crowds of 50 or more sign up for these events that include 10 whiskies sharing a common denominator, such as cask strength, a new import or malts from defunct distilleries.

"I call them Whisky Challenges, not so much tastings," points out Ian. "Everyone receives a sheet with the names and descriptions of the whiskies and their designate of Lowland, Highland and Island categories. Participants earn points for correctly identifying each whisky and region. Everybody learns something, tastes some great malts and has a bit of fun."

Pear, Cashel Blue & Endive Salad with Walnuts

Ted's Choice A nutty brown ale such as Newcastle Brown Ale or a strong brown ale like the Belgian Gouden Carolus ("Golden Charles").

Makes 4 servings

If a salad can boast harmony, then this classic combination positively sings. Not only is Cashel Blue a component in the salad, it is also used with great success in the simple dressing that accompanies it. The ripe pears and sharp blue cheese contrast beautifully with the crunch of the sugared walnuts.

1/3 cup (75 mL) extra virgin olive oil

1/2 cup (125 mL) fresh walnut halves

2 tsp. (10 mL) granulated sugar

sea salt and freshly ground black pepper

1/4 lb. (125 g) Cashel Blue cheese

1 tbsp. (15 mL) walnut oil

1/2 tsp. (2 mL) Dijon mustard

3 tsp. white wine vinegar

2 tsp. (10 mL) finely chopped chives

2 large, ripe pears

juice of 1/2 lemon

3–4 Belgian endive

Warm a bit of the olive oil in a small sauté pan set over medium-low heat. Gently sauté the nuts until they become slightly toasted and fragrant — don't let them burn. Add the sugar and stir together to coat the nuts. Keep stirring and tossing the nuts with the sugar until the sugar starts to caramelize the nuts. Add a little salt and pepper to taste and stir again. Transfer to a plate to cool and set to one side.

Using a heaping spoonful of the cheese, make the dressing by mashing the cheese with a fork in a small bowl. Blend in the rest of the olive oil and a little walnut oil (reserve the rest), mustard and vinegar. Taste for seasoning, and then add the chives and blend together. Set to one side.

Core and slice the pears (peel them if you prefer) into a little bowl. Toss together with the lemon juice and reserved walnut oil. Set to one side.

Trim the ends of the endive and slice across the width into thick slices. Add the slices to the reserved dressing and toss together. Arrange on individual salad plates. Place a portion of dressed pears and the remaining crumbled cheese on each, followed by a few walnuts. Serve immediately.

Sheridan's Cheesemonger

There are two shops with this name in Ireland. The original is found in Co. Galway and the other is in Dublin. Brothers Seamus and Kevin Sheridan offer a collection of some of Ireland's best farmhouse cheeses as well as selected European farmhouse cheeses. The shop in Dublin is in the centre of the city and is filled with all manner of great cheeses, salamis, Connemara honey, homemade jams and other farm products.

Poached Eggs with Mushrooms on Toasted Pain de Campagne

Ted's Choice A strong Belgian-style golden ale, such as Duvel, or a darker version of a golden ale, Maudite from Unibroue.

Makes 4 servings

One day in Brittany, Ted and I cycled from our cottage through little villages, by woodland streams, over small stone bridges and along countless country roads. Although we had a substantial backpacked lunch of local cheese, paté, gherkins, good bread and wine, we were starving when we returned, bike-weary and thirsty. This dish proved to be the perfect antidote, simple yet satisfying due to the quality of the local mushrooms and wonderful bread. If you're a dab hand at poaching eggs, you might not want to follow this foolproof method, but it does result in perfect poached eggs. The vinegar helps the whites of fresh eggs to keep their shape and form while poaching.

6 tbsp. (90 mL) white wine vinegar

3 cups (750 mL) water

8 large fresh eggs (free range, if possible)

4 tbsp. (60 mL) olive oil

1 tbsp. (15 mL) butter

Measure 4 tablespoons (60 mL) of the vinegar into the water in a large measuring cup or a bowl with a spout. Break the eggs carefully into this mixture and let sit for 20 minutes or so.

In the meantime, heat a sauté pan with the olive oil and butter. When the butter has melted, add the mushrooms, toss to coat with the oil and butter mixture and give them the odd stir as they cook.

Bring a skillet or shallow pan of water to the boil along with the remaining vinegar and a little salt. Now, reduce the heat to very low. Very carefully drain off almost all the water in which the eggs have been sitting, and then slip them into the hot water in the pan. Poach the eggs for 3–5 minutes. Toast the bread. Season the mushrooms with salt and pepper to taste. Butter the toast. Spoon the mushrooms (and any accumulated juices) over the toast and top with two poached eggs per serving. Add salt and pepper, sprinkle each serving with chives and serve immediately.

1 ¼ lb. (600 g) assorted wild mushrooms, wiped clean and, if large, roughly chopped

4 thick slices of rustic country bread

4 tbsp. (60 mL) butter

sea salt and freshly ground black pepper

4 tbsp. (60 mL) finely chopped chives

Anglesey Eggs

Ted's Choice A traditional farmhouse dry cider.

Makes 4 servings

On the Welsh island of Anglesey, children used to recite a little playground rhyme each year on the Monday before Easter. As they banged wooden clappers they would chant — in Welsh — "Clap, clap, an egg for little boys on the parish . . ." While it may not have much of a ring to it in English, it obviously did in the melodious Welsh tongue. The following dish is one that showcases eggs with the classic Welsh vegetable, leeks. This is a lovely addition to an Easter or early spring brunch. See the recipe for Scots Eggs for the best way to hard boil an egg, page 72.

4 large Yukon Gold potatoes, peeled, halved

3 large leeks, rinsed well, trimmed, thinly sliced

1/4 cup (60 mL) butter

6 large eggs, hard-boiled, quartered

2 1/2 tsp. (22 mL) dry mustard

1/4 cup (60 mL) butter

1/4 cup (60 mL) unbleached all-purpose flour

2 1/2 cups (625 mL) whole milk

4 oz. (125 g) grated Caerphilly or sharp Cheddar cheese

sea salt and freshly ground pepper to taste

Place the potatoes in a medium-sized saucepan, cover with cold water, add a good bit of salt, loosely cover and bring to the boil. Reduce heat and simmer until potatoes are tender, about 15–20 minutes. About 7 minutes before the potatoes are cooked, put the leeks in a steamer and steam over the potatoes, uncovered, for about 6–7 minutes until tender. Transfer the leeks to a clean tea towel and pat dry. Drain potatoes, return saucepan to a very low heat to thoroughly dry them out. Remove from the heat and mash with a potato masher. Add 1/4 cup/60 mL of butter, the mustard and the steamed leeks and beat all the ingredients together until you have created a light, fluffy mass. Season with salt and pepper to taste, cover with a clean tea towel and a lid and set to one side while you prepare the cheese sauce.

Preheat oven to 400F (200C). Melt the remaining 1/4 cup/60 mL of butter in a saucepan over low heat.

Whisk in the flour and let cook for a minute or two; remove from heat if mixture begins to colour. Add milk gradually, whisking in as you do so. Increase heat and cook until mixture comes to a gentle boil and thickens. If too thick, add a little additional milk. Add all but 2 tablespoons/30 mL of the cheese and stir in well to melt. Season with salt and pepper to taste.

Lightly butter a shallow gratin dish. Spoon the potato mixture around the outside. Fill the centre with the quartered eggs. Cover all with the cheese sauce and use rest of the cheese for the top. Bake for 20–25 minutes until golden brown and heated through.

Leeks and the Welsh

Ever wondered why the leek has such a strong association with Wales? According to legend, the country's patron saint, St. David, ordered his soldiers to attach leeks to their battle helmets against the pagan Saxons so they could easily identify one another.

Glamorgan Sausages with Onion Chutney

Ted's Choice Felinfoel Brewery's Double Dragon Ale.

Makes 4 servings

Not sausages in the strict sense, these savoury, sausage-shaped cheese fritters were traditionally based on a Welsh sheep's cheese called Glamorgan. No one seems to produce that lovely old cheese any longer, so these days pubs and home cooks use either the more readily available Caerphilly or a sharp Cheddar. Just keep in mind that you need a big-flavoured cheese that becomes creamy and rich when melted. Store any remaining chutney in a glass jar with a non-reactive lid and keep refrigerated.

For the chutney:

2 tbsp. (15 mL) butter

2 tbsp. (30 mL) olive oil

1/2 cup (125 mL) granulated
   sugar

5 red onions, peeled, finely
   chopped

1 clove garlic, finely chopped

1/4 cup (60 mL) finely chopped
   ginger root

2 tsp. (10 mL) fresh thyme
   leaves, finely chopped

1/2 tsp. (2 mL) ground cumin

1/2 tsp. (2 mL) ground coriander

pinch ground cloves

1/3 cup (75 mL) sherry vinegar

1/3 cup (75 mL) balsamic vinegar

2 tbsp. (30 mL) red pepper jelly

2/3 cup (150 mL) dry red wine

sea salt and freshly ground
   pepper to taste

In a large saucepan, melt the butter with the olive oil over low heat. Add the sugar and stir to dissolve completely. Add the onions all at once and stir to coat with the butter and sugar mixture. Add the garlic, ginger, thyme, cumin, coriander and cloves, mix together well and cook until onions are quite soft, 15–20 minutes. Add the vinegars, red pepper jelly and wine and work into the onion mixture. Continue to cook at a simmer for another 20 minutes or so, until mixture is thickened. Season with salt and pepper. Let mixture cool before using.

In a mixing bowl, combine the cheese, onions, parsley, thyme, dry mustard and salt and pepper. Mix together well then add the fresh breadcrumbs and egg yolks. Blend together, adding a little milk, if necessary, if mixture is too dry. Beat egg whites until light and frothy. Form the cheese mixture into sausage shapes. Dip each in flour, shaking off the excess, then into the beaten egg whites and finally the breadcrumbs. Repeat until all the cheese mixture has been shaped. Heat enough oil to shallow-fry the sausages in a large skillet placed over medium-high heat. Fry the sausages for 5–7 minutes, turning occasionally, until crisp and golden brown on all sides. Serve with the onion chutney.

For the sausages:

8 oz. (250 g) grated Caerphilly, Cheshire or sharp Cheddar

3 green onions, white part only, roughly chopped (reserve the green part for salads, etc.)

3 tbsp. (45 mL) finely chopped flat-leaf parsley

1 tbsp. (15 mL) fresh thyme leaves, finely chopped

1 1/2 tsp. (7 mL) dry mustard

sea salt and freshly ground pepper to taste

1 cup (250 mL) fresh breadcrumbs

3 large eggs, separated

milk, as needed

flour, as needed

1 1/2 cups (375 mL) fine dry breadcrumbs

vegetable oil for frying

Felinfoel Brewery

This Welsh brewery is the oldest in the country, famous for its Double Dragon, the "national ale of Wales." Although it started out as an inn producing its own beer, the popularity of what became known as Felinfoel beer eventually led to the beer being produced for other inns in the area. Because of its connections with the tin-plate industry, Felinfoel was the first brewery in the UK to offer beer in conical cans sealed with a standard crown seal in 1935. Double Dragon – sold under the name Welsh Ale in North America – is a malty bitter with an aroma of apples and a sharp, crisp taste.

DOUBLE-BAKED DUBLINER SOUFFLÉ

Ted's Choice A wheat beer such as Maeve's Crystal Beer from the Dublin Brewing Company.

Makes 8 servings

We loved the individual cheese soufflés we were served in a pub just outside Dublin in Co. Wicklow where we stopped for lunch. I thought they were based on good Cheddar until our server told us about Dubliner Irish cheese. Similar to Cheddar, creamy, gold-toned Dubliner is Irish cheese at its best. Ask for it at a reputable cheesemonger and, if the shop doesn't have it, ask for any Irish (or Scottish) Cheddar. Serve these make-ahead soufflés with a sprightly, well-dressed green salad and sweet little ripe tomatoes. You will need 8 ceramic ramekins, sprayed with a little non-stick cooking spray, for this recipe.

1/4 cup (60 mL) butter

1/4 cup (60 mL) unbleached all-purpose flour

1 3/4 cups (425 mL) whole milk

1/2 cup (125 mL) grated Dubliner cheese

5 large eggs, separated (egg whites should be at room temperature)

1 tbsp. (15 mL) dry mustard

sea salt and freshly ground pepper to taste

1 1/4 cups (310 mL) whipping cream, approx.

1/3 cup (75 mL) grated Dubliner cheese

Preheat oven to 375F (190C). In a saucepan, melt the butter over medium heat, whisk in the flour and cook for a few minutes before gradually whisking in the milk. Bring to a gentle boil, whisking all the while, until mixture thickens, about 3–5 minutes. Remove from the heat and allow to cool a little. Stir in the cheese, egg yolks, mustard and a little salt and pepper. Blend together well.

In a separate bowl, whip the egg whites until stiff. Gently fold the egg whites into the yolk mixture, and then evenly distribute the mixture among the ramekins. Place the ramekins in an ovenproof dish or roasting pan. Pull out the oven rack and place the dish or pan on it. Carefully pour in just enough water to come halfway up the sides of the ramekins. Slide the rack back into the oven and bake the soufflés for 20 minutes when they should be puffed up and golden brown.

Pear, Cashel Blue & Endive Salad
with Walnuts — Page 74

Remove from the oven to cool and fall slightly. When cool, run a knife around the edge of each soufflé and turn out onto a baking sheet lined with parchment paper. (You may cover loosely with plastic wrap and refrigerate, or freeze, at this stage if you wish.)

When needed, preheat oven to 425F (220C). Pour a little cream over each, sprinkle with the remaining cheese and reheat in the oven for 5–7 minutes, a little longer if soufflés are frozen, about 10 minutes.

Dublin Brewing Company

We like to think of the Dublin Brewing Company as David to the giant that is Guinness (Uncle Arthur as the brewing conglomerate is nicknamed). This small craft brewery is very much a hands-on facility, founded in 1996 and situated in historic Smithfield Market, an area with a long history of brewing and distilling. Even more significant is the fact that the D.B.C. is directly across the River Liffey from Guinness, not the first time that Guinness has had any competition; at one time, towards the end of the eighteenth century, there were 12 breweries in operation along Dublin's river, producing a host of different beers. There is a long, well-documented history involving Guinness using its strength and power to buy up competitors right, left and centre until they effectively dominated the industry, which makes the success of D.B.C. all the more significant. Born in Scotland, Canadian Liam McKenna was chosen from eight hundred applicants to become the new brewmaster for the company. While McKenna was there, the company inaugurated Beckett's Gold, a honey-amber brew, aromatic and refreshing; the rich, red-hued 1798 Revolution Ale, brewed with roasted barley and two types of crystal malt; Maeve's Crystal Wheat, a light ale; and the renowned D'Arcy's Dublin Stout, a terrific ale that won Best Stout and Best Overall Product in Ireland at the 1998 Stockholm Beer Festival. A newer member of the D.B.C. family is Wicked Apple Organic Cider, a medium-dry cider, with a tart, cleansing quality. At the time of writing, McKenna is a consultant to the Canadian brewing industry.

Gower Peninsula Piperade with Cockles

Ted's Choice A fresh-tasting Albariño from Galicia or Portuguese Alvarinho.

Makes 4 servings

In Brittany's fishing port of Guilvinec, fishermen offer wicker baskets filled with all manner of wonderful things from the sea — fresh fish like skate and sardines, fat, pink langoustines, crabs, lobster, cockles, oysters and scallops. Inspired by the wealth of seafood, I made this dish for supper using fresh cockles, a bivalve that has always been popular with the Irish. The lovely old song about Dublin's Molly Malone, the world's best-known fishmonger, sings its praises. This dish is actually more Spanish than it is French, yet it is on the menu in the award-winning Fairyhill Hotel and Restaurant located in the Gower Peninsula in Wales. Popular in each place, it can be made using fresh cockles or clams, langoustines (prawns), shrimp, bits of lobster tail or just about any shellfish at all. In Spain it is more likely to include chorizo or ham. Most supermarkets carry small glass jars of imported English double cream. If you can't find it, use whipping cream, although the dish won't be quite so creamy. Serve with a watercress and fresh fennel salad dressed with lemon juice and olive oil.

4 thick slices rustic bread

2 cloves of garlic, halved

1/2 cup (125 mL) olive oil, approx.

8 eggs

2/3 cup (150 mL) double cream

sea salt and freshly ground black pepper

1 red bell pepper, roasted, cut into strips

1 yellow bell pepper, roasted, cut into strips

Rub the bread with the cloves of garlic. Heat olive oil in a skillet and when hot, fry the bread on both sides until golden brown. Transfer the bread to paper towels to drain well. Keep warm. Break eggs into a mixing bowl and whisk together with the double cream, salt and pepper. Pour off most of the olive oil in the pan (reserve for another use). Add all but four pepper strips to the pan (reserving for garnish), add the egg mixture and gently start to scramble the eggs with the peppers. When half cooked, add the cockles (or clams or shrimp), and cook a little longer until the eggs are cooked but the mixture is still creamy and moist and the seafood is cooked, just a few minutes.

To serve: place a piece of bread on each of four warmed plates, top with egg mixture, sprinkle each with the chives and garnish with reserved peppers.

1/2 cup (125 mL) cockles
   (or equivalent amount of clams
   or chopped shrimp)
1/4 cup (60 mL) finely chopped
   chives

Talisker

Robert Louis Stevenson called Isle of Skye's Talisker single malt "king o' drinks," an apt description for this whisky born on the west coast of Skye. This is MacLeod territory and at one time the head of the clan, the laird of Dunvegan Castle, received whisky in lieu of rent from the distillery. There are still members of this clan working at the distillery today. Because of its proximity to the sea, Talisker has a seaweedy, peppery, peaty flavour. Interesting to note that a vatted malt (a blend of single malt whiskies of different ages, either from the same or different distillery) called Poit Dubh (named after the "black pots" in which illicit whisky was once made) from Skye has a Talisker component, as does Te Bheag, another lovely blended whisky from Skye.

Fromage Blanc with Fresh Herbs

Ted's Choice A dry Rosé — Rosado — from Spain.

Makes 4 servings

You can approximate the lovely taste of simple fresh young cheese known in Brittany and throughout France as *fromage blanc* by combining readily available cottage cheese and a few other easily obtainable ingredients. I've also made it with well-drained ricotta. Look for the block-style cottage cheese, sold wrapped in wax paper and plastic, not the tub variety. Vary the fresh herbs as you wish. This is lovely on a hot summer day with cold ham, fresh-picked greens, ripe tomatoes and a bit of balsamic vinegar for the cheese.

1 lb. (500 g) solid cottage
   cheese, drained if necessary
1 cup (500 mL) sour cream
1 large clove garlic, very finely
   minced
2 tbsp. (30 mL) finely chopped
   chives
3 tbsp. (45 mL) finely chopped
   parsley
2 tbsp. (30 mL) finely chopped
   chervil
1 tbsp. (15 mL) finely chopped
   dill
sea salt and freshly ground white
   pepper to taste
sliced baguette

Combine all the ingredients, except the baguette, and blend together thoroughly. Spread out on a sheet of wax paper or plastic wrap and roll into a fat, sausage shape. Chill thoroughly before serving with slices of baguette.

Whisk(e)y & Cheese

Everyone knows about the happy relationship between fine wine and great cheese, but great single malt whisky also has a lot to offer towards the enjoyment of good cheese. Depending on the malt (in this case, Scotch and Irish) and the cheese (we found hard and semi-hard cheeses to be most accommodating with whisky), this partnership can be exceptionally harmonious. Try some of these couplings:

- Manchego with Ardbeg or Bruichladdich
- Sharp Cheddar with Linkwood, Balvenie (Portwood) or Redbreast
- Parmigiano-Reggiano with Glenkinchie or Longmorn
- Cashel Blue with Bushmills Single Irish Malt Whiskey

Sticky Onion Tart with Teifi Valley Cheese

Ted's Choice An amber-toned beer such as the Best Bitter from the Welsh Tomos Watkin Brewery.
Makes 4–6 servings

From the Association of Welsh Cheesemakers, this recipe, which could be thought of as an onion *tarte tatin*, features the Gouda-like Teifi cheese combined with slow-cooked onions. If you can't obtain Welsh cheese, use a good-quality Gouda. It's the quality of the milk from this verdant region that makes the cheese so good.

2 tsp. (10 mL) butter

1/4 cup (60 mL) butter

3/4 cup (150 mL) granulated
  sugar

2 large red onions, sliced

3 cloves garlic, thinly sliced

sea salt and freshly ground black
  pepper

2 tbsp. (30 mL) balsamic or
  sherry vinegar

1/2 pkg. frozen puff pastry,
  thawed

8 oz. (250 g) Teifi or Gouda
  cheese, sliced

to serve: freshly ground black
  pepper, finely chopped parsley

 Preheat oven to 425F (220C). Use the 2 teaspoons of butter to grease an 8-inch (20-cm) cake pan.

In a large sauté pan, combine the remaining butter with the sugar over medium heat, stirring to dissolve the sugar completely. Add the vinegar and stir into the sugar mixture. Add the onions and garlic to the sugar mixture, allowing them to sit atop the mixture. Increase heat slightly, place a lid on the pan and allow onions to cook until slightly caramelized on the bottom. Remove from the heat and cool slightly.

Lightly dust a work area and roll out the pastry to make a circle large enough to cover the base of the cake pan. Use a spatula to scrape the onion mixture over the base of the buttered cake pan. Top with the pastry, tucking down the edge all around. Bake in the oven for 25 minutes or until pastry is puffed and golden. Remove from the oven and invert onto a baking tray. Preheat broiler. Arrange the slices of cheese over the surface and place beneath the hot broiler until the cheese is golden brown. Sprinkle with freshly ground black pepper and a bit of chopped parsley and serve.

Le Gallois – Y Cymro

Padrig Jones is the head chef of Le Gallois – Y Cymro in Cardiff, his hometown. After working with superstar chef Marco Pierre White in London, Jones returned home and joined forces with his caterer sister Elen to open this dining room, which features some of the finest cooking in Wales. The name of the restaurant translates as "Welshman" in French (and in Welsh). Jones says the menu reflects both cultures and leans towards modern European, so you'll find the likes of roasted foie gras with rhubarb relish, caramelized scallops with glazed pork belly, double rib of Welsh lamb with cassoulet of French beans and wild garlic and local venison with celeriac *dauphinoise*. In addition to wonderful sweets (mango *tarte tatin*, a carpaccio of blood oranges with carrot and orange sorbet, yum), homemade ices and sorbets, and a selection of Welsh and European cheeses are always on hand. Great wine list, too.

Cheddar Buck Rabbit with Back Bacon

Ted's Choice A dark stout or porter like Propeller's London Porter, from the Propeller Brewery in Halifax, Nova Scotia.

Makes 2 servings

In eighteenth-century Scotland, the word *rabbit* was used in recipes to describe a dish that, in fact, contained no meat at all and *buck* signified that the dish included an egg. Welsh *rabbit* or *rarebit* is another example of a dish eaten when times were a little lean. However, there is nought that is lean about this sumptuous treat for two. If ever there was a dish to help soak up pints of stout, this is it. Make this for yourself and one other fellow pub crawler.

4 oz. (125 g) grated sharp
  Cheddar

2 tbsp. (30 mL) butter

1/4 tsp. (1 mL) dry mustard

pinch of cayenne

1/4 cup (60 mL) stout

sea salt and freshly ground
  pepper to taste

6 slices of back bacon, cooked,
  kept warm

2 large eggs, poached

2 thick slices of rustic country
  bread

Preheat broiler. In a little saucepan, combine the Cheddar, butter, mustard, cayenne and stout and melt together over a low heat, stirring frequently. Season with a little salt and pepper and leave on a very low heat. Poach the eggs as described on page 77. While the eggs are poaching, toast the bread and place on two oven-proof serving plates. Use a slotted spoon to lift the eggs out of the water, drain, and lay on top of the toast. Pour the reserved cheese sauce over the eggs. Place beneath the hot broiler just for a minute until the surface is bubbling and hot. Serve immediately with the bacon.

Bruichladdich Islay Single Malt Whisky

"The lad's back," read the headline in a local Islay newspaper in May 2001, a happy reference to the fact that the famed Bruichladdich (brook-LADDIE) had been reopened. Formerly owned by the American Jim Beam group, the distillery lay closed and quiet since 1994 until a consortium of shareholders put together the necessary funds to bring it back. It's now under the direction of master distiller and Islay native Jim McEwan, twice winner of the "Distiller of the Year" title and the former Chief Distiller at neighbouring Bowmore.

This brings the number of working distilleries on the island to seven: Bowmore, Lagavulin, Ardbeg, Laphroaig, Bunnahabhain and Caol Ila, an astonishing number for such a small island. The valuable old casks that were part of the distillery purchase were then bottled as 10-year-old, 15-year-old and 20-year-old Bruichladdich. A magnificent 30-year-old vintage is available only at the distillery. This is now the only Islay distillery owned and run by a small, singularly Scottish, company. Here is what the company has to say about the 15-year-old: "A real honest old-style whisky flavour is immediately apparent. Lots of sweet malt, digestive biscuits, butterscotch, tropical fruit. Lashings of oak and a sprinkle of sea spray and dry seaweed remind you of the 15 years maturing by the ocean . . . full of style and sophistication, it lingers gently on the palate."

CHAPTER 4

Grains, Greens & Roots

Sublime potatoes! that, from Antrim's shore

To famous Kerry, form the poor man's store;

Agreeing well with every place and state —

The peasant's noggin, or the rich man's plate.

Much prized when smoking from the teeming pot,

Or in turf embers roasted crisp and hot.

Welcome, companion to flesh, fowl or fish;

But to the real gourmands, the learned few,

Most welcome, steaming in an Irish stew.

– Anon

Oats, barley, rye and buckwheat, cabbages, kale, leeks, onions, beans, carrots, beets, turnips, rutabagas, parsnips and potatoes – the grains, greens and root vegetables related to Celtic lands are rustic and real, life-sustaining stuff. Oats were consumed as porridge, used in baking, in the form of dumplings and savouries, in soups, stews, desserts and beverages. Finely ground oatmeal was even used to coat fresh fish before frying, an inspired bit of cooking that continues to this day as modern chefs cling to the best of the past. Barley was, and is, of course, a vital ingredient in the brewing of ale and whisky, but it was also used in the kitchen in all manner of soups, stews and breads.

More than any other European country, Ireland embraced the potato, cultivating it extensively, as a field crop and staple. Praties, as potatoes were called, were mainly the food of the poor in Ireland. Eventually, potatoes at least partially began to replace oats — on which the people had relied heavily as a staple, especially during those years when the oat harvest was less than expected. The potato was unfussy; it didn't require wonderful soil conditions or special tools, and it absolutely thrived on rain, of which Ireland had plenty. Most importantly, it was nourishing. During the early 1800s, households across Ireland consumed an average of about five pounds (2.3 kg) of potatoes per person a day, constituting 80 percent of their diet. Other famines related to field crops — including the potato — caused hardship and death in Ireland, but nothing came close to the wretched devastation wrought by the three-year blight of *Phytophthora infestans*. Although this deadly fungus struck Spain, France, indeed all of Europe, it devastated Ireland with particular ferocity from one end of the island to the other. This passage is from Mary O'Brien's *The Farm by Lough Gur:*

> It was heart-breaking . . . to see poor people tottering to the door, half-fainting, swaying on their skeleton feet, as they held out little bags for the crust or a spoonful of flour — all we had to give them. One old man was found dead in the turnip garden, too weak to pull it up . . . little children died on the floor of the cabin where they

slipped from the weak arms of their mother . . . it wasn't only star-vation, more died from typhus and other diseases brought about by want, than lack of food. Corn, which came at last, and maize meal, sent from America, saved those who were still alive.

Besides the experiences of my childhood, some of my fondest memories of potato eating came about during our trip to Ireland. There was great pleasure, to be sure, in eating locally grown, fresh-dug potatoes, even in the simplest preparations. But there was something more. For those with Irish roots, eating potatoes in Ireland evokes serious feelings for many reasons. Not the least of these is the impact this simple yet vital food had on the country and, indeed, the world in general. At one time, this vegetable meant the difference between sustenance and starvation for an impoverished people, my people. My dad used to recite something his mother told him: *"The sauce of the poor man is a little potato eaten with the big one,"* a reference to the fact that the poor could only manage to put one food on their table.

So, on our journey from Ulster to Cork, I ate potatoes on average about three times a day, in every conceivable form. In the morning, I would tuck into the famous Ulster Fry with its requisite speckled brown potato bread fried in a bit of bacon fat. I had potatoes in soups or in the form of a big, crusty baker topped with cheese and onions. Great with a good pint. Lunch might bring a glorious tumble of chunky, golden chips with fresh fish. On one occasion, when we stopped for a midday meal at a lovely old pub called Treacy's in Portlaoise, I showed hesitation between chips and "creamed" (mashed) potatoes. Noticing my dilemma, our server said, "How about a little of both, then?" I couldn't have been happier. At dinner in the evening, there they would be again in the form of the most luxurious, satin creamy mash I have ever tasted. As I ate, I thought of the farmers who planted, nurtured and cultivated them, and about my ancestors who may have died for want of them. And I felt grateful for having the experience in the country where they were grown.

Baby Beetroots with Cream & Chives

Breton *Chou Farci*

Char-grilled Potato & Chorizo Salad

Fresh Watercress & Radish Salad

Artichoke & Potato Gratin

Escalivada Tostadas

Celtic Country Peas & Lettuce

Tortilla de Patate

Ballymaloe Mustard Mash

Deane's Char-grilled Asparagus on Toast with Truffle Oil

Colcannon

McCann's Oatie Pilaf

Patrick Guilbaud's Baby Vegetables à la Grecque

Wild Mushrooms with Hazelnuts & Cream

Gaelic Greens with Bacon & Potatoes

Cornish Onion, Parsnip & Potato Cakes

Three-Root Purée

Baby Beetroots with Cream & Chives

Ted's Choice A Lowland malt, such as Bladnoch.

Makes 4 servings

Inspired by a side dish we enjoyed at an old hotel dining room in Brittany, this is an especially good accompaniment to roast pork or chicken. Try it, too, with thick-cut fillets of halibut, tuna or salmon. The vibrant hue of the finished dish provides a startling colour contrast. If you grow your own beets — or beetroot, as this lovely old vegetable is traditionally called — you won't have a problem obtaining baby beets. Look for them at farmers' markets. You could also use larger beets cut into quarters for this dish.

1 lb. (500 g) baby beets, trimmed (leave the root tip intact)

1 small shallot, minced

1 tbsp. (15 mL) butter

1 tbsp. (15 mL) olive oil

juice of 1 small lemon

sea salt and freshly ground pepper to taste

1 cup (250 mL) whipping cream

1/4 cup (60 mL) crème fraîche

1/4 cup (60 mL) finely chopped chives

Bring a large saucepan of water to boil over high heat. When it has come to the boil, add the beets and salt to taste. Reduce heat to medium high and cook the beets until tender, about 30 minutes. While they are cooking, combine the butter and the oil in a skillet (large enough to eventually hold the beets) over medium high heat. Add the shallot and cook gently for a few minutes until softened. Test the beets with the tip of a paring knife to see if they are tender at the centre. Drain and place in cold water for a few minutes. Peel the beets while they are warm and trim if necessary. Transfer beets to the skillet and add lemon juice; toss beets around a bit and season with salt and pepper. Pour the cream into a measuring cup and then blend in the crème fraîche with a fork or whisk. When well blended, slowly add the cream mixture to the beets. Stir it gently into the beet mixture and then allow the beets to cook, over low heat, with the cream for 5 minutes or so, until the cream has

taken on the colour of the beets. Pour everything into a
warmed serving dish, sprinkle with the chives and serve
immediately.

Crème Fraîche

It's easy to make your own crème fraîche if you can't buy it.
Warm 1 cup (250 mL) of whipping cream gently. Remove from
the heat and combine with 2 tablespoons (30 mL) of
buttermilk or sour cream in a glass bowl. Mix well, cover and let
stand at room temperature (the top of your refrigerator is a good
place) overnight. Give it a good stir once it has thickened, cover
and refrigerate until needed. It will continue to thicken once
chilled and will keep well for up to 10 days in the refrigerator.

Bladnoch Lowland Malt Whisky

This distillery takes its name from the River Bladnoch that flows into Solway Firth, right
on the border with England in the southwest region of Scotland. Just like the history of
distilling itself, Bladnoch has Ulster roots. Owner Raymond Armstrong is from Northern
Ireland, and while looking for vacation property he found and bought this distillery that
was mothballed in 1993 by United Distillers. This is the second time the distillery has
had an Ulster connection because long before this, Bladnoch was owned by the
Belfast firm William Dunville & Co. The old farm distillery also operates a Whisky
School where visitors can take part in the process of whisky-making over the course
of three days. The distillery website is www.bladnoch.co.uk.

Breton Chou Farci

Ted's Choice An Irish "red" ale, such as Dublin Brewing's Revolution Red Ale. A red ale is an Irish version of pale ale, less hoppy with malty, buttery, caramel flavours derived from a longer boiling of the wort (the solution of grain sugars strained from the mash tun). Or, try Deanston Single Malt.

Makes 4 servings

Cabbage is a staple of the Celtic kitchen, and it is used in everything from soups and salads to stews and in dishes like this one that features it filled with another favourite food of the Celts — pork. If you prefer, you could also combine the filling ingredients to make traditional cabbage rolls. You will need a square of double-folded cheesecloth large enough to enclose the cabbage completely for this recipe.

1 small Savoy cabbage

1 lb. (500 g) lean ground pork

1/2 cup (125 mL) finely chopped
  mushrooms

2 thin slices wholegrain bread,
  soaked in a little milk

1 tsp. (5 mL) sea salt

freshly ground pepper to taste

1/2 cup (125 mL) finely chopped
  chives

1 egg, lightly beaten

2 tbsp. (30 mL) melted butter

Place a large saucepan of water on to boil over high heat. Pull off and discard any tough outer leaves and cut out and discard as much of the bottom core as you can. When it has come to the boil, plunge the whole cabbage into the water and blanch for about 5–10 minutes or until the leaves begin to separate fairly easily. Then, transfer the blanched cabbage to cold water for a few minutes. Drain and separate the leaves — you will need 10–12 leaves. (If you have remaining cabbage, reserve for another use.) Retain the blanching liquid in the saucepan.

In a mixing bowl, combine the pork with the mushrooms, bread, salt, pepper and chives. Mix together with a fork, then blend in the beaten egg and mix again. If the mixture seems a little dry, add a little of the milk used to soak the bread and mix again.

Spread out the cheesecloth on a work surface. Place two cabbage leaves (curly edge up) in the centre of the cheesecloth and spread a thin layer of the pork mixture over the leaves. Cover with another leaf, add another layer of meat and repeat until the leaves and meat are used, ending with a layer of cabbage. Gather the four corners of the cloth together, twist together, and then tie with kitchen string. (This helps to compact the leaves and keep the round shape.)

Return the saucepan containing the blanching liquid to the heat and bring back to a boil. Add a little salt and lower the wrapped cabbage into the water (there should be enough water to cover the cabbage). Reduce heat and simmer the cabbage, covered, for about 1 hour.

Preheat oven to 400F (200C). Lightly butter a large baking dish. Remove the cabbage from the cheesecloth and place in the dish. Drizzle with butter and place in the oven until it begins to brown lightly over its surface, about 20 minutes or so. Cover with foil if it is beginning to colour too quickly. Serve cut into wedges.

Chef Patrick Jeffroy

One of Brittany's most popular contemporary chefs, Patrick Jeffroy adheres to traditional culinary values while creating his own particular brand of innovative cuisine. His hotel-restaurant in Plounérin, near Morlaix, a river port in Finistére, earned a Michelin star after one year. Now he is the chef in residence at the L'Hotel de Carantec, a lovely inn on the Bay of Morlaix, the perfect venue for a chef renowned for his ways with fresh fish and seafood.

CHAR-GRILLED POTATO & CHORIZO SALAD

Ted's Choice A "fresh" red from Ribeiro D.O., Spain, perhaps labelled "Pazo."

Makes 4–6 servings

A sunny, Spanish dish that works perfectly on a hot summer day, all this grilled salad needs are some cool, ripe tomatoes, buttery lettuce and good, crusty bread to make it complete. Easily doubled.

1 ½ lb. (680 g) small new
   potatoes, scrubbed

½ lb. (250 g) chorizo sausage

4 green onions, trimmed

¼ cup (60 mL) extra virgin olive
   oil

1 tbsp. (15 mL) sherry vinegar

1 tbsp. (15 mL) balsamic vinegar

sea salt and freshly ground
   pepper to taste

¼ cup (60 mL) finely chopped
   basil

Preheat grill to medium-high. Halve the potatoes, place in a saucepan, cover with cold water, add a little salt to taste and bring to the boil. Cook for just 10 minutes, drain, and set to one side to cool.

Slit the sausage in half lengthwise and place in a large bowl. Add the potatoes, and onions and the olive oil. Toss the vegetables and sausage together with the oil to coat thoroughly.

Transfer vegetables and sausage to the grill and cook for 6–15 minutes until vegetables are tender and everything is nicely charred. Brush with a little additional olive oil, if necessary, as everything cooks.

Transfer vegetables and sausage back to the bowl. Snip green onions into pieces with kitchen shears and add to the bowl. Sprinkle vinegars over everything, add salt and pepper to taste and toss together well. Add chopped basil and toss again and serve.

Fresh Watercress & Radish Salad

Ted's Choice With smoked fish, try a wheat beer or a lighter Islay malt like Bunnahabhain "with a hint of Islay peat."

Makes 4 servings

Watercress is not an ingredient generally associated with Spanish cooking and, indeed, it is not popular anywhere in the country except for the northwest coast in Galicia. Here it is used to make unusual — but very good — little *albondigas* or meatballs that, when finished, are always served with this fresh-tasting salad. Ancient watercress, with its small, peppery, iron-rich leaves is grown and enjoyed all over Ireland where, it is believed, it is best to pick that which is found growing beside a spring. This is very good with any smoked fish. Don't trim away all the stem because it has a lovely, flavourful crunch.

Combine all the ingredients for the dressing together in a small mixing bowl. Whisk together well until thickened. Cut through the watercress with a sharp knife once or twice. Combine the watercress in a salad bowl or large mixing bowl with the radishes and onion. Add half of the dressing, toss together well, and then add remaining dressing and repeat. Serve immediately.

For the dressing:

1/4 cup (60 mL) extra virgin olive oil

juice of 1 small lemon

1 egg yolk

1 tsp. (5 mL) wholegrain mustard

1 tbsp. (15 mL) finely chopped flat-leaf parsley

sea salt and freshly ground pepper to taste

For the salad:

2 bunches watercress, washed, dried, trimmed

6 large radishes, very finely sliced

1/2 small red onion, very finely sliced

Artichoke & Potato Gratin

Ted's Choice Artichokes are tough on any wine, but avoid reds at all costs because the chemical known as cynarin in artichokes makes them taste metallic. Go for a nice, clean lager instead.

Makes 6–8 servings

Beautiful artichokes are just one of Brittany's favourite vegetables. The Bretons seem to have a particular way with *artichauts*, often growing them to enormous proportions, larger than any I have seen elsewhere. The following recipe is an approximation of a dish we had in a little restaurant in Morlaix, a town renowned for its busy outdoor market. Besides a wealth of fresh produce, the market offers an incredible array of fresh seafood, including oysters, crabs, scallops, langoustines, sea urchins and endless varieties of fish. You'll need a sizable amount of cooked artichoke hearts for this preparation. If you are unaccustomed to preparing fresh globe artichokes, you may substitute good-quality frozen or jarred artichoke hearts. If using the latter, rinse, drain and dry them well before using. Or try the following method for preparing your own.

1/4 cup (60 mL) olive oil

2 leeks, trimmed, well rinsed, sliced (use all of the white and half of the green portion)

4 large Yukon Gold potatoes, scrubbed, thinly sliced

sea salt and freshly ground pepper to taste

4 cups (1 L) sliced, cooked artichoke hearts

1/4 lb. (125 g) Gruyère cheese, grated

In a large skillet, heat half of the oil over medium-high heat. Sauté the leeks in the oil for about 10 minutes. Add the remaining oil and the sliced potatoes, salt and pepper. Stir to mix the ingredients well and to coat the potatoes with oil. Cover and let cook over low heat for about 10 minutes. Use a metal spatula to flip the potatoes over, and then add the artichokes. Cover and cook for 15–20 minutes until the potatoes are cooked through. Turn the vegetables over again and use the spatula to press down on the potatoes, breaking them up a little as you turn them. Let cook for another minute or so and turn them again, continuing to break them up as you do so. Preheat oven broiler to high.

Distribute the cheese over the top of the vegetables and slip beneath the broiler for about 5 minutes, when the cheese should be melted and golden brown. Serve immediately.

Artichokes — The Heart of the Matter

Slice off any remaining stem to create a flat base. Snap off and discard any tough, outer leaves that may be at the base. Now, cut off the top inch or so of the artichoke and use kitchen shears to snip off the prickly tips of each leaf. Rinse the artichoke well. Use a fresh lemon wedge to rub all the cut surfaces of the artichoke to prevent discolouration. Steam or boil the artichokes in lightly salted water (add the juice of a lemon to the water, too) for 30–40 minutes, depending on their size, or until a leave pulls out easily. Transfer cooked artichokes to paper towels and place them upside down to drain for a few minutes. (The base of each leaf is edible and the best way to eat the leaves is to pull them off, dip them in any accompanying sauce, and draw them through your teeth.) With a spoon, scoop out the pale, small leaves at the bottom and also the fuzzy choke in the centre. Now you have reached the real meat of the artichoke — the heart and bottom.

Escalivada Tostadas

Ted's Choice A chilled Spanish white made from the Albariño grape. This wine has a fresh, crisp, appley flavour, very similar to the *vinho verde* of Portugal, where this grape is called *alvarinho*.

Makes 4–6 servings

When they roast vegetables like this in Spain they call it *escalivada*, a lovely name for this colourful mixture of eggplant, peppers, onions and zucchini that can be roasted in the oven or cooked on an indoor or outdoor grill. Use good extra virgin olive oil — preferably from Spain — for this dish. You can vary this by presenting it in a shallow ceramic bowl as part of an antipasto spread, tossing with pasta or serving over rice.

1 small eggplant, trimmed

1 red bell pepper

1 green bell pepper

1 medium red onion, peeled, quartered

1 zucchini, trimmed, sliced lengthwise

juice of 1 small lemon

1/4 cup (60 mL) extra virgin olive oil

2 tbsp. (30 mL) finely chopped parsley

1 tbsp. (15 mL) finely chopped thyme

sea salt and freshly ground pepper to taste

1 baguette, sliced into 1/2-inch (1-cm) slices

additional extra virgin olive oil for brushing

Preheat oven to 500F (260C). Place the eggplant, peppers, onion and zucchini in a shallow roasting pan. Drizzle over about 2 tablespoons (30 mL) of the olive oil and toss together. Roast in the hot oven for about 20 minutes, turning the vegetables over a couple of times throughout the roasting time. Remove the pan from the oven and let vegetables cool slightly. Reduce oven temperature to 350F (180C). When cool enough to handle, skin the peppers, removing the seeds and core. Peel the eggplant, slice in half and, using a spoon, remove the seeds. Roughly cut the eggplant, peppers, onion and zucchini and transfer to a bowl. Add the remaining olive oil, lemon juice, parsley, thyme, salt and pepper and toss together. Let sit for a few minutes at room temperature to allow flavours to develop.

Place the slices of bread on a baking sheet. Lightly toast in the oven for about 5 minutes in total, turning once. Remove from the oven and lightly brush with a bit of olive oil. Spoon a little of the vegetable mixture on each toast and serve.

Celtic Country Peas & Lettuce

Ted's Choice A mature red burgundy or a Pinot Noir from Oregon.

Makes 4–6 servings

An old-fashioned yet still very popular side dish, this is as likely to be found in Ireland as it is in Brittany or Wales. Nothing in the least sophisticated about this, it's just very good. Best when made with the season's first peas, but small frozen peas will work too.

Discard any discoloured lettuce leaves, and then stack the remaining lettuce leaves in a pile and cut into thin strips. Add the butter to a large skillet or saucepan and melt over medium heat. Add the onions and cook slowly; don't let them brown. Add the peas, lettuce, parsley, salt and pepper and stir together well. Place a round of buttered parchment or wax paper on top of the vegetables, pressing it into place. Cook very slowly for another 10 minutes. Remove the paper and stir in the cream. Let it heat through gently for another minute or so before serving.

1 head butter or Boston lettuce, washed, dried
1/4 cup (60 mL) butter
4 skinny green onions, trimmed, finely chopped
1 lb. (500 g) fresh-shelled peas
1/4 cup (60 mL) finely chopped flat-leaf parsley
sea salt and freshly ground pepper to taste
1/4 cup (60 mL) cream

Tortilla de Patate

Ted's Choice Go for a Manzanilla sherry. Manzanilla is a dry *fino* sherry, with a salty tang from the proximity to the sea. Serve cool in a slender glass (in Spain these are called *copitas*).

Makes 4 servings

We tasted Spain's best potatoes in Galicia, in many different forms but none more appealing than when combined with onions, eggs and good Spanish olive oil. Cut the finished tortilla into little squares and top each with a little bit of roasted red pepper and you've got the perfect *tapa*.

1 medium onion, finely chopped

4 medium Yukon Gold potatoes, peeled, cut into 1/8-inch (2-mm) slices

3/4 cup (175 mL) olive oil, preferably Spanish

1/2 tsp. (2 mL) sea salt

1/2 tsp. (2 mL) freshly ground pepper

5 large eggs

sea salt to taste

1 roasted red bell pepper, chopped

Combine the onion and potatoes in a large bowl. Toss together well. Heat the oil in a heavy 9-inch (22.5-cm) skillet over medium-high heat. Add potato mixture in layers, adding salt and pepper to each layer, until all the potatoes and onion are stacked.

Reduce heat to medium-low. Cook potatoes, turning often, for 15–20 minutes or until tender, watching that they do not brown. Using a slotted spoon, transfer potato mixture to a paper towel–lined plate. Drain, patting with more paper towels. Let cool slightly. Pour the cooking oil into a bowl and set to one side.

Lightly whisk the eggs together with a little salt in a bowl. Add the potatoes and stir well into the egg mixture. Let this sit for about 10 minutes at room temperature.

Wipe skillet clean and replace 1 tablespoon (15 mL) of cooking oil to the skillet. Place over medium heat. When oil is hot, add potato mixture. Cook, shaking skillet occasionally, for about 4 minutes or until tortilla is brown on the bottom.

Place a large round plate upside down over the skillet and flip the tortilla out to turn it over. Slip it back into the skillet and continue to cook, pressing down on it and shaking the skillet, for about another 4 minutes. Transfer to a cutting board and let cool to room temperature. Then, cut into small squares, top each with a bit of roasted pepper and serve.

Spanish Spuds

"The best potatoes in Spain are grown in Galicia. They are called *cachelos* and are very tasty potatoes," says my Spanish-born friend Teresa Barrenechea, chef and author. When I heard those words, I knew I had found yet another Celtic similarity. It made sense to me that the Celtic province of Galicia in northwest Spain would have wonderful potatoes like Ireland, Brittany and Canada's East Coast. The first time I enjoyed these Spanish spuds I was in a restaurant specializing in seafood. Casa Rosita in Cambados, Galicia, served the freshest seafood I have ever eaten. Most memorable for me was *lenguado* — baby sole — simply pan-fried in a little olive oil, spritzed with a bit of lemon and served with a tumble of sweet little potatoes. They were remarkable.

BALLYMALOE MUSTARD MASH

Ted's Choice With any potato dish, an Irish beer is the call. Look for an Irish ale or a Best Bitter.

Makes 6 servings

This is how they make the wonderful, creamy, satin-like mashed potatoes I so enjoyed at Myrtle Allen's lovely Ballymaloe House Hotel in County Cork. Certainly, it doesn't hurt that the potatoes are some of the best in the world, the cream and butter are rich and luxurious and the eggs fresh-laid. Failing those details, you'll still be thrilled with the results. These are the best. In Ireland, they always cook potatoes in their skins and peel them before mashing. I'll leave the question of peeling before or after up to you.

6–8 large Yukon Gold potatoes
sea salt to taste
2/3 cup (150 mL) butter
3/4 cup (175 mL) whipping cream, gently heated until hot
1 extra large egg, beaten
1 1/2 tsp. (7 mL) dry mustard
sea salt and freshly ground white pepper

Peel the potatoes and quarter them (if you are cooking them within their skins, scrub them well before quartering). Place in a large saucepan and just cover with cold water. Stir in a good bit of salt. (Taste the water at this point. You should be able to taste the salt slightly; if not, add a bit more salt.) Cover the saucepan loosely and place on high heat. When the water has just come to the boil, reduce heat to medium, put the lid completely on the saucepan and boil gently for about 20 minutes. Test one of the potatoes with the tip of a paring knife. When the potatoes are tender all the way through, remove them from the heat and drain, keeping them in the saucepan. Return the saucepan to the heat, turning it down as low as possible or off entirely so that you're just using the residual heat in the burner. Shake the saucepan over the burner a few times, until no moisture remains and potatoes are quite dry.

Now, add the butter all at once and mash it well into the potatoes for a few minutes. When potatoes are well mashed, add the hot cream and continue to mash well into the potatoes. Using a wooden spoon or flat whisk, blend in the beaten egg and mustard until no traces of egg or mustard remain and the mass of potatoes is silky and smooth, adding a little more butter or cream to achieve this. Taste and add a little more salt and white pepper if you wish. Serve hot with a bit more butter.

Gilding Seared Salmon

It hardly needs to be said that wonderful salmon needs little in the way of embellishment. But this is a lovely little sauce to use with seared or grilled salmon. Start by pan-searing salmon fillets in a hot skillet, about 3 minutes per side, longer if you prefer. Lightly sauté shallots in a little butter, add about a cup of good fish broth and reduce somewhat. Add a shot glass of whisky, a cup of cream and a spoonful of Dijon mustard. Whisk together to blend and add a spoonful of butter to enrich. Use the recipe on page 110 for Ballymaloe Mustard Mash as a base for the salmon, lightly spoon a little of the sauce over the salmon and top everything with a few frizzled (deep-fried) leeks. Garnish with a little fresh watercress.

Champ

Before I visited Ireland, I was familiar with only one version of champ, the comfort dish of Irish peasant origin so beloved by my dad. Mum would make it for him whenever he'd enjoyed a little too much ale, and at those times she would embellish the original dish somewhat by nestling a halved, soft-boiled egg into the mound of spuds mashed with hot milk and green onions. It would be set before him dusted with salt and white pepper with a lovely knob of butter melting in the centre. These days champ can be found on menus not only in stylish Irish restaurants but also in London, New York and Toronto. And there are numerous regional variations in Ireland — made by combining the potatoes with either parsley, nettles, dulse, chives, peas or leeks.

DEANE'S CHAR-GRILLED ASPARAGUS ON TOAST WITH TRUFFLE OIL

Ted's Choice Wheat beer or a dry white Bordeaux with a blend of Semillon and Sauvignon, or a good Sauvignon Blanc from the Loire Valley.

Makes 2–4 servings

Michael Deane's Belfast restaurant offers a menu that surely is one of the best examples of the new Irish cuisine, combining, as it does, the wonderful local produce and contemporary styles and foods. This preparation is inspired by one dish I had there, sans toast. Choose plump lengths of asparagus for this recipe, which is, by the way, easily increased.

1 lb. (500 g) plump asparagus

2 tbsp. (30 mL) olive oil

1/4 tsp. (1 mL) sea salt

1/4 tsp. (1 mL) freshly ground pepper

1–2 tbsp. (15-30 mL) truffle oil

2–4 thick slices of crusty bread, toasted or grilled, buttered

1/4 lb. (125 g) Parmigiano-Reggiano cheese, at room temperature

Preheat grill to medium high. Snap off the ends of the asparagus by gently bending each stalk (it will naturally break where the best part of the stalk meets the woody bit). Discard the ends or reserve for making stock. Blanch asparagus in boiling, salted water for 30 seconds; drain and transfer to a shallow dish. Drizzle the asparagus with the oil and season with the salt and pepper. Toss all together. Place asparagus in a grill basket and grill over medium-high heat, turning occasionally, for 15–20 minutes or until tender and lightly charred.

Meanwhile, prepare the toast and keep warm. Use a potato peeler to shave the cheese into large pieces. Lay the grilled asparagus over the toast, drizzle with the truffle oil and arrange pieces of cheese over each serving. Serve immediately.

COLCANNON

Ted's Choice How about Big Rock McNally's Extra Ale from Calgary, Alberta. (Ed McNally's forebears left Ireland during the potato famine.)

Makes 4–6 servings

Colcannon is a traditional dish from Ireland that was always served on October 31, All Hallows Eve, the ancient Celtic New Year's Eve. Small charms used to be added to this dish for children to discover. While this generously flavoured dish is also known as bubble and squeak — for the sounds that came from the pan as it cooked — some say that this name should only be used when meat is included. A great way to utilize leftover cabbage and mashed spuds, this is perfect with roast pork, good sausages or hefty slices of smoked ham.

Combine the butter and olive oil in a large skillet over medium-high heat. Add the onion and cook for a few minutes until softened, but not to the point that they lose their bright green colour. Add the cabbage and toss together with the onion. Add the potatoes to the pan, breaking them up roughly with a fork as you combine them with the cabbage mixture. Season with salt and pepper. When the potatoes are heated through, transfer to a warmed serving dish. Sprinkle over the chopped parsley, and then make a well in the centre of the colcannon and add the knob of butter to melt over all. Serve at the table from the dish.

1/4 cup (60 mL) butter

1 tbsp. (15 mL) olive oil

4 green onions, chopped

2 cups (500 mL) cooked cabbage

3 cups (750 mL) mashed potatoes

sea salt and freshly ground pepper

finely chopped parsley

knob of butter

McCann's Oatie Pilaf

Ted's Choice Bushmills Black Bush Irish Whiskey. Made with 80–90 percent single malt, with a touch of soft grain whiskey to spread the sweet maltiness throughout, this whiskey is aged in *oloroso* sherry casks.

Makes 6 servings

From the people at McCann's, the magnificent makers of the world's greatest oatmeal. This recipe just won't work without their famous steel-cut oats. Wonderful with pan-seared salmon or chicken.

1 cup (250 mL) McCann's Steel-cut Irish Oatmeal

3 tbsp. (45 mL) olive oil

1 large onion, finely chopped

1/2 fennel bulb, finely chopped

1 stalk celery, finely chopped

1 clove garlic, minced

1 tbsp. (15 mL) finely chopped parsley

1/2 tsp. (2 mL) each, finely chopped thyme and marjoram

3 cups (750 mL) warm chicken broth (lightly salted)

sea salt and freshly ground pepper to taste

1 cup (250 mL) frozen small peas, thawed

1 small red bell pepper, seeded, finely chopped

1 small green bell pepper, seeded, finely chopped

Preheat oven to 400F (200C). Distribute the oats evenly over the surface of a baking sheet with raised edges. Place in the oven and toast for 5 minutes being watchful that the oats don't burn. Remove from the oven and set to one side.

Heat olive oil in a heavy saucepan placed over medium-high heat. Add onion, fennel, celery, garlic and herbs and sauté for 5 minutes or until vegetables are softened. Add oats and stir to combine well with the vegetables. Add the broth and increase heat to bring the mixture to a boil. When it has come to a boil, reduce heat to allow it to simmer. Add salt and pepper to taste. Cover and let simmer for 25 minutes or so, until all the broth has been absorbed and the oats are just tender. Remove from the heat and stir in peas and peppers. Serve hot.

Glamorgan Sausages with
Onion Chutney – Page 80

Escalivada Tostadas — Page 106

Bushmills Distillery

The little town of Bushmills in Country Antrim, Northern Ireland, is home to the whiskey distillery of the same name — the oldest licensed whiskey distillery in the world, established in 1608. Take a one-hour guided tour and whiskey-tasting and then head over to Bushmills Inn.

Touristy it may be, but anyone with Irish roots owes it to themselves to stop at this lovely old inn, even if just to sit by the open turf fire and enjoy a glass of Irish. The dinner menu may include beef tenderloin flame-licked using that same whiskey or fresh salmon from the River Bush, described as being "within casting distance." For obvious reasons, this is *the* place to order an Irish coffee — the best you've ever had.

Greywalls Country Hotel

Not far from where we were wed in Scotland in East Lothian is the magnificent Greywalls Country Hotel. There are many excellent golf courses in this area —10 within an 8-mile radius, in fact — but Greywalls must be the most famous, with a past guest list that includes Jack Nicklaus, Arnold Palmer and Lee Trevino. Even more impressive for Ted was the fact that Robert Bruce (descended from *the* Bruce), who was Lord Lieutenant of Shetland, stayed at Greywalls each year during the month of June. Edward VII stayed as a guest before World War I.

Designed by the Edwardian architect Sir Edwin Lutyens, Greywalls was built in 1901. The house overlooks Muirfield Golf Course and the Firth of Forth. A family home for most of its history, this lovely old house has been owned and cared for by three generations of the same family. It has been restored, extended and converted over the years but retains the original grace and character. We loved the comfort and quiet of the panelled library, the fireplace lit with a log fire — the perfect place to relax with a single malt after a meal in the dining room. On the menu, peat-smoked Shetland salmon with asparagus and hollandaise, carpaccio of yellow fin tuna niçoise, cutlet of Scottish lamb and braised Angus beef with a parsnip mash, and a selection of Scottish cheeses with homemade oatcakes and quince jelly.

Patrick Guilbaud's Baby Vegetables à la Grecque

Ted's Choice A lighter style Sauvignon Blanc from Touraine in the Loire Valley.

Makes 4 servings

The two-Michelin-starred restaurant Patrick Guilbaud in Dublin is found within the splendid Merrion Hotel, one of the city's best addresses. It is renowned for its "modern classic cuisine" that utilizes an incredible variety of local ingredients — fresh fish, meat, game and seasonal produce and dairy products prepared with integrity and style. This simple yet impressive dish that showcases the season's first vegetables is a case in point.

1 cup (250 mL) extra virgin olive oil

1 cup (250 mL) dry white wine

juice of 2 lemons

2 tbsp. (30 mL) coarsely cracked coriander seeds

1 bay leaf

sea salt and freshly ground pepper to taste

4 baby onions, peeled, left whole

5 baby carrots, lightly scraped if necessary

2 baby turnips, lightly scraped if necessary

1 slender leek, trimmed, rinsed, cut into thirds

1/2 red bell pepper, seeded

1 small fennel bulb, trimmed, halved

1/2 cup (125 mL) mushrooms, wiped clean, halved

8 baby corns

1/4 cup (60 mL) snowpeas

1/2 cup (125 mL) cauliflower florets

Add the oil, wine, lemon juice, coriander seeds, bay leaf, salt and pepper to a large, heavy saucepan and bring to the boil over high heat. Cook each group of vegetables separately in the hot liquid, just until tender. Use the tip of a paring knife to test. As they become tender, use a slotted spoon to transfer to a bowl. When all the vegetables have been pre-cooked, return all of them to the hot liquid in the saucepan. Remove from the heat, cover and let them stand to infuse for one hour at room temperature. When ready to serve, transfer the vegetables to a serving platter, pour the liquid through a sieve, discarding solids. Pour as much of the braising liquid as you desire over the vegetables and serve. (May be served warm, at room temperature or chilled.)

Wild Mushrooms with Hazelnuts & Cream

Ted's Choice When I think mushrooms, I think Pinot Noir.

Makes 4 servings

While almonds are always associated with Spain, hazelnuts hold a special meaning for the Spanish. According to legend, the Virgin Mary is said to have once taken shelter beneath a hazelnut bush during a storm, and now it is believed that lightning will never strike this bush, nor will a snake make its home there. I first enjoyed this combination (without cream) as a side dish to pork in Galicia, but then had something very similar (but with the addition of rich cream) served over thick-cut toast in a little café in Brittany. Enjoy this simple dish as an accompaniment to fish, chicken or pork or toss it with cooked pasta or served over rice or other grains. If you wish, add a little rehydrated porcini mushroom to the fresh mushrooms.

Combine the olive oil and butter in a large skillet and set over medium-high heat. When butter has melted, add the shallots and garlic and cook for a few minutes until softened. Add the mushrooms and stir to coat well with the oil and butter mixture. Cook the mushrooms for 5 minutes or so, until softened. Add the nuts and thyme and stir well into the mushroom mixture. Now, add the cream and stir well into the mushrooms, adding a little more if the mixture seems too thick. Season with salt and pepper and serve hot.

3 tbsp. (45 mL) olive oil

3 tbsp. (45 mL) butter

2 shallots, finely chopped

2 cloves garlic, finely chopped

1 lb. (500 g) assorted wild mushrooms (brown, portobello, chanterelles, morels)

1/2 cup (125 mL) hazelnuts, toasted, chopped

1 tbsp. (15 mL) fresh thyme

1 cup (250 mL) cream

sea salt and freshly ground pepper to taste

Porridge of Champions

"Chief of Scotia's foods," is how Robbie Burns described porridge. You know porridge is taken seriously in Scotland when you discover that an annual competition for the best porridge maker is held each year. The winner receives the Golden Spurtle Award, £200 and the title "Master Porridge Maker of the World." The year we travelled to Scotland to wed and then honeymoon in Islay, the reigning champion was Scott Chance, owner and chef at the lovely Harbour Inn in the wee town of Bowmore, home also to the world-famous Bowmore Distillery. Of course, I had a bowl of his award-winning porridge at breakfast. It was outstanding and creamy, very, very creamy, a result of the constant stirring with the spurtle — the traditional tapered wooden implement used just for stirring oatmeal and named for the sound oatmeal makes when it is cooking and spluttering. Now oatmeal in Scotland, Ireland and Wales is not of the North American rolled oats variety (an invention of the Quaker Oats Company, by the way). Oatmeal is graded pinhead (the largest), rough, medium-rough, medium, fine and super-fine.

Duncan Hilditch, chef and proprietor of the Ecclefechan Bistro in Carrbridge on Speyside in the Scottish Highlands, was another porridge-making winner. Not sure which grade he used, but here is his winning recipe:

> Take one cup of oatmeal and put into a saucepan with four cups of cold water. Stir gently over a medium heat until it reaches simmering point, lower the heat and continue to stir — to avoid any lumps — for five minutes. Add half a teaspoon of salt and two teaspoons of sugar and half a cup of buttermilk or cream. Give a final good stir and serve in a warm bowl.

Duncan says to serve it with brown sugar and double cream and I couldn't agree more.

Moira Caton is another winner of the Golden Spurtle Award for the Best Bowl of Porridge Served in Fife, a fact that makes the visitors to Arisaig, her B&B in Cupar, Fife, (www.cuparbedandbreakfast.com) quite happy, I'm sure. Moira says, and I concur, "What you add to your porridge is your choice and purely subjective, but I don't think all the new-fangled ways of cooking in other flavours enhances it. It just ends up tasting like a pudding [dessert] which was never its intention."

Moira uses three types of oats, of varying sizes, all from Scott's Porage Oats, which are milled just outside Cupar. The porridge competition takes place every year in St. Andrews at the Scottish Food and Drink Festival. Even if you can't find Scott's products, try a variety of different-sized oats as Moira does. Herewith her recipe for one portion:

Two tablespoons Scott's Old Fashioned Porage Oats, 1 tablespoon Scott's Porage Oats and 1 tablespoon Scott's Medium Cut Oats. Cover with filtered tap water and soak overnight in a saucepan. Bring gently to the boil, stirring constantly to avoid lumping. Slowly add more filtered water as required to reach desired consistency. Now, allow to simmer with lid on over a gentle heat for no less than 10 minutes. During simmering, and NOT before, add a pinch of good rock salt to bring out the nutty flavour of the oats. Serve with your favourite type of milk or cream, topped with brown sugar, molasses or honey. [I sometimes add a little cinnamon – delicious!]

By the way, in France only the Bretons eat porridge. According to tradition, it takes considerably longer to make than in Scotland. They say it is best made over a three-day period. Two days to soak the oats, one hour to cook the *peux*, as the porridge is called. It then must be cooked (boiled) nine times (!) before eating with butter and sour milk or buttermilk. At the restaurant that bears his name in Plounérin, however, Breton chef Patrick Jeffroy prepares *bouilie d'Avoine*, a sort of very thin oatmeal porridge that he sautés with roasted bacon.

Gaelic Greens with Bacon & Potatoes

Ted's Choice Bowmore "Dawn" 15-year-old Single Malt Whisky. It spends 12 years in bourbon casks and then two or three years in a port cask.

Makes 4–6 servings

Growing up in Toronto, I had a best friend named Patsy O'Shea. Whenever I visited her house, her Dublin-born dad would play his fiddle while the aroma of this country-style supper wafted from the kitchen. You can use thick-cut strip bacon if you wish, but I think this dish is best made with lean back bacon. Serve with fiery prepared mustard or mustard pickle.

6 slices thick-cut back bacon, cooked

2 tbsp. (30 mL) butter

1 onion, chopped

3/4 cup (175 mL) chicken broth or water

1 lb. (500 g) kale, trimmed, coarse stems removed, chopped

3 medium-sized potatoes, scrubbed (peel only if necessary), diced

2 tbsp. (30 mL) malt vinegar

sea salt and freshly ground pepper to taste

1/4 cup (60 mL) finely chopped chives

Cut the bacon into strips, set to one side and keep warm. Melt the butter in a large skillet over medium-high heat and sauté the onion until softened, about 5 minutes. Add the broth or water, the chopped kale and the potatoes, stir to combine and bring to the boil. Cover, reduce heat slightly and cook until potatoes are tender and most of the liquid has evaporated, 12–15 minutes. Remove from the heat and stir the vinegar into the mixture. Add the reserved bacon and toss together. Season to taste and sprinkle with chives before serving hot.

Cornish Onion, Parsnip & Potato Cakes

Ted's Choice If serving this with ham, have either a Mortlach or the Balvenie Double Wood with nutty, spicy flavours.

Makes 4–6 servings

Many years ago, I lived in a tiny village in the Cotswolds, in England's West Country. Often we would make the short trip to beautiful Cornwall, a place I grew to love. One of my favourite authors, D.H. Lawrence, in a letter to a friend wrote, "I like Cornwall very much. It is not England. It is bare and dark and elemental, Tristan's land. . . . It is old, Celtic, pre-Christian."

These crisp little patty-cakes from Cornwall (a variation of which are also enjoyed in Wales) are very good with ham.

Melt the butter in a small saucepan over medium heat. Add onion and cook until soft, about 5 minutes. Combine the parsnips and potatoes in a mixing bowl and scrape into the mixture the contents of the saucepan. Add a portion of the flour, the salt, pepper, nutmeg and eggs and mix the ingredients together well. If it appears too wet, add additional flour until the mixture is of the right consistency to form little cakes. Shape them into rough little patties (they shouldn't appear perfect), about 1/2-inch (1-cm) thick. Coat each lightly with the breadcrumbs. Heat vegetable oil in a frying pan and fry the patties until crisp and golden on both sides, about 2–3 minutes per side. Transfer to paper towels to drain. Keep warm until ready to serve.

2 tbsp. (30 mL) butter

1 onion, finely chopped

3 large parsnips, peeled, cooked, mashed

3 medium-size floury potatoes, peeled, cooked, mashed

1/4 cup (60 mL) unbleached all-purpose flour (approx.)

sea salt and freshly ground pepper to taste

pinch of ground nutmeg

2 eggs, lightly beaten

1/2 cup (125 mL) dry breadcrumbs

1/2 cup (125 mL) vegetable oil for frying (approx.)

THREE-ROOT PURÉE

Ted's Choice If serving this dish to accompany roast pork or turkey with an onion and herb stuffing, try a New World Sauvignon Blanc from Canada or New Zealand.

Makes 4 servings

While the individual root vegetables that make up this triumvirate — turnips, rutabagas and carrots — are rather humble, in unison they are quite sophisticated. Use a food processor to achieve the smoothness required.

1 small rutabaga, peeled, cut into small chunks

3 white turnips, peeled, cut into small chunks

3 carrots, peeled, cut into small chunks

sea salt to taste

2 tbsp. (30 mL) butter

2 tbsp. (30 mL) crème fraîche

1/2 tsp. (2 mL) ground nutmeg

sea salt and freshly ground pepper to taste

Combine the vegetables in a large saucepan and cover with boiling water. Add salt and bring to a boil, reduce heat, cover loosely and cook until tender, about 15–20 minutes. Drain well and add the cooked vegetables to the bowl of a food processor. Add all the remaining ingredients and purée until smooth. Taste for seasoning and serve while still hot.

Bunnahabhain Distillery

If you're curious about the wonderful whiskies from beautiful Islay, the island that is known as the Queen of the Hebrides, start with the exceptionally smooth Bunnahabhain (bunna-HA-venn). Boasting just a trace of the peat for which Islay malts are renowned, this is a delicate malt with a light to medium body and a fruity, full finish. Bunnahabhain is Gaelic for "mouth of the river" and this Islay distillery is indeed located at the mouth of the River Margadale in a remote cove. The water used in the making of this gentle whisky rises through limestone and is piped to the distillery, which means it doesn't pick up any big peat influence along the way, just a trace amidst other distinctive characteristics. Bunnahabhain is one of the components in Black Bottle, a unique blend containing all the Islay malts.

Babbity Bowster

This Glasgow establishment is housed on Blackfriars Street just off High Street in a splendid building on the site of a former monastery. Today this combination café-bar-restaurant-hotel is a very popular place for lunch, dinner or just a good pint on the patio. The "Schottische" restaurant menu is tied to the seasons and features local foods and produce. As for the lovely-sounding name, apparently the *babbity bowster* was a popular dance in the eighteenth-century, at the time the building was constructed. Spoken with a Glaswegian accent, the words *bob at the* become *babbity*, while *bowster* meant "bolster or large pillow." Some sly naughtiness is implied by the name because the menu states: "We leave you to decide who may have performed a bobbing dance at the edge of the bed and for what reasons . . . some things never change!"

CHAPTER 5

FROM LAKE, RIVER & SEA

. . . our exquisite fragile and delicate forms are reared by the ocean and rocked by storms.

– Anon

That evocative quote perfectly describes not only the magnificent bounty of fish and seafood so common to every one of the Celtic countries, but also the land itself. In each place – Scotland, Ireland, Wales, Brittany, Galicia, Isle of Man and Cape Breton – the Celtic elements are all inextricably linked with a seafaring past. The influence of, and proximity to, the sea, is omnipresent. It seems to have shaped the lives of Celtic people forever as evidenced by this line from poet Sir Walter Scott: *"It's nae fish ye're buying, it's men's lives."*

The assortment of fish, shellfish and seafood is astounding. With this sort of inspiration, chefs from all of these countries create memorable dishes on a daily basis, some that are simply accented and reminiscent of the past and others that have a more contemporary influence.

Toni Vicente, whose restaurant in Santiago de Compostela bears his name, is one such chef. Clearly influenced by the styling of fellow Spanish chef Ferran Adria, he served us some of the most innovative *nueva cocina* in Spain, as evidenced by delicate pieces of pan-roasted angler fish (monkfish) served with a "spaghetti" of zucchini and warm cherry tomatoes. Paper-thin slices of *polpo* (octopus) are edged with coarse salt and smoked paprika — a Galician tradition — but innovatively served as part of a modern tapas plate with salmon mousse placed in a porcelain spoon and a miniature *croquetta*.

When we visited the beautiful Ballymaloe Cookery School in County Cork, founder Darina Allen showed me a copy of her *Irish Traditional Cooking*, a wonderful book that features recipes culled from Ireland's heritage. In it I found this reference to a "typical Irish seafood platter that, with the odd replacement, could just as likely be found in Brittany, Galicia, Scotland or Wales." Darina says this should serve six people as a "substantial starter": 6 sea urchins, 18 Dublin Bay prawns, 18 mussels, 18 cockles, 18 roghans, 12 palourdes (the last two are types of clams), 6 native Irish oysters, periwinkles. Served with homemade mayonnaise, fresh lemon and sprigs of wild watercress or fennel seaweed, it was almost identical to a memorable menu from Casa Rosita, a restaurant in Galicia, and another in Cancale, Brittany.

An embarrassment of riches from the sea, indeed.

Lobster *à l'Armoricaine*

Scallop & Shrimp Sausages

Cape Breton Lobster Rolls with Chips & Aïoli

Loch Fyne Smoked Salmon Salad with Cucumber & Radish

Ballycotton Fish Pie with Champ

Hot-smoked Salmon Fillets Wrapped in Filo with Watercress Cream

Readers Newfie Cod Cakes with Bonavista Tartar Sauce

Galician Hake with Chorizo & Sherry Vinegar

Scallops in a Galician Style with Saffron Rice

Shanks *Fritto Misto*

Turbot & Shellfish in Terracotta

Musselburgh Mussels in *Beurre Breton* with Toast

Cancale Oysters in Cream with Leeks

North Berwick Salmon Fishcakes with Lemon Butter

Char-grilled Squid with Rice Noodles in a Chile & Cilantro Vinaigrette

Dunbrody Crisp Potato-wrapped Brill

Grilled Oysters with Bacon & Smoked Salmon

Lobster à l'Armoricaine

Ted's Choice An unpeated malt like Tobermory from the Isle of Mull or another lightly peated malt, the beautifully named Ledaig — means "safe haven" in Gaelic.

Makes 4–6 servings

The Celts had a special word that they used to describe Brittany's wildy beautiful coastal areas — *Armor*. And this is the root word for what is probably Brittany's most renowned seafood preparation, known as *homard à l'Armoricaine*, a luxurious dish comprised of shelled lobster chunks, shallots and tomatoes in a sauce of wine and cream. Absolutely heavenly. Serve this over simple cooked rice with a sprinkling of fresh chopped parsley.

Lobster in Galicia is no less outstanding. I remember a main course at lunch I enjoyed in the little town of Cedeira that involved shelled lobster in combination with small red potatoes and lots of watercress dressed in a lemony mustard vinaigrette to which had been added plenty of finely chopped mint.

3 live lobsters, about 2 lbs. (1 kg) each

1/4 cup (60 mL) extra virgin olive oil

1 medium onion, finely chopped

3 shallots, finely chopped

2 cloves garlic, minced

1 cup (250 mL) finely diced carrots

1 cup (250 mL) finely diced green beans

2 tomatoes, chopped

2 tbsp. (30 mL) tomato paste

1 1/2 cups (375 mL) dry white wine

1/2 cup (125 mL) dry sherry

Follow the directions on the opposite page for preparing the live lobsters. When all the meat has been removed, cut it into good-sized pieces and set to one side until ready to combine with the finished sauce. Retain the tomalley (the green-coloured liver), coral (roe or eggs) and the shells.

Pour the oil into a large skillet and set over medium heat. Add the onions, shallots and garlic and cook for 10–12 minutes until softened. Now, add the carrots, green beans, tomatoes, tomato paste, wine, sherry and a scant cup of water and mix to combine everything well. Reduce heat and allow mixture to simmer for about 10 minutes.

Break up the lobster shells with a mallet or rolling pin. Add the crushed shells to the sauce in the skillet, stirring them in well. Continue to cook the sauce slowly until it is reduced and thickened. Pour the whole mixture through a sieve and press against the solids to extract as much flavour as possible from everything. Discard solids. Return the liquid to the skillet and set to one side for a minute. Combine the reserved tomalley and coral with the butter, cayenne, salt and pepper in a small bowl and mix together to form a paste. Place the skillet holding the sauce on low heat. Stir in the paste mixture and the reserved lobster pieces and cook for a couple of minutes to heat through. Add the cream, stir well into the lobster mixture and allow to heat through before serving as described above.

3 tbsp. (45 mL) butter, at room
   temperature
1/2 tsp. (2 mL) ground cayenne
sea salt and freshly ground
   pepper to taste
1/4 cup (60 mL) whipping cream

Lobster Know-How

You need 3 live lobsters for this recipe, about 2 lbs. (1 kg) each (or, 2 lobsters weighing about 3 lbs./1.5 kg each). Put a large pot of water on to boil – you will need at least a gallon (4 L) of water for each lobster and you should cook them one at a time, for about 9–10 minutes each. The water should be briskly boiling before you add the lobster. As soon as the water starts to return to the boil, reduce the heat to allow the lobster to poach slowly. This will ensure that the flesh doesn't toughen or become rubbery. Have an ice bath ready and place the boiled lobster in it to chill for a few minutes before removing the meat.

Scallop & Shrimp Sausages

Ted's Choice A Chardonnay preferably non-oaked, such as Niagara's Henry of Pelham.

Makes 6 servings

Here is a sort of seafood *boudin blanc*, a variation on a dish we enjoyed in Brittany. Serve it with steamed baby potatoes, tiny peas and pearl onions — that's how we had it in France. You will need a food processor for this recipe.

1 1/4 lb. (680 g) uncooked medium shrimp, peeled, deveined

1 lb. (500 g) bay scallops, rinsed, dried

2 tbsp. (30 mL) olive oil

2 tbsp. (30 mL) butter

1/4 lb. (125 g) mushrooms, wiped clean

1 shallot, minced

1/4 cup (60 mL) fresh bread-crumbs

1 tsp. (5 mL) sea salt

1 tsp. (5 mL) Chinese chile sauce

2 tsp. (10 mL) lemon zest, minced

2 tbsp. (30 mL) fresh chopped chives

2 egg whites

1 1/2-2 cups (375-500 mL) whipping cream

non-stick cooking spray

In a large skillet, warm the oil and sauté 3/4 lb. (375 g) of the shrimp for 1 minute, just until they turn pink. Remove with a slotted spoon to a cutting board. When cool enough to handle, chop coarsely with a sharp chef's knife and set to one side.

Add the butter to the skillet and melt over medium heat. Add the mushrooms and shallot and sauté for about 3 minutes until softened. Transfer this mixture to the bowl of a food processor. Add breadcrumbs, remaining uncooked shrimp, scallops, salt, chile sauce, lemon zest and chives. Pulse the mixture a few times until it is puréed.

Add the egg whites to the mixture and pulse again to incorporate. Start adding the cream through the feed tube as the motor is running to achieve a thick purée. You may not use all the cream.

Using a spatula, scrape the mixture into a bowl and stir in the sautéed chopped shrimp. Cut heavy aluminum foil into 6 pieces, about 6x8-inches (15–20 cm) each. Butter the inside of the foil and divide the seafood mixture onto each piece, placing it lengthwise down the centre of each piece. Roll up and seal the ends by folding up and pinching together.

Bring a large pot of water to the boil. Add the foil-wrapped sausages and lower the heat to a gentle simmer. Cover the pot and simmer the sausages for 15 minutes. Remove from the heat and let sausages stand in the water for another 10 minutes.

Remove from the water with tongs and carefully unwrap each. (You can keep them warm at this point in a lightly buttered dish. Cover with wax paper and a lid.) Serve by slicing each one into rounds and placing overlapping on a dish with the recommended accompaniments as described above.

Albariño

The lovely grape from Galicia – green Spain – Albariño is a refreshingly fragrant and fruity white wine with a characteristically crisp, slightly minerally finish that brings to mind the granite soils of this coastal region. Absolutely wonderful with fresh fish and shellfish, young green vegetables or on its own as an undemanding aperitif. Another popular easy-quaffing wine from Portugal, *vinho verde,* is based on the same grape.

Cape Breton Lobster Rolls with Chips & Aïoli

Ted's Choice A Best Bitter, like the one from the Halifax-based Propeller Brewery.

Makes 4 servings

When we travelled to Cape Breton, we saw signs everywhere for lobster rolls — outside little cafés, diners and even at that familiar joint with the golden arches. Lobster is obviously a specialty in Nova Scotia and I can't think of a nicer way to showcase it than in these overstuffed rolls. The aïoli is really meant for the accompanying chips, but use some of it in the lobster mixture, too. If you don't choose to make it, use a good-quality mayonnaise in its place.

For the aïoli:

4 cloves garlic, minced

2 large egg yolks

2 tbsp. (30 mL) fresh lemon juice

1/2 tsp. (2 mL) sea salt

1/4 tsp. (1 mL) freshly ground pepper

3/4 cup (175 mL) extra virgin olive oil

1/2 cup (125 mL) chopped fresh parsley

Combine the garlic, egg yolks, lemon juice, salt and pepper in a blender or food processor. Pulse on and off a few times until blended. With the motor running, gradually drizzle in the olive oil. Continue to blend until the mixture becomes creamy and thick. Transfer the mixture to a bowl and combine with the parsley. Cover and refrigerate for about half an hour before using.

Combine the lobster with the celery, aïoli or mayonnaise to taste in a bowl and season with a little salt and pepper. Distribute lettuce among the split and toasted rolls and follow with the lobster mixture. Serve immediately with the following chips and remaining aïoli.

Peel the potatoes and slice them into thick, lengthwise pieces, about 2-inches (5-cm) long and 1/2-inch (1-cm) wide. Add to a bowl of cold water as you work. Once they are all cut, leave in the water for at least 15 minutes. Heat the oil to 350F (180C). Drain the chips and pat dry with a clean tea towel. Make sure they are completely dry. Carefully add the potatoes, in batches, to the hot oil and fry until they are just beginning to colour and are soft. Lift the chips from the fat and drain them on paper towels. They can sit at this point for some time, or at least 10 minutes, before the second fry. When you are ready, increase the heat so that the oil reaches 400F (200C). Return the pre-cooked chips to the oil and cook for the second time, again in batches, until the chips are crisp and golden, about 3–5 minutes. Serve at once.

For the lobster roll:
3 cups (750 mL) cooked lobster meat, cut into bite-sized pieces
1/4 cup (60 mL) finely chopped celery
aïoli or mayonnaise, as needed to bind
sea salt and freshly ground pepper to taste
4–6 leaves romaine lettuce, shredded
4 good-quality rolls (shaped like hot dog buns), split and toasted

For the chips:
6 large floury potatoes
vegetable oil

Loch Fyne Smoked Salmon Salad with Cucumber & Radish

Ted's Choice Oban West Highland 14-year-old Single Malt.

Makes 4 servings

It was my Ted who first told me about Loch Fyne in Argyll and the incredible smoked salmon he had enjoyed there. So, en route to Islay we stopped at Loch Fyne restaurant and oyster bar to wander through their shop and then to the restaurant to have lunch. It took forever to decide what to order — there were pan-fried king scallops in a white wine and garlic sauce served with red Swiss chard, *bradan rost* (salmon roasted in the smoke kiln) served hot with whisky and horseradish sauce, smoked haddock chowder, char-grilled halibut, their intensely flavoured Loch Fyne kippers, and a staggering array included in their shellfish platter. We settled on their pristine oysters served alongside hot sausages (dubbed a "traditional oyster fisherman's meal") and their Loch Fyne Ashet, a cold platter that included *bradan rost*, smoked salmon, their incredible *bradan orach* (a traditional, strongly smoked salmon) and *gravad lax* with a fresh dill sauce. As my dad would have said, what a feed. This preparation that showcases good-quality smoked salmon makes a pretty first course for a summer lunch or dinner. You will need a 3-inch (7.5-cm) biscuit or cookie cutter to use as a mold. Or, fill a similar-sized cup with the mixture and turn it over onto each plate to form a little mound. Serve with warm crusty rolls.

1/2 large seedless cucumber

6 radishes, trimmed

6 oz. (170 g) smoked salmon, cut into thin strips

2 tbsp. (30 mL) sour cream

1 tbsp. (15 mL) cream

1 tbsp. (15 mL) creamed horseradish

Slice off and reserve a 1-inch (2.5-cm) piece of the cucumber. Slice the remaining cucumber in half lengthwise and use a small spoon to scrape out and discard the seeds running down the centre. Cut the halves of cucumber into matchsticks. Reserve one or two of the radishes for garnish and slice the remaining radish into similar matchstick lengths. Place the cucumber and radish matchsticks in a bowl, cover with plastic wrap and refrigerate until well chilled.

Half an hour before serving, combine the radish and cucumber with the salmon, sour cream, cream, horse-radish, dill, lemon and pepper. If necessary, add a little additional sour cream or cream to achieve a mixture that will hold together. Divide this mixture into four portions. Set out four serving plates. Arrange a few baby spinach leaves attractively in the centre of each. Place the cutter in the centre of the spinach leaves and add one of the portions of salmon mixture to the centre, gently pressing it into the cutter. Pat the surface of the mixture down with the back of a spoon. Carefully remove the cutter, wipe clean if necessary and repeat with remaining mixture. Slice the remaining cucumber and radish into very thin slices and use them to garnish the top of each serving by arranging them in alternate slices atop each one. Drizzle a little olive oil over each serving, making sure to include the spinach leaves. Garnish each with a lemon wedge and serve.

2 tbsp. (30 mL) finely chopped dill
1 tsp. (5 mL) minced lemon zest
freshly ground pepper to taste
4 cups (1 L) baby spinach leaves
to garnish: extra virgin olive oil for drizzling and 1 lemon, quartered

Ye Old Peacock Inn, Newhaven, Edinburgh

When we hailed a black cab in Edinburgh and told the driver the name and address of the fish restaurant that was our destination, he told us, "Ye don't want to go there. I'll take you to a place where ye'll get a real fish supper," and so he did. This lovely old place beside Newhaven Harbour specializes in freshly caught Scottish haddock and lots of it. Gargantuan lengths of impeccable fish are treated to shatteringly crisp batter and sided with great chips and are very reasonably priced. Portions range from "ladies size" to "the whale," an astonishing full pound of battered haddock. Old-fashioned and very, very good. Moral of the story: always take the advice of an Edinburgh cabbie.

Ballycotton Fish Pie with Champ

Ted's Choice An Orvieto from Umbria.

Makes 6–8 servings

When we visited the famed Irish country house hotel of Ireland's food maven Myrtle Allen in Co. Cork, she kindly told us to make sure to visit the tiny village of Ballycotton, just down the road from her hotel. This lovely fishing village on the southern coast of Ireland was originally a typical, rather sleepy little spot, complete with whitewashed houses, a few shops, a pub and post office. Then, during the summer of 1995, Ballycotton was chosen as the location for a film starring Marlon Brando and Johnny Depp. The villagers' excitement knew no bounds until the dream ended when funding for the film ran out. But that fifteen minutes of fame (coupled with the town's proximity to Ballymaloe and the internationally renowned Ballymaloe Cookery School) helped to put this fishing community on the map. Today — while it could hardly be called bustling — it is home to several good restaurants and a nice hotel overlooking the bay.

Each day, as weather permits, the fishers land their catch in the tiny harbour, and the variety and range of fish they catch is truly amazing. Myrtle told us it includes flat and round fish, squid, monkfish, shrimp, crab, lobsters, crayfish and tiny periwinkles. "We don't complete writing the dinner menu for Ballymaloe's dining room until the kitchen learns what the fishers have brought home that day," says Myrtle. The following recipe is from Myrtle's daughter-in-law and the owner of the famous Ballymaloe Cookery School, Darina Allen, who says, "Many different types of fish may be used for a fish pie, so feel free to adapt this recipe a little to suit your needs. Periwinkles would be a good and cheap addition and a little smoked haddock is tasty also."

For the pie:

2 small onions, peeled, quartered

1 small carrot, scraped, sliced

1 small bay leaf

1 sprig fresh thyme

Place the onions, carrot, bay leaf, thyme, peppercorns and milk into a saucepan. Bring to a boil over medium-high heat, then reduce heat and let simmer for 3–4 minutes. Remove from the heat and then leave to infuse for 10–15 minutes before straining (discard solids) and setting to one side.

Place the eggs in a small pan, bring to the boil, then remove from the heat and let stand for 10–12 minutes. Refresh under cold water, peel and roughly chop. Melt half the butter in a small frying pan over medium heat and sauté the mushrooms for a few minutes until softened. Season with salt and pepper and set to one side. Place all the fish in one layer (do in batches if necessary) into a large wide pan or skillet and cover with the infused milk mixture. Season generously with salt and pepper. Cover and simmer gently for 3–4 minutes until the fish is just cooked. Using a slotted spoon, carefully transfer the cooked fish to a large plate and, if necessary, remove any bones or skin from the fish. Try not to break up the pieces of fish. Pour the liquid in the pan through a sieve into a measuring cup and set to one side.

In a large pan, melt the remaining butter and whisk in the flour to form a roux. Cook over low heat for half a minute, and then pour in the cooking liquid in the measuring cup into the roux, whisking as you do so until the mixture is thick and smooth. Remove from the heat and add the cream, parsley, eggs, mushrooms (and any liquid that has accumulated in their pan), fish and mussels or shrimp, if using. Stir gently to combine. Season to taste and spoon this mixture into a large oven-proof dish (or into individual serving dishes) and set to one side as you prepare the potato topping.

3 black peppercorns

2 cups (500 mL) milk

4 large eggs

1/4 cup (60 mL) butter

1 cup (250 mL) sliced mushrooms

2 1/2 lb. (1.25 kg) fillets of cod, haddock, hake, salmon or pollock, or a mixture

18 fresh mussels, washed, debearded, cooked, or 6 oz. (185 g) medium shrimp, peeled, deveined, cooked (either are optional)

2 tbsp. (30 mL) unbleached all-purpose flour

1/4 cup (60 mL) whipping cream

2 tbsp. (30 mL) finely chopped parsley

sea salt and freshly ground pepper

For the champ:

3 lb. (1.5 kg) floury potatoes

1 tsp. (5 mL) sea salt

6–8 green onions, trimmed, finely chopped

1 1/4 cups (310 mL) milk

1/4 cup (60 mL) butter

sea salt and freshly ground pepper to taste

Cut the potatoes into even chunks and cover with cold water, add the 1 teaspoon (5 mL) of salt and bring to a boil. Cook the potatoes for about 20 minutes or until tender. While the potatoes cook, warm the milk in a saucepan over gentle heat, add the onions, bring to a boil, reduce the heat and simmer for a few minutes. Remove from the heat and let stand for 5 minutes. Drain the potatoes, return them to a low heat and shake the pan over the element for a minute or so to make sure they are quite dry. Then, cover with a clean tea towel and let stand for 10 minutes until cool enough to handle. Peel and mash them, then add the onions and milk mixture, and finally beat in the butter with a wooden spoon. Season to taste. (At this point the dish can be prepared in advance, loosely covered with plastic wrap and refrigerated until ready to put in the oven.)

Preheat oven to 350F (180C). Spoon the champ over the fish and bake for about 30 minutes (increase cooking time a little if reheating from cold) until it is bubbling round the edges and the potato is beginning colour in places. If you wish, turn on the oven broiler to brown the top.

Guinness

In 1759 Arthur Guinness signed a nine-thousand-year lease at an annual rent of £45 to take over the St. James Gate Brewery, which had been silent for 10 years. There wasn't a lot happening brewing-wise in Dublin at the time and the quality of what was available was poor. In the rural areas of Ireland, it was virtually non-existent, with most folk favouring whisky, gin and potent poteen over anything. That was all to change with the introduction of Uncle Arthur's black ale. Guinness was styled after an ale called porter, fashionable in London at the time and named for the Billingsgate and Covent Garden market porters who were especially fond of it. Once Arthur Guinness moved away from ales and developed his own recipe for porter, the black stuff became so popular that it wasn't long before it was synonymous with all things Irish. The next time you're in a reputable pub that knows how to take care of their Guinness, order a pint and, as you're waiting for it to settle, watch the lovely, rapid cascade of bubbles that, apparently defying the natural laws of gravity, travel downward in your glass. More than one beer expert has claimed that this little phenomenon occurs when the faster rising bubbles push the slower ones down.

Perhaps because of its colour and perceived weight, some believe Guinness to be a strong stout, high in alcohol. But, in fact, at 4.1 percent alc. it is considerably lower than many popular ales. So, to repeat one of their more famous advertising campaigns, *Don't be afraid of the dark*.

Today the massive Guinness brewery, related buildings and property take up 65 acres in Dublin and the stout known as Guinness, renowned for its unique malty flavour and ultra-creamy head, is exported to more than 120 countries. Besides the famous stout, the company also owns Harp Lager and Smithwick's Ale.

Hot-smoked Salmon Fillets Wrapped in Filo with Watercress Cream

Ted's Choice An Ardbeg or Talisker single malt. And maybe a drop or two of water to "release the serpents"!

Makes 4 servings

Salmon and watercress — two distinctly Celtic foods — are combined in this quite contemporary first course that could almost be thought of as a Celtic spring roll. The accompanying sauce is a beautiful brilliant green and works well with any fish. Great for St. Patrick's Day dinners.

For the salmon:

1/2 small white onion, finely chopped

1 tbsp. (15 mL) butter

1 lb. (500 g) smoked salmon fillets (or unsmoked), skinned

2 tbsp. (30 mL) olive oil

2 tbsp. (30 mL) fresh lemon juice

1 tbsp. (15 mL) finely minced lemon zest

sea salt and freshly ground pepper to taste

1/3 cup (75 mL) butter (plus a little extra for greasing)

3 sheets frozen filo pastry, thawed

For the watercress cream:

2 tbsp. (30 mL) olive oil

1 shallot, finely chopped

4 tbsp. (60 mL) dry white wine

Preheat oven to 425F (220C). Melt the tablespoon (15 mL) of butter in a small pan and sauté the onion for 5 minutes or until softened. Set to one side to cool. Cut the salmon into 1/4-inch (.6-cm) strips. Toss in a bowl along with the oil, lemon juice, zest and seasoning. Mix together. Scrape the onion into the bowl with the salmon and mix to combine.

Use some of the butter to grease a baking sheet. Melt the remaining butter and set to one side. Lay one sheet of filo pastry on a dry work surface. Use a pastry brush and paint with butter, cover with the second sheet, apply more butter, and then repeat with the third sheet, brushing once again with the butter. Use a sharp chef's knife to cut the pastry layers in half lengthwise to make two equal-sized squares. Divide the salmon mixture into 8 equal portions. Using one portion, arrange the salmon in a line near one end of one of the pastry square. Encase the salmon by folding in the two side edges, brush with a little more butter, and then roll the salmon up to fully enclose it. Transfer the salmon package to the baking sheet, seam-side down and repeat with remaining salmon and filo pastry to make eight packages. Brush all the salmon packages with remaining butter and bake in the oven for about 15 minutes or until packages are crisp and golden brown.

While they are baking, prepare the sauce: add the olive oil to a saucepan and gently sauté the shallot until softened. Add the wine, increase the heat and allow the mixture to come to a boil. Boil until the mixture is reduced by half, add the crème fraîche and boil again until reduced once more and thickened. Add the watercress and parsley leaves and as soon as they are wilted (30 seconds or less), purée with a hand-held blender or transfer to a regular blender or food processor. Season to taste. Keep warm.

To serve: Allow two salmon packages per person. Use four small ramekins to serve as holders for the watercress sauce and place next to the packages on each plate.

1 cup (250 mL) watercress leaves (strip them from the stems)

2 tbsp. (30 mL) flat-leaf parsley leaves

1 ¼ cups (300 mL) crème fraîche (see Chapter 4, page 99, to make your own)

How to Hot-smoke Salmon

You will need a large cast iron skillet or a wok, a lid to cover it, and a circular cake rack just large enough to fit within the skillet. The very best Scottish smoked salmon is produced with the wood from oak barrels used in the aging of whisky. Failing that, the best choices are hardwoods and fruitwoods. Use woodchips (or sawdust) to minimize the amount of smoke. First, fold a sheet of heavy-duty foil to form a double layer large enough to cover the bottom of the skillet, and then set it to one side. Place the skillet on high heat for about 10 minutes until it is very hot. Use a paring knife to pierce the foil in a few places, sprinkle the skillet with a good layer of soaked woodchips (or about 3–4 tablespoons/45–60 mL of sawdust) and quickly cover with the foil. Spray the cake rack with non-stick cooking spray (or oil it) and place it over the foil. Then arrange the fish fillets (no more than 4) on the rack and immediately cover with the lid. Reduce heat slightly (the pan must be very hot to be effective). One-inch (2.5 cm) fish fillets will be hot-smoked in about 15–20 minutes. Alternatively, hot-smoke the salmon for 10 minutes, remove from the heat and let rest for 15 minutes, and then sear in a hot skillet to complete the cooking.

Readers Newfie Cod Cakes with Bonavista Tartar Sauce

Ted's Choice Try Cave Spring Cellars Chardonnay Estate Bottled.

Makes 8 servings

This is a variation on a recipe devised by my good friend and fellow cookbook author, Chef Ted Reader. Ted and I collaborated on *The Sticks & Stones Cookbook: The Art of Grilling on Plank, Vine and Stone*. A popular book, it received a Silver Cuisine Canada book award. In the original recipe, Ted cooked the cod cakes on slabs of preheated granite, but you can also fry them on a griddle or a cast iron pan or bake them in a 425F (220C) oven for 12–15 minutes until heated through and cooked. The accompanying sauce is from Ted's mum, Astrida Reader, who emigrated from Latvia to Newfoundland where she met Ted's dad, Alex. Obviously, she learned quickly how to cook Newfoundland-style.

For the tartar sauce:

2 cups (500 mL) mayonnaise

1/2 cup (125 mL) zucchini relish

1 tsp. (5 mL) coarsely ground
   black pepper

1 tbsp. (15 mL) fresh lemon juice

2 tsp. (10 mL) chopped dill

sea salt to taste

In a mixing bowl, whisk together the mayonnaise, relish, pepper, lemon juice and dill. Season with salt to taste. Cover and refrigerate for 1–2 hours to allow flavours to develop.

If you plan to cook the cod cakes in the oven, preheat to 425F (220C). Place the cod in a large mixing bowl and shred into small pieces with your fingers. Add remaining ingredients and blend together with a fork. Shape mixture into eight round cakes.

Spray a baking sheet with non-stick cooking spray (or line with parchment paper). Lay the cod cakes on the sheet and bake for 12–15 minutes until heated through and cooked. Serve with the tartar sauce and mixed baby greens.

For the cod cakes:

2 lb. (1 kg) fresh cod fillets
3 green onions, finely chopped
1 small red onion, diced
1 red bell pepper, seeded, diced
1 tbsp. (15 mL) barbecue seasoning
1 tbsp. (15 mL) chopped dill
1 cup (250 mL) mayonnaise
1 tbsp. (15 mL) fresh lemon juice
1 1/2 cups (375 mL) coarsely crushed soda crackers
sea salt and freshly ground pepper to taste

Rodney and the Oyster

One of the best places in Toronto to enjoy pristine oysters, Dungeness crab, fresh fish and just about anything else from the sea is at Rodney Clark's unpretentious restaurant. Clark was born in Prince Edward Island and so naturally knows a thing or two about oysters. He says — and we concur — that the oyster is at its best naked, without any condiments. As for what goes best with the bivalves, Clark says it depends on the oyster. Different oysters need different beer. If the oyster in question is particularly strong-tasting, opt for stouts, porters or strong ale — which is exactly the coupling you'll get in Galway Bay when their local oysters are teamed with a creamy-headed Guinness. Milder, sweeter varieties, like Canada's East Coast oysters, will be better suited to a pale ale or a wheat beer.

Galician Hake with Chorizo & Sherry Vinegar

Ted's Choice Albariño, certainly, but also try a white Rioja.

Makes 4 servings

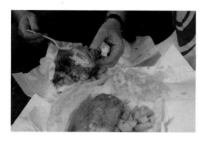

I adore hake, a wonderfully flavourful fish that enjoys great popularity in Spain. One of the best fish suppers I have ever had — and I've had a few — came from the Dublin fish shop known as Leo Burdock's. Ted opted for the cod and I had a huge length of delicious hake that was crisply battered and served with terrific chips. We took our treasures across the road and sat within the grounds of a churchyard and wolfed down our suppers. Man, was it good. In Galicia, this is how we grew to love this fish — shallow-fried in olive oil and teamed with little waxy, slightly crushed potatoes, chunks of chorizo and a simple yet effective sauce based on Spanish *oloroso* and sherry vinegar.

1 lb. (500 g) new waxy potatoes, scrubbed

3 tbsp. (45 mL) extra virgin olive oil (preferably Spanish)

2 tsp. (10 mL) drained capers

4 hake (or haddock) fillets (about 5 oz/155 g each)

2–3 tbsp. (15–30 mL) unbleached all-purpose flour

sea salt and freshly ground pepper to taste

1 tsp. (5 mL) paprika

1/4 lb. (125 g) chorizo sausage, outer skin peeled, diced

1/3 cup (75 mL) *oloroso* sherry (medium-sweet)

1 tbsp. (15 mL) sherry vinegar

Place the potatoes in a saucepan, just cover with boiling water, add a little salt to taste and cook for 20 minutes, or until tender. Drain well, return to a very low heat and shake the pan over the heat for a few seconds to thoroughly dry them. Using a wooden spoon or a pestle, gently crush each potato a little against the sides of the pan (this will help the potatoes to absorb the other flavours). Add 1 tablespoon (15 mL) of the olive oil and the capers, give it a bit of a stir and cover with a lid to keep warm. Combine the flour with a little salt, pepper and the paprika, mix to blend well, and then use to lightly dust the fish fillets, shaking off the excess. Heat remaining oil in a skillet and place over medium-high heat. Place the fish fillets in the pan and cook for 3 minutes on each side or until crisp and pale golden brown. (If you have to work in batches to avoid overcrowding do so; but keep cooked fish warm in a low oven or covered on top of the stove.) Transfer fish to a paper towel–lined plate. Pour off most but not all of the oil. Add the chorizo and cook briefly for just under a minute, at which point it should be crisp. Add the sherry and the vinegar and stir, scraping up the little bits clinging to the pan. Cook until the mixture is reduced somewhat and is beginning to thicken. As soon as it does, remove from the heat and whisk in the butter. Arrange the fish on a large serving platter and spoon the sauce and chorizo over the fish. Arrange the potatoes around the fish and sprinkle all with the parsley and chives. Serve immediately or just warm.

2 tbsp. (30 mL) butter, diced
2 tbsp. (30 mL) chopped parsley
1 tbsp. (15 mL) chopped chives

The Star(fish) of the Galway International Oyster Festival

Young Patrick McMurray owns the popular Starfish Oyster Bed and Grill in Toronto, reason enough to like the guy. After he won the title "World Champion Oyster Shucker" at the Galway International Oyster Festival in September 2002, up against 14 other competitors from all over the world, well, we don't understand why he wasn't made honorary mayor when he returned home. This championship is a very big deal in Galway. In the 48 years of its existence it had never been won by a Canadian and only once before was it won by a non-European (an American in 1976). Apparently, the Galway oyster is a lot trickier to open than others, but not for Patrick. And it's not just getting the danged things open in record time that the judges look for. They must be well opened without flaws. Points are awarded primarily for the speed of opening 30 oysters. And, just like in hockey, penalties may be imposed for a number of reasons — an oyster not severed from its shell, an oyster with blood, an oyster with shell or grit on its flesh, cut flesh of an oyster, an oyster not presented upright or any oysters not opened or presented. Whew. Who did Patrick beat? Australia, the UK, Ireland, Sweden, USA, Germany, Switzerland, Finland, Japan, Northern Ireland, Norway and Denmark. Good on ya, Patrick.

Scallops in a Galician Style with Saffron Rice

Ted's Choice A dry Rosado from Spain or a Viognier.

Makes 4 servings

Scallops are very typical of Galicia where chefs and home cooks alike prefer to treat them simply to allow their distinctive flavour to shine through. This dish is a perfect example and is even more appealing when served over the accompanying colourful rice. Sadly, it is very difficult (or impossible) for North Americans to obtain either of Spain's legendary hams, whether in the form of *jamón serrano*, a generic term for mountain-cured ham, or the truly wonderful *jamón ibérico*, derived from the happy, black-footed, acorn-eating Iberian pigs. In this dish, good-quality cured ham or prosciutto may be used in its place. Look for Spanish olive oil for this dish. Serve with wedges of fresh lemon for squeezing at the table. Begin by preparing the rice.

For the saffron rice:

2 tbsp. (30 mL) olive oil

1 tbsp. (15 mL) butter

1 small onion, minced

1 cup (250 mL) short-grain rice (preferably Spanish, but any quality short-grain rice may be used)

1 cup (250 mL) chicken broth

1 cup (250 mL) water

few strands of saffron, crushed

sea salt and freshly ground pepper to taste

In a Dutch oven or similar heavy-based saucepan, combine the oil and butter over medium-high heat. Add the onion and cook until softened, about 5 minutes. Stir in the rice and ensure that it is well coated with the other ingredients, and then add the broth, water, saffron and salt and bring the mixture to a boil. Reduce the heat to very low, cover and let simmer for 15–20 minutes until the rice is cooked. Let stand for 5 minutes before serving.

Pat the scallops dry and lightly sprinkle both sides with salt. Heat the oil in a heavy skillet over high heat. Just as the oil begins to smoke, add the scallops and sear them quickly on both sides for about 20 seconds per side — no longer, as they will be returned to the skillet later. Transfer to a warm platter. Return the skillet to the heat, add the garlic and onion and sauté for a few minutes until softened, about 5–6 minutes. Add the parsley and saffron, and then return the scallops to the pan along with the ham and wine. Bring the mixture to a gentle boil, reduce heat and cook for no longer than 3 minutes, less if you like. Serve over the rice.

For the scallops:
1 1/2 lb. (680 g) sea scallops
sea salt to taste
3 tbsp. (45 mL) olive oil
2 cloves garlic, minced
1 large onion, finely chopped
1/4 cup (60 mL) chopped parsley
few strands of saffron
1/4 cup (60 mL) good-quality
    cured ham or prosciutto
1/4 cup (60 mL) dry white wine

La Lonja de Portonova

The fish and seafood public auction in Portonova, Galicia, is an amazing event. Held very late at night, this is where chefs, restaurateurs, shop and hotel owners gather to bid on seafood that has just been brought back from the sea. Restaurants like Casa Rosita in Cambados that specialize in the very best of simply prepared, locally caught seafood vie with others eager to get the best at the best price. I saw mussels, clams, baby sole – *lenguado*, the massive crabs known as *centolla*, barnacles, oysters, octopus, shrimp, lobster, hake, tuna, monkfish, brill, turbot, sea bass, cod, sardines, eel and the huge scallops, perfect for *vieiras de Santiago* – St. James's baked scallops, a dish offered in just about every restaurant in Santiago on St. James's Day.

Shanks Fritto Misto

Ted's Choice A Pinot Grigio or Chenin Blanc.

Serves 4

When this vibrantly colourful dish was brought to my table at Chef Robbie Millar's restaurant called Shanks, I let out a little gasp. It was so beautiful, so striking in colour and form, yet really so simple. *Fritto misto* is Italian for a "mixed fry," which can include pieces of vegetable, seafood, fish or cheese. Use extra virgin or simply virgin olive oil for the deep-frying.

2 large eggs, separated

3/4 cup (150 mL) all-purpose flour, sifted

pinch of salt

1 cup (250 mL) sparkling water (club soda is fine)

1 large red onion, peeled, separated into rings

1 fennel bulb, trimmed, cut into chunks

1 red pepper, seeded, cut into chunks

1 large zucchini, sliced

8–10 large shrimp, peeled, deveined, tails intact

Half fill a large, deep, heavy saucepan or deep-fat fryer with enough oil to achieve a depth of about 3–4 inches (7.5–10 cm). Preheat oven to 200F (95C) in readiness to keep food warm. Heat oil to 350F (180C). As it is heating, mix the egg yolks, flour, salt and water together in a mixing bowl. In another bowl, whisk the egg whites until they form soft peaks and fold into the flour mixture. Dip the vegetables and shrimp into the batter a few at a time, letting excess batter drip into the bowl, and carefully drop into the hot oil. Deep-fry in batches for 2–3 minutes, stirring until vegetables and shrimp are pale golden in colour. Drain on paper towels and keep warm in the oven as you repeat the process with remaining vegetables and shrimp. Serve immediately with lemon wedges and good salt and pepper.

Turbot & Shellfish in Terracotta

Ted's Choice A fresh "joven"-style red from Galicia.

Makes 4–6 servings

Turbot is in plentiful supply in the northwest corner of Spain and here it is combined, in classic Galician style, with fresh shellfish and tomatoes. Best cooked within the lovely brick-coloured terracotta ovenproof dish, you can also use any good ceramic or glass casserole in its place. Now you may think that the quantity of olive oil is excessive, but the Spaniards produce some of the world's greatest olive oil and use it lavishly as it adds so very much to the flavour and quality of the finished dish. Have lots of good, crusty bread on hand to serve with this.

Preheat oven to 400F (200C). Heat the oil in a large skillet over medium-high heat. Add the garlic and onion and cook for a few minutes. Add tomatoes, a little salt and pepper and the paprika and mix well into the onion mixture, reduce the heat and simmer for 15 minutes or so.

Lay the slices of turbot in the oven dish and place the scallops, clams or mussels and shrimp on and around the fish. Pour the sauce over all and place in the oven for 15–20 minutes. At this point the fish and shrimp will be cooked through and the shellfish opened. (Discard any that have not opened.)

Remove from the oven and pour the white wine over the fish, garnish with the parsley and serve immediately.

1 1/2 cups (375 mL) olive oil (preferably Spanish)

2 cloves garlic, crushed

3 medium-sized onions, chopped

2 cups (500 mL) chopped plum tomatoes (fresh or canned)

sea salt and freshly ground pepper to taste

2 tsp. (10 mL) paprika

3 1/4 lb. (1.5 kg) turbot fillets, cut into 1-inch (2-cm) slices

12 sea scallops

12 clams or mussels, in their shells

1 lb. (500 g) small shrimp, peeled, uncooked

1/2 cup (125 mL) dry white wine

1/4 cup (60 mL) chopped parsley

Musselburgh Mussels in Beurre Breton with Toast

Ted's Choice From Belgium, Gueuze Lambic "Mort Subite" — a perfect and classic match with mussels.

Makes 4 servings

Musselburgh, in East Lothian not far from Edinburgh, is so-called because of a famous mussel bed that was found long ago at the mouth of the River Esk. This is a quiet little town that has always been renowned for its mussels and mussel eaters. I think they would be pleased with my version of hot buttered mussels licked with a savoury butter made in a Brittany style. The butter works wonderfully well to complement any shellfish. Use the mussel cooking liquid for other soups, chowders or sauces.

4 1/2 lb. (2 kg) mussels, cleaned as described on the opposite page

4 cloves garlic, roughly chopped

1/4 cup (60 mL) chopped parsley

1 cup (250 mL) dry white wine

2/3 cup (150 mL) water

1 shallot, minced

1/2 cup Muscadet

1 large clove garlic, minced

1 tbsp. (15 mL) finely chopped parsley

1 tbsp. (15 mL) finely chopped tarragon

1/2 cup (125 mL) butter, diced

sea salt and freshly ground pepper to taste

Place the cleaned mussels in a large, wide pan. Sprinkle the chopped garlic and the parsley over the mussels. Then pour over the white wine. Bring the pan to the boil, cover with a lid, and cook, shaking the pan frequently, for a couple of minutes until the mussels have opened. Discard any that have not opened. Let mussels cool slightly until you are able to handle them. Then, remove the mussels from their shells and discard shells. Keep warm while you make the butter.

Strain the cooking liquid through a fine sieve, wipe the pan clean and return the liquid to it. Place over medium-high heat and bring to the boil again. Let it continue to boil until it has reduced by half. Now, add the shallot, the Muscadet, garlic, parsley and tarragon and allow the mixture to return to the boil. Let it boil gently for a few minutes, then start to whisk in the butter until all of it has been incorporated. Add the reserved mussels, season with salt and pepper. Pour into individual soup bowls and serve immediately garnished with hot (unbuttered) toast.

Mussels 101

Most of the mussels sold commercially these days have been pretty well cleaned for us, including the removal of any barnacles stuck to the shell and the removal of their little beards. The technical term for this, by the way, is the byssus, which attaches the mussel to the rock or rope on which it grows. Pour your mussels into a clean sink and cover with lots of cold water. Drain, rinse again in another lot of water and drain again. (It's not a good idea to let them sit overly long in fresh water or they will die.) Discard any mussels that do not close when tapped firmly or any with broken or cracked shells. You might also want to discard any mussels that feel much heavier than the others as they may be filled with sand. The simplest preparation? Transfer mussels to a large, wide pan and add chopped onions or shallots, fresh herbs, garlic cloves, chopped tomatoes, white wine, beer or broth. Bring to the boil, cover with a lid and, shaking the pan frequently for a few minutes, cook until the mussels have all opened, discarding any that have not.

Scottish Mussels to Spain

Galicia is renowned for the quantities of mussels it harvests each year and, in Ireland, barely a menu exists without mussels on it somewhere. I've had them bathed in cream in Brittany, teamed with leeks in a saffron-hued sauce and served over squares of puff pastry in Wales and baked with fresh herbs in Edinburgh. On the northern Scottish Isle of Lewis some of the best mussels in the world are harvested. There are what skilled fishers call "grade A fishing grounds" here, which means that the mussels can be eaten straight out of the pristine water without risk. Along with oysters, mussels have been native to this area for centuries, although today the business of "growing" mussels is much more precise. As with hake and cod, the Spaniards must have an insatiable appetite for mussels. Besides their own, they regularly buy Scottish mussels, which are slow-grown owing to the colder water temperature, and so sweeter and better flavoured.

In old Scotland, mussel brose was a common dish: place mussels in a saucepan, add water, cover and heat until they open. Strain the cooking liquid into a basin. Shell the mussels. Lightly toast some oatmeal and reserve. Heat some milk along with the cooking liquid and season with a bit of salt and pepper, and then add the mussels to the liquid. Put the oatmeal into a large basin and add some of the milk mixture, stirring it quickly so that it forms little clumps, like tiny dumplings, and then add to the soup.

Cancale Oysters in Cream with Leeks

Ted's Choice Muscadet.

Makes 4–6

Brittany's Cancale is *the* place to enjoy oysters in France. The seaside town is home to a vast farm of oyster beds where individual restaurants send their little vans right out onto the sand bar to collect the sumptuous oysters for their waiting chefs. I lost track of the numbers of Belon oysters Ted and I slurped while sitting astride the sea wall, happily chucking our shells — as thousands had done before us — over the side.

1/4 cup (60 mL) butter

1 clove garlic, minced

2 leeks, trimmed, rinsed and thinly sliced (use all of the white part and half of the green)

2 tbsp. (30 mL) Pernod

24 oysters, shucked and the liquour reserved

2 cups (500 mL) milk

2 cups (500 mL) whipping cream

sea salt and freshly ground pepper to taste

In a large saucepan, melt the butter over medium heat. Add the garlic and leek and sauté for about 6–7 minutes until softened; don't allow it to brown. Stir in the Pernod, oyster liquour, milk, cream and seasoning. Bring the mixture very carefully to a gentle boil, and then lower the heat immediately and let simmer for about 5 minutes.

Carefully slip the oysters into the cream mixture. Remove the pan from the heat, cover and let stand for about 8 minutes, or just until the edges of the oysters are beginning to curl. Serve immediately in warmed soup plates.

How to Open an Oyster

Open oysters with an oyster knife, inserting it between shells at pointed end. Remove any broken shell, sever the muscle at the hinge if still attached and discard the flatter shell half. If not consuming straightaway, cover with a damp cloth and place in the refrigerator until ready to use.

Championship Garlic Oysters

This recipe is from Patrick McMurray. These are served in many places in Ireland, the best of which is Moran's of the Weir, in Clarenbridge. For an appetizer for four, I recommend 4 to 6 oysters per person. Use a nice cooking oyster, something that will take the heat. To be true to the recipe, use Belon oysters if you can find them because they are as close to Galway native oysters as we can get in Canada. Shuck the top off and leave the meat attached to the bottom shell. (Ingredient amounts are loose — depending how garlicky you like it.)

In a bowl, mix together butter, breadcrumbs, garlic and a drop of Pernod. Mix until you have a spreadable consistency. Spread this mixture over each oyster in the shell, filling all of the shell.

Place the oysters beneath a hot broiler for a few minutes, until the butter is bubbling and breadcrumbs are golden brown. Remove from the oven, place on a tray. Serve with brown bread, butter and Guinness.

North Berwick Salmon Fishcakes with Lemon Butter

Ted's Choice We had a couple of pints of Tennent's Lager, well chilled.

Makes 4 servings

On May 1, our wedding day in Scotland, Ted and I had a prenuptial lunch at a little pub in the town of North Berwick, very close to the beautiful castle in which we were married — Ballencreiff. I figured I should order something substantial to eat, especially since we would be toasting ourselves post-ceremony with single malts and bubbly. No one appreciates a fainting bride. So, I opted for fat little salmon cakes like these. (By the way, Ted had a plate of mince and tatties and bashed 'neeps. And just in case you need a translation, that's savoury minced beef in gravy, potatoes and mashed turnips.) Add a little watercress and a wedge of lemon to each serving of the fishcakes. I have also had salmon and other cakes made of fish that are dipped in fine oatmeal before frying. This unmistakable Celtic ingredient helps to give the exterior a lovely crunchy coat.

For the fishcakes:

- 1 lb. (500 g) cooked salmon fillet, skinned, cooled
- 1 1/2 cups (375 mL) mashed potato
- 1 tbsp. (15 mL) ketchup
- 1 tsp. (5 mL) Worcestershire sauce
- 1 tsp. (5 mL) dry mustard
- 3 tbsp. (45 mL) chopped parsley
- 3 tbsp. (45 mL) chopped chervil
- 2-3 tbsp. (30-45 mL) unbleached all-purpose flour
- 1 tbsp. (15 mL) olive oil
- 1 tbsp. (15 mL) butter

Place the salmon in a bowl and break it up gently with your fingers. Reserve half of the salmon and place in another bowl. Mix half of the salmon with the mashed potato, ketchup, Worcestershire sauce, mustard, parsley and chervil. Use a fork to blend everything together well. Now, add the remaining salmon and mix in gently so as not to break up the fish too much.

Lightly flour your hands and shape the salmon mixture into four cakes; they should be fat and substantial, not flat and thin. Place on a plate, cover with plastic wrap and refrigerate for about half an hour.

Preheat oven to 400F (200C). Lightly flour the fishcakes, shaking off the excess. Heat the oil and butter in a frying pan and when butter has melted and begins to foam, add the fishcakes and fry for 3–4 minutes on each side, until they are golden brown. If the frying pan is ovenproof, slip the whole pan into the oven to bake the fishcakes for 12–15 minutes until they are heated through. Or, use a baking dish for the fishcakes.

Place the butter and cream in a small saucepan and place over low heat. Add the lemon juice and onion and simmer the mixture over very low heat. It should heat through but never boil. Season to taste.

To serve: Pour a little of the sauce on a plate, lay the fishcakes over part of the sauce and use more sauce to drizzle over the fishcake.

For the sauce:
1/4 cup (60 mL) butter
1/2 cup (125 mL) whipping cream
3 tbsp. (45 mL) fresh lemon juice
1 thin green onion, trimmed,
   finely chopped
sea salt and freshly ground
   pepper to taste

CHAR-GRILLED SQUID WITH RICE NOODLES IN A CHILE & CILANTRO VINAIGRETTE

Ted's Choice A Cava or dry Rosé.

Makes 4 servings

This dish is inspired by one created by Paul Rankin, one of Ireland's best-loved chefs who, along with his wife and fellow chef Jeanne (a former Winnipegger), helped to turn the fine dining scene in Belfast into a reality. They opened their first restaurant, Roscoff, in 1989, at a time when there was a serious shortage of restaurants with any sort of culinary pedigree in that city. A brief two years later, Roscoff was awarded a Michelin star, one of the first (and at the time, only) restaurants in Ireland to do so. Today, Paul and Jeanne are the owners of Cayenne, a hip and very contemporary restaurant in Belfast whose menu reflects the diverse tastes and styles of authentic fusion cooking.

For the vinaigrette:

2 tbsp. (30 mL) fresh ginger, minced

1/4 cup (60 mL) rice wine vinegar

1 tbsp. (15 mL) soy sauce

2 tbsp. (30 mL) Asian chile sauce

1 bunch cilantro, washed, dried, leaves pulled off, roughly chopped

sea salt and freshly ground pepper to taste

2/3 cup (150 mL) extra virgin olive oil

1/4 cup (60 mL) sesame oil

Combine the ginger, vinegar, soy sauce, chile sauce and cilantro leaves in the bowl of a food processor. Pulse a few times to blend and then add the two oils gradually with the motor running until smooth. Season with salt and pepper, pour into a measuring cup, cover with plastic wrap and reserve until needed.

Preheat a grill to hot (alternatively, the squid may be seared in a cast iron pan or stove-top grill). Place the squid in a bowl and toss together with the olive oil, salt and pepper.

Place the prepared noodles in a bowl and toss with the sesame oil.

In the centre of a single serving platter or individual plates, arrange the noodles and surround with the salad greens.

Now, quickly grill the squid for about 45 seconds on the hot grill, turning once or twice. Remove with tongs to the platter or plates. Pour the reserved vinaigrette over the squid, garnish with sesame seeds and cilantro and serve immediately.

For the squid and noodles:

1 lb. squid, cleaned and cut into 1 1/2-inch (3.8-cm) pieces

1/4 cup (60 mL) olive oil

sea salt and freshly ground pepper

6 oz. (185 g) rice noodles, prepared according to package directions

2 tsp. (10 mL) sesame oil

4 cups (1 L) mesclun mix (or baby spinach)

to garnish: 3 tbsp. (45 mL) sesame seeds, toasted

fresh cilantro sprigs

Tangling with Squid

Paul Rankin describes in simple terms how to prepare squid for cooking – give it a go:

Separate the head and tentacles from the body and discard the stiff cartilage quill. Cut the head off just above the eyes and reserve the tentacles. Remove the purplish skin and rinse the meat thoroughly in cold water. Cut the body into pieces. Coat the squid pieces in a little oil and season with salt and pepper.

I'd like to add that, when grilling squid, remember the cardinal rule: do not overcook. Squid takes no time at all to cook on a hot grill. If you leave it past the allotted time, it will toughen and become undesirably rubbery. When this happens, leave it for a while longer and, miraculously, it will tenderize itself – but do try to keep to the recommended cooking time. This is one of those dishes that all comes together very quickly at the end, so have everything else ready as recommended and then grill the squid precisely as directed.

Dunbrody Crisp Potato-wrapped Brill

Ted's Choice A lighter Chardonnay from the Mâconnais area of France.

Makes 6 servings

The following recipe uses brill, a favourite flat fish in the UK. It is enjoyed for its flavourful white flesh that is excellent poached, steamed or fried. Brill may be more difficult to obtain in North America; if that is the case, substitute haddock, cod or sea bass.

Clarified butter (also known as *drawn butter*) is butter that has been slowly melted, evaporating most of the water and separating the milk solids (which generally sink to the bottom of the pan) from the golden liquid above it. Any foam is skimmed off and discarded, and then the clear, golden, clarified butter may be used for frying as it has a higher smoke point once the milk solids have been removed. This is also known as *ghee* in East Indian cooking.

4 brill fillets, about 5 oz. (150 g) each, skinned

3 large (long) waxy potatoes, peeled

3/4 cup (175 mL) clarified butter

2 tbsp. (30 mL) olive oil

2 large leeks, trimmed, rinsed well, finely chopped

1/2 tsp. (2 mL) curry powder

4 tbsp. (60 mL) dry white wine

1 cup (250 mL) cream

sea salt and freshly ground pepper to taste

Check the brill fillets for any pin bones and remove with tweezers. Trim the fillets to form neat, uniform pieces. Lightly season and set aside.

Using a vegetable peeler, or mandoline, cut long, shaved lengths of potato. The slices should be even and thin enough to fold without snapping, but not so thin that they are translucent.

Heat half of the clarified butter with half of the oil in a frying pan until hot but not smoking. Blanch the potato strips in the fat, a few at a time, for about 2 minutes until just softened but not coloured. (You may need to replace the butter and oil occasionally if it starts to burn.) As the potato strips are cooked, keep them warm so that they do not become hard and stiff.

Wrap each fish fillet in potato strips, overlapping each strip by half, to make four neatly wrapped parcels.

(You may need to use two potato strips per row, depending on the thickness of the fish.) Place in the refrigerator to chill and set for 1 hour. Remove and brush lightly with a little more clarified butter, then return to the refrigerator.

Heat about 2 tablespoons (30 mL) of the clarified butter in a saucepan and gently cook the chopped leeks for 5–7 minutes until softened. Just before they are done, add the curry powder and stir well. Stir in the wine and cook for 2 minutes. Season and pour in the cream. Simmer for a further 5 minutes to reduce. Keep warm.

Heat a large non-stick frying pan. When hot, add the fish parcels to the dry pan. Cook for about 3 minutes on each side until golden brown and crisp. Drain on paper towels. Spoon small mounds of the leek mixture on to serving plates and place the fish parcels on top. Serve immediately.

Dunbrody House, County Wexford, Ireland

County Wexford is in Ireland's sunny southeast, an area that welcomes vacationers and day-trippers from within and without the country. Take a tour around the Hook Peninsula via the coast road that will bring you to Hook Head, and the oldest lighthouse in Europe, circa 1172, perched on the edge of a sandstone cliff overhanging the sea. A short drive from here is Dunbrody House, an idyllic 1830s Georgian manor. Set on two hundred acres of green parkland, the manor house enjoys a reputation as one of Ireland's best-loved country house hotels. Owned and operated by the thirtysomething Kevin and Catherine Dundon, this outstanding property defines comfortable luxury, rather like an overstuffed, but beautiful, loveseat. Bedrooms are spacious, filled with light and colour, each one different in its own way. The thread that runs through them, and indeed through the whole house, is the warmth emanating from the owners and staff. Chef Kevin worked for many years in Canada acquiring a number of awards before returning to Ireland to work in Dublin. Not surprising then that the dramatically appointed dining room overlooking the gardens serves some of the best food in Ireland. Directly across from the entranceway to the house is the bright, new Dunbrody Cookery School. Here the chef conducts classes at all levels, offering packages that include accommodation at the hotel and daily classes.

Three years ago, Dunbrody House was a bit of a ruin, overgrown and neglected. Today it is a member of the Best Loved Hotels of the World association, Small Luxury Hotels of the World, and is listed in Ireland's Blue Book, a prestigious collection of Ireland's best.

GRILLED OYSTERS WITH BACON & SMOKED SALMON

Ted's Choice My favourite, Veuve Clicquot-Ponsardin Vintage Champagne (or non-vintage depending on what day of the week it is . . .).

Makes 4 servings

We had huge grilled oysters in Brittany and again in Edinburgh at a lovely little restaurant where they were teamed with bacon and silky Scottish smoked salmon. A little over-the-top, but everybody needs something like this once in a while. Serve with fresh lemon wedges and thin slices of good whole wheat bread.

See the sidebar in this chapter on page 153 on how to open an oyster. Choose 12 of the deepest oyster shells for this recipe.

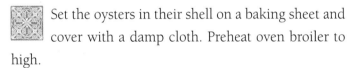 Set the oysters in their shell on a baking sheet and cover with a damp cloth. Preheat oven broiler to high.

Prepare the hollandaise: combine egg yolks, cold water and vinegar in a saucepan set over a larger pan filled with hot, simmering water. (The pan containing the egg mixture should not actually come into contact with the hot water.) Whisk the egg yolks until they are smooth and thick. Now, start to whisk in the melted butter, a little at a time, until it has all been absorbed and your sauce is creamy, thick and a rich, golden colour. Add a little pepper to taste.

Evenly distribute the crumbled bacon and strips of salmon over each oyster. Spoon out a generous amount of hollandaise to cover each, then place the baking sheet beneath the hot broiler.

Broil for just 2 minutes until the sauce is golden brown. Serve immediately.

12 large oysters, shelled

3 egg yolks

1 tbsp. (15 mL) white vinegar

1 tbsp. (15 mL) cold water

1 cup (250 mL) butter, melted

freshly ground pepper to taste

8 lean strips of bacon, cooked, crumbled

8 slices smoked salmon, cut into strips

Seared Salmon with Ballymaloe
Mustard Mash — Page 110

Scallops in a Galician Style with Saffron Rice — Page 146

CHAPTER 6

İɴ ᴛʜᴇ Cᴀᴜʟᴅʀᴏɴ & Pᴀɴ

*A good chicken and a noble piece of ham, with a little shoulder of lamb,
small to have the least of grease, and then a paste of the roes of trout
with cream, a little butter and the yolk of egg, whipped tight and poured
in when the chicken, proud with a stuffing of sage and thyme, has been
elbowing the lamb and the ham in the earthenware pot until all three
are tender as the heart of a mother.*

*In with the carrots and turnips and the goodness of marrow bones,
and in with the potatoes. Now watch the clock and every fifteen minutes pour in a noggin of brandy and with the first a pint of home-brewed
ale. Two noggins in, and with the third, throw in the chopped bottoms
of leeks, but save the green leaves until ten minutes from the time you
sit to eat, for you shall find them still a lovely green.*

*Drink down the liquour and raise your eyes to give praise for a
mouth and a belly, and then start upon the chicken.*
– How Green Was My Valley by Richard Llewellyn

Irish stew, Scots broth, the hearty bean and pork stew known in Galicia as *fabada*, Brittany's *pot-au-feu* and Canadian East Coast chowders are just a few of the classic Celtic meals prepared in one pot. These preparations are a legacy from another time, long ago. The Celtic kitchen of old boasted but two vital pieces of equipment: a bakestone and a cast iron cauldron with a lid. Filled with combinations of meat and vegetables, or fish, seafood and wild herbs, these heavy pots were hung from an overhead rafter with chains and placed over an open peat fire to cook slowly. These dishes enjoy the longevity they do simply because they are as comforting and delicious as they are economical and sustaining.

Though doubtless born from a need to make the most of little, individual ingredients like lamb shanks, pork hocks, beef brisket and oxtails are now regularly featured on the menus of the world's most significant dining rooms. Chefs that proudly boast the new Celtic cooking, like Ireland's Richard Corrigan at the Lindsay House in London and Michael Deane of Deane's in Belfast, have helped to elevate and refine this former peasant country cuisine, without losing the roots of what originally made it so good and so very memorable.

Fadò's Modern Dublin Coddle

Brittany's *Pot-au-Feu* with Buckwheat Dumplings

Kerveller Lamb & Flageolet Beans

Cotriade Bretagne

Rabbit in Cider with Dijon

Galician *Fabada*

Scottish Highland Chicken with Whisky & Cream

Scots Barley Broth with Skirlie Dumplings

Stout Irish Beef Carbonnade

Distiller's Arms Pork Hocks with Carrickfergus Champ

Allen's St. Patrick's Day Lamb Shanks in Guinness

East Coast Chowder with Potatoes & Dulse

Oxtails in Red Wine with Parsnip Purée

Fadò's Modern Dublin Coddle

Ted's Choice Go Guinness.

Makes 8–10 servings

"A feed of coddle" is dear to the hearts of Dubliners, invoking much the same emotional response as Irish stew. Enjoyed by James Joyce, Sean O'Casey and a cast of thousands, coddle used to be the traditional Saturday night repast, set before the man who had spent quality time with his mates over a number of pints of the black stuff. Traditionally, floury potatoes, onions, bacon and sausages were combined in a large heavy pot — potatoes on the bottom, chopped onions on top, thick-cut slices of bacon and sausages on top with water just to cover and lots of freshly ground pepper. This is then set to cook slowly for about an hour at which point the coddle (which, by the way, means "to cook slowly") receives a handful of chopped parsley before serving with soda bread and butter. Definitely good solid fare for any who may be, uh, ale-ing.

Fadò Restaurant at the Mansion House in Dublin is housed in an historic building adjacent to the Lord Mayor's residence. The kitchen, under the direction of executive chef Derek McLoughlin, specializes in what he calls "modern Irish" cuisine. This recipe for an updated coddle, complete with piped herby mash, is a perfect example of that genre. This is a big dish that would be perfect to feed a crowd on St. Patrick's Day. By the way, *fadò* is an Irish Gaelic word meaning "long ago."

For the parsley-chive butter:
1/2 cup (125 mL) butter, softened
2 tbsp. (30 mL) chopped parsley
2 tbsp. (30 mL) chopped chives
sea salt and freshly ground
  pepper to taste

In a bowl, combine the butter, parsley and chives and cream together until well blended. Season with salt and pepper to taste. Cover with plastic wrap and reserve until needed.

Place the corned beef and the bacon in a large Dutch oven or similar heavy pot with a lid. Add cold water just to cover, and then add the bay leaves, thyme and a few whole peppercorns. Cover and bring to the boil over high heat, reduce heat and cook slowly for about 90 minutes, skimming regularly. Now add the sausages and carrots, pushing them down and around the meat, and cook for another 10 minutes, adding a little more water if the level has reduced a great deal. Add potatoes, celery and quartered onions and cook until vegetables are tender, about 15–20 minutes. Remove the potatoes and transfer to a bowl. Cover with a clean tea towel and keep warm for a few minutes. Remove all the remaining vegetables and transfer to the centre of a large warmed platter and keep warm. Use tongs to transfer the beef and bacon to a cutting board and slice thickly. Arrange on top of the vegetables and keep everything warm while you prepare the potatoes. Mash the potatoes with the parsley-chive butter and the cream until smooth. Use a piping bag fitted with a large nozzle to pipe the mashed potatoes around the meat and vegetables or just spoon it round. Sprinkle everything with chopped parsley and serve immediately.

For the coddle:

2 lb. (1 kg) corned beef brisket
2 lb. (1 kg) whole back bacon
2 bay leaves
2 sprigs fresh thyme
a few whole peppercorns
1 lb. (500 g) good-quality pork sausages
4 stalks celery, trimmed, roughly chopped
4 carrots, scraped, roughly chopped
4 small onions, quartered
2 lb. (1 kg) floury potatoes, peeled
1 cup (250 mL) cream, heated
1/2 cup (125 mL) chopped parsley

Of Mash & Men

As with most brewing and distilling operations, the by-products of these operations — spent grain, mashed malt or barley — are recycled as feed to farm animals, most especially pigs. In the days when there were hundreds of illegal ale- and whisky-making operations in Scotland, Ireland and Wales, this was also a clever way to hide the evidence of distilling from the excise man. Recycling at its very best.

Brittany's Pot-au-Feu
with Buckwheat Dumplings

Ted's Choice A Bavarian weisse (wheat) beer like Schneider Weisse.

Makes 8–10 servings

It wasn't until I experimented with this recipe — and the one before — that I realized how strongly similar they were, in form and content. Although versions of *pot-au-feu* are certain to be found throughout France, in Brittany this complete meal disguised as soup is teamed with the robustness of dumplings that are based on white buckwheat flour, the same flour used in the making of the area's famous crepes. Note that the finished dumplings won't resemble the form you may be used to, i.e., a soft, round shape. The batter is poured into a thin tea towel (or layers of cheesecloth), and tied into a sort of pouch that is then placed on top of the *pot-au-feu* and simmers along with it as it cooks. When it is cooked it rather resembles a crumbly, savoury stuffing. If you prefer, seasoned cooked bulgur, barley or another grain could be served alongside instead of the dumplings.

In France, a very meaty salt pork is available and it is used in this dish, something that you will be hard-pressed to find in North America. It is not traditional but, as a substitute, use short ribs of beef. You will need your very largest stockpot for this recipe.

2 lb. (1 kg) short ribs of beef, trimmed of excess fat

1 lb. (500 g) length of smoked pork sausage

1 fresh ham hock

1 smoked ham hock

4 small white onions, left whole

1 *bouquet garni*: 2 bay leaves, 6 sprigs parsley, 2 celery tops, 2 sprigs thyme, tied in a bundle with kitchen twine

6 black peppercorns

Place beef ribs, sausage, ham hocks, onions, *bouquet garni* and peppercorns in the stockpot. Cover with cold water and bring to a boil over high heat. When it has come to the boil, reduce heat to medium and let boil gently for about 20 minutes. Then reduce the heat a little and use a metal spoon to remove any foam that has risen to the surface. Let the pot boil gently over medium heat, loosely covered, for about an hour.

Prepare the dumpling mixture by combining the flour and salt in a large mixing bowl. Make a well in the centre and whisk in the milk and egg. You should have a rather thick batter. Use a clean thin cotton tea towel to line another bowl, and then scrape the batter into it. Gather the ends together and tie securely with kitchen twine. Add this to the pot, placing it atop the meat. Reduce heat a little to allow it to simmer, uncovered, for an hour, continuing to skim the surface as necessary.

Now add the carrots, potatoes, leeks and turnips to the meat in the pot. Continue to simmer until vegetables are just tender, but not completely cooked through. Add cabbage wedges and cook everything for another 15 minutes.

Preheat oven to low. Using tongs, transfer the dumpling pouch to a colander to drain and rest until it is cool enough to handle. Transfer vegetables and meat to a large platter and keep warm in the oven. Pour the cooking liquid through a sieve, discard solids, and pour the liquid into a clean saucepan. Place over high heat and let the liquid reduce somewhat for 10 minutes or so. Season to taste.

Take the meat from the oven and transfer to a cutting board. Slice meat as you wish (discarding any bits you don't want) and rearrange on the platter. Carefully unwrap the dumpling pouch and transfer to a bowl. Fluff the cooked mixture with a large fork. Pile it onto a corner of the serving platter with the vegetables in another corner. Pour some of the reduced cooking liquid over the meat, vegetables and dumpling. Pour the rest into a little jug to be poured at table. Serve immediately.

4 cups (1 L) white buckwheat flour

1 tbsp. (15 mL) sea salt

4 cups (1 L) milk

1 egg

3 large carrots, peeled, and cut into thick diagonal chunks

8 small potatoes, scrubbed

2 leeks, trimmed, rinsed, cut into 2-inch (5-cm) lengths

2–3 small white turnips, peeled and quartered

1 medium green cabbage, cored and cut into wedges

sea salt and freshly ground pepper to taste

Kerveller Lamb & Flageolet Beans

Ted's Choice A full-bodied red from the Rhone, such as a Crozes-Hermitage or Gigondas.

Makes 6–8 servings

I made this one day in our little cottage kitchen in Brittany after I had spied some wonderful lamb in the local supermarket and my favourite beans, the sweet little pale green beans known as *flageolet* that are a classic accompaniment to lamb in France. Soon the entire cottage filled with the wonderful aromas of slow-cooked lamb and garlicky beans. What a good dinner this is. Look for boneless shoulder of lamb as it really makes the dish. You can often find it in the form of frozen shoulder chops in your supermarket freezer. If so, you can choose to cook the meat on the bone or off, as you wish — however, the bones will certainly add even more flavour. Flageolet are small, tender French kidney beans that are not always easy to find. Look for them in dried form in specialty food shops. You may also see them in canned form. If you do, they are ready to use and may be added, after draining and rinsing, towards the end of the lamb's cooking time.

1 1/2 cups (375 mL) dried flageolet beans, soaked in cold water overnight

1 *bouquet garni*: 1 bay leaf, 3 sprigs parsley, 2 sprigs thyme, tied in a bundle with kitchen twine

1 medium onion, studded with a whole clove

1 medium carrot, peeled, chopped

2 lb. (1 kg) shoulder of lamb, trimmed of excess fat and cut into 1 1/2-inch (3.8-cm) pieces

Drain the beans and transfer to a heavy-based saucepan along with the *bouquet garni*, onion and carrot. Add enough cold water to cover the beans completely (don't add salt as this will encourage the beans to split open) and place on a high heat. When the water has come to the boil, reduce heat and simmer for about 45–60 minutes until they are just cooked. (They will cook further with the lamb.)

Pat the meat dry with paper towels and give it a good seasoning with the salt and pepper. Sprinkle the sugar over the pieces of meat (this will help it to brown). Heat half the oil in a Dutch oven or similar heavy-based pot with a lid and add a third of the lamb. Sear the pieces on all sides using tongs to turn the meat as it browns and transfer to a plate. Continue until all the lamb has been browned, adding a little more of the oil as needed. Make sure the oil is heated well before adding another batch of lamb. Return all the lamb to the pot and sprinkle with the flour, stirring it well into the meat for a few minutes. Add the brandy, if using, and use it to scrape up any bits clinging to the bottom of the pot. Now, add the wine, tomato paste, tomatoes, garlic, herbs and a bit of sea salt and lots of freshly ground pepper. Give everything a good stir, bring to the boil, reduce the heat, cover loosely and simmer for 1 hour, checking it occasionally to see that it is not boiling rapidly.

Drain the beans, discard the *bouquet garni* and the onion. Add the beans to the lamb and simmer together until the lamb is tender, about another 45 minutes. Remove and discard any herb stalks and the bay leaf. Adjust seasoning. Serve the beans and lamb together in shallow soup plates.

sea salt and freshly ground
   pepper to taste
2 tsp. (10 mL) sugar
1/4 cup (60 mL) olive oil
3 tbsp. (45 mL) unbleached
   all-purpose flour
1/4 cup (60 mL) brandy (optional)
2 cups (500 mL) dry white wine
1 tbsp. (15 mL) tomato paste
2 ripe plum tomatoes, quartered
4 cloves garlic, crushed
1 sprig parsley
1 sprig thyme
1 branch rosemary
1 small bay leaf

Salt of the Sea

Brittany's famous sea salt is just one of the reasons to visit the Guérande peninsula, the lovely little village of the same name and Kervalet, Batz-sur-Mer and Saillé. Paludiers is the name given to the salt marsh workers who, from June to September, toil at harvesting some of the world's greatest salt. As has been done since Roman times, they trap the seawater in shallow beds called *oeillets*, left to evaporate then raked into huge mounds. This is the grey *sel de mer* – crystallized sea salt.

But the salt most prized by chefs and food lovers is the *fleur de sel*, which is collected from the very top of the beds as the water evaporates. Packed in little cloth bags, this salt is also sold in combination with bits of dried seaweed from the estuary, a wonderful intensely flavoured mixture designed to season fish and other seafood.

COTRIADE BRETAGNE

Ted's Choice A Trappist beer like Chimay Première.

Makes 6–8 servings

The artist Monet spent several months in Brittany and he wrote about the enjoyment derived from this particular bouillabaisse. After we tasted our first *cotriade* in the port of Concarneau, I knew I would never be able to duplicate the exact tastes at home — especially since much of the gleaming fish had been taken from the boat to the restaurant's waiting chef minutes after docking. However, I did repeat the experience in Galicia where the ingredients (and the delivery time!) were almost completely identical. In each case, the finished broth was served separately, ladled out of a tureen, with the fish and shellfish on the side. This rustic seafood stew takes its name from *côte*, meaning "coast." It will only be as good as the individual fish and shellfish you use. The fresher, the better. Take the time to make the fish stock because it is integral to the success of the finished dish. Traditionally, this is served with fried bread, a little grated cheese and a bowl of rouille, the spicy sauce made of chiles, garlic, fresh breadcrumbs, olive oil and some of the fish stock.

1/4 cup (60 mL) butter

1 tbsp. (15 mL) olive oil

3 carrots, peeled, finely chopped

3 onions, finely chopped

2 leeks, trimmed, rinsed (use all the white part and a bit of the green), finely chopped

4 cloves garlic, minced

1 1/2 lb. (750 g) waxy potatoes, peeled, diced

3 lb. (1.5 g) assorted fish (hake, haddock, halibut, red snapper, monkfish, sea bass or cod are good choices)

Combine the butter and olive oil in a large soup pot set over medium-high heat. Add the carrots, onions, leeks and garlic and sauté until softened, about 12–15 minutes. Add the potatoes and continue to cook until the potatoes are just tender, another 7–8 minutes.

While the potatoes are cooking, cut the fish into 2-inch (5-cm) pieces. Add the fish to the pot along with the thyme, saffron, fish stock, salt and pepper. Cover the pot and cook for about 5 minutes. Using a slotted spoon, carefully transfer the cooked fish and vegetables to a warmed platter and keep warm. Retain the broth in the pot.

In another saucepan, combine the wine and shallots and bring to a boil over high heat. Add mussels and shrimp, reduce heat to medium, cover and cook just until the mussels open and the shrimp is pink. Shake the pan occasionally. Discard any mussels that don't open and transfer the mussels and shrimp to the platter with the fish and vegetables. Add the cooking liquid to the fish broth in the pot, bring back to the boil briefly, and then pour the combined liquids through a sieve into a warmed tureen, discarding solids. Portion the fish, shellfish and vegetables onto individual serving bowls and ladle a little of the broth over each. Serve the additional broth at table, in separate smaller bowls if you wish.

2 sprigs thyme

pinch of saffron

8 cups (2 L) hot fish stock

sea salt and freshly ground pepper to taste

2 cups (500 mL) Muscadet (or other dry white wine)

2 shallots, finely chopped

1 lb. (500 g) mussels, scrubbed, debearded

1/2 lb. (250 g) jumbo shrimp, peeled, deveined

Taking (Fish) Stock

Plan to make the fish stock early in the day. Ask the fishmonger for a good assortment of non-oily fish heads, bones, bits and pieces to equal about 2 lb. (1 kg). Put all of it into your biggest stockpot. You can also add shells and any trimmings from the fish used in this recipe. Roughly cut an onion (skin and all), an unpeeled lemon, a carrot and celery stalk, a few black peppercorns and crushed cloves of garlic, a good bit of sea salt, a couple of bay leaves and sprigs of fresh thyme and parsley.

Now, cover all of this with at least 10 cups (2.5 L) of cold water and bring to a boil. Lower the heat and let it bubble away for no longer than 30 minutes, skimming the foam that will occasionally rise to the surface. Strain through a fine sieve into a bowl and discard solids.

Rabbit in Cider with Dijon

Ted's Choice A traditional farmhouse dry cider, or as close to that as you can get.

Makes 4 servings

This is the way they enjoy rabbit in Brittany. Farm-raised rabbit is tender and quite delicious, but care still needs to be taken so as not to dry out the delicate meat. In this preparation, the rabbit retains moisture because of the broth, cider and mustard. Serve with fresh fava or green beans and sturdy mashed potatoes. Make sure to use dry (alcoholic) cider.

2 tbsp. (30 mL) olive oil

2 lb. (1 kg) rabbit, sectioned into
    8 pieces

1 onion, finely chopped

4 cloves garlic, chopped

1 cup (250 mL) dry cider

1 tsp. (5 mL) sea salt

1/2 tsp. (2 mL) freshly ground
    pepper

1 *bouquet garni*: 2 bay leaves,
    6 sprigs parsley, 2 celery tops,
    2 sprigs thyme, tied in a
    bundle with kitchen twine

3 cups (750 mL) chicken broth

3 tbsp. (45 mL) Dijon mustard

Warm the olive oil in a large skillet set over high heat. Add rabbit pieces in batches and brown well on both sides, turning the pieces over as they brown. Transfer pieces to a plate and set to one side.

Add the onion and garlic to the skillet and sauté until softened and just beginning to colour, about 6 minutes. Return the rabbit and any accumulated juices to the skillet, followed by the cider, salt, pepper and *bouquet garni*. Bring to a gentle boil and cook over medium heat until the liquid is reduced by half, about 10 minutes.

Add the chicken broth and let mixture return to the boil, and then reduce heat to medium. Let simmer, uncovered, for about 45–50 minutes or until meat is quite tender.

When cooked, transfer the meat to a large, warmed serving platter and keep warm. Pour the sauce through a sieve into a saucepan. Discard *bouquet garni* and press the solids through the sieve. Whisk in the mustard and taste for seasoning. Heat through thoroughly, pour over the meat and serve immediately.

Galician Fabada

Ted's Choice A Spanish Tempranillo.

Makes 4 servings

The bean stew known as *fabada* is made in various forms throughout Spain, sometimes with black beans, or the wonderful white beans from Asturia or chickpeas, which are popular in Galicia. Now, I once brought home from Spain all the authentic ingredients — including the wonderful sausage and ham — necessary to make real *fabada* at home. I thought I would pass muster at Canada Customs because everything had been sealed in an airtight, plastic pouch. Well, the vigilant officials at the airport didn't agree with me and, sadly, my prized package of foodstuffs was confiscated. Moral of the story: enjoy *fabada* in the country of origin. Failing that, make this reputable substitute that features chickpeas and spicy chorizo sausage.

Drain and rinse the chickpeas. Place them in a large pot with the broth, tomato juice and water. Add additional water, if necessary, to cover. Bring to a boil over high heat. Reduce heat and simmer for 1 1/2 hours, until tender.

Meanwhile, warm the oil in a skillet set over medium-high heat. Sauté the onion until soft, about 5 minutes. Cut the sausages into chunks and add them to the skillet. Continue to cook for about 20 minutes, turning the sausage chunks over to brown and cook evenly. Add the garlic halfway through the cooking time.

When the sausages are cooked and the chickpeas are tender, scrape the contents of the skillet, including the juices, into the pot containing the chickpeas. Stir to combine well. Stir in the strips of red pepper, the tomato paste and the paprika. Simmer for another 10 minutes.

2 1/2 cups (625 mL) dried
  chickpeas, soaked overnight
1 cup (250 mL) chicken broth
1 cup (250 mL) tomato juice
1 1/2 cups (375 mL) water
2 tbsp. (30 mL) olive oil
1 large onion, chopped
1/2 lb. (250 g) chorizo sausage
  (or other spicy sausage)
1/2 lb. (250 g) mild sausage
2 cloves garlic, finely chopped
1/2 cup (125 mL) roasted red
  pepper strips
1 tbsp. (15 mL) tomato paste
1 tsp. (5 mL) paprika
sea salt and freshly ground
  pepper to taste

Scottish Highland Chicken with Whisky & Cream

Ted's Choice The Famous Grouse blended whisky, which, by the way, includes these three whiskies in the blend: Glenrothes (for fragrance), Highland Park (for a light smokiness) and Macallan (for unmistakable richness and backbone).

Makes 4–6 servings

The Scottish tradition of cooking chicken in an enclosed pot is known as *stoved* or *stovies*, a word that derives from the French *étouffée* that describes cooking in a covered or closed vessel. When I make this, I cut the chicken up the back, remove the backbone (keep it for stocks) and spread the two halves out, flattening the bird. This is what the Irish call *spatch-cock*, an abbreviated term for "dispatch the cock," which indicated a quick, efficient method of grilling or cooking the bird. In fact, it does help the chicken to cook quickly and more evenly. If you don't have a roasting pan with a lid, enclose the pan with foil. Serve this comforting dish with Brussels sprouts and mashed potatoes.

3 lb. (1.5 kg) chicken, excess fat trimmed, cut down the back
sea salt and freshly ground pepper to taste
1/4 cup (60 mL) olive oil
2 tbsp. (30 mL) butter
1/3 cup (75 mL) blended Scotch whisky, warmed
1/2 cup (125 mL) chicken broth
1 cup (250 mL) whipping cream
1/4 cup (60 mL) chopped parsley

Preheat oven to 400F (200C). Pat the chicken dry with paper towels and rub all over with salt, pepper and half the olive oil. Combine the remaining oil and butter in a lidded roasting pan and place over medium heat. When butter is foaming, place the chicken, breast-side down, in the pan and brown for about 4–5 minutes, then turn and brown on the other side for the same length of time. Drain off most of the fat. Return the pan with the chicken to the heat and, working quickly, pour the whisky over it and then set alight. Let the flame die down and then add the broth. Cover the chicken with the roasting pan lid (or tuck foil all the way around) and transfer to the oven to bake for about 45–50 minutes.

When the chicken is cooked, transfer it to a cutting board to rest. Drain off some of the accumulated fat and then set the pan on a medium-high heat. Add a spoonful of water to loosen bits clinging to the bottom of the pan, and then add the cream, stirring as you do so. Bring to a boil and let cook for about 2–3 minutes. Add the parsley to the sauce and keep warm. Section the chicken and serve the sauce at table with the chicken.

Highland Park

On a windswept Scottish island that sees months of bleak, rainy weather, it's no wonder that the enjoyment and drinking of fine whisky is woven into the thread of Orkney islanders life. Highland Park is the most northerly distillery of Scotland, just a fraction further north than Scapa, with the added distinction of being one of the few remaining that still malt their own barley, as does Islay's Bowmore. Highland Park has its own peat banks and, like Bowmore and all the other distilleries on that island, its malt is dried over peat, as it has been for centuries, because that was the only substance available for fuel. The distillery then blends 20 percent of this peated malt with imported, unpeated malt. (By the way, it is Highland Park that supplies the smokiness to the blended Famous Grouse whisky.) Canadian troops were among those stationed on Orkney during World War II who used Highland Park's washbacks as bathing tubs; one would hope this means they have remained faithful to the spirit. Highland Park 12-year-old is an outstanding example of what this distillery is renowned for — a delicately balanced malt with the signature "catch." It may be rare, but if ever you have the chance to try Highland Park's 18- or 25-year-old, don't hesitate.

Speyside Whisky Festival

Held each year at the beginning of May, the Speyside Whisky Festival provides opportunities to tour some of Scotland's most esteemed distilleries, meet the experts in the whisky industry and, the best part, taste some stellar malts. There is great fun to be had during the evenings, fuelled by malt and music and the company of fellow whisky lovers from around Scotland and the world. Visit www.spiritofspeyside.com for more information.

Scots Barley Broth with Skirlie Dumplings

Ted's Choice St. Andrew's Ale from Belhaven Brewery.

Makes 6 servings

I could have placed this traditional recipe in the chapter dealing with soups, but once you've prepared it I think you'll agree that it belongs here, with hearting, rib-sticking dishes. *Skirlies* (also known as skirl-in-the-pan or mealie pudding in some parts of Scotland) are substantial dumplings that really resemble the buckwheat dumplings of Brittany. The difference is that skirlie dumplings are made with oatmeal. Originally made with beef suet, the name derives from the sound made when the suet hit the hot pan, which some thought sounded like the "skirling" of bagpipes. You can also use this mixture, unshaped, to accompany grilled or roasted meat, chicken or fish. Ask your butcher to chop the meat for you. You may either make the dumpling mixture ahead of time or prepare it as the lamb is cooking.

For the skirlies:

1/4 cup (60 mL) butter

2 onions, finely chopped

1 1/2 cups (375 mL) oatmeal

1/3 cup (75 mL) chopped parsley

sea salt and freshly ground
  pepper to taste

Place the butter in a skillet and, when melted, add the onions. Cook until golden brown, about 7 minutes. Add the oatmeal and mix it well into the onion mixture. Cook for about 10 minutes, stirring the oatmeal to help it absorb the butter mixture. Remove from the heat and add the parsley. Let cool for a few minutes, then shape the mixture into little balls. Set to one side until ready to place atop the simmering broth.

Put the lamb into a large soup pot and cover with the water and bay leaf. Add salt and pepper and bring to a boil over medium-high heat. Let the pot boil for a few minutes, removing any foam that rises to the surface. Now add the barley and peas, reduce the heat and let cook slowly for about 1 1/2 hours. At the end of this time, remove the lamb to a plate and let cool for a few minutes. When cool enough to handle, cut the meat from the bones and trim excess fat. Discard fat and bones. Return the meat to the pot and add the carrots, onion, peas, leek and turnips and add a little more salt and pepper. Bring to the boil, then reduce heat to a simmer and cook until everything is tender, about another 35 minutes. During the last half of the cooking time, add the skirlie dumplings to float on the surface of the broth to heat through. Add the chopped parsley and serve.

For the broth:

2 1/2 lb. (1.25 kg) shoulder or
    neck of lamb (on the bone)
    cut into chunks
8 cups (2 L) water
1 bay leaf
sea salt and freshly ground
    pepper
1/2 cup (125 mL) pearl barley
1/2 cup (125 mL) dried peas
3 carrots, peeled, diced
1 medium onion, chopped
1 leek, trimmed, rinsed, white
    part only, chopped
2 white turnips, scrubbed, diced
2 tbsp. (30 mL) chopped parsley

The Witchery by the Castle

I couldn't resist the name of this restaurant that sits on the Royal Mile just downhill from Edinburgh Castle. Set in the midst of a beautifully preserved medieval tenement, this is the venue where those women perceived to be witches met their fiery end.

Figuring if I had lived at that time, I probably would have been branded thusly, I decided this was the spot to commemorate our last evening in this beautiful old city. The Witchery is a very dramatic place, all heavy tapestries and tall candles, gilded ceilings, the whole accented with a sort of theatrical romance. A recipient of a *Wine Spectator* award for its wine list — 137 pages in length — the restaurant features a menu that includes whisky-cured salmon, boned roasted quail, platters of Scottish seafood and those sumptuous oysters from Loch Fyne, for starters. Mains include Aberdeen Angus beef, rump of lamb, Gressingham duck and a lovely grilled lobster served with some of the best chips you're likely to have.

Stout Irish Beef Carbonnade

Ted's Choice Murphy's Irish Stout.

Makes 4–6 servings

There is very little difference between a good Irish stew (lamb or beef) and a carbonnade from Northern France, especially since they both include beer. Stout — Murphy's Stout or Guinness — helps to flavour the finished dish and provide the dark colour required for a classic carbonnade. Although you could certainly use lamb for this recipe, stewing beef (especially on the bone) also makes a great carbonnade. Serve with little whole boiled potatoes and young carrots, tossed with butter, chives and parsley.

2 tbsp. (30 mL) olive oil

2 lb. (900 g) stewing beef, cut
  into chunks

3 tbsp. (45 mL) sugar

1 large onion, chopped

2 tbsp. (30 mL) unbleached
  all-purpose flour

2 cups (500 mL) hot beef broth

1 1/2 cups (375 mL) Murphy's
Irish Stout

2 tbsp. (30 mL) red wine vinegar

2 bay leaves

sea salt and freshly ground
  pepper to taste

Heat the oil in a heavy skillet or frying pan set over medium-high heat. Pat the meat dry with paper towels and season with a little salt and pepper. Sear the meat on all sides, turning with tongs as the meat browns. Transfer the meat to a Dutch oven or similar heavy pot. Add the sugar to the skillet and let it cook until it becomes dark brown and caramelized. Add the onion and flour and stir together until well blended. Now add the broth and the beer and bring the mixture up to a boil, cook for a minute or two, and then add the vinegar, bay leaves and salt and pepper. Pour this hot mixture over the beef in the Dutch oven. Give it all a good stir, then cover, reduce the heat and let simmer gently for 1 1/2 to 2 hours until the meat is tender.

Once the meat has cooked, pour the liquid into a saucepan and bring to the boil again. Reduce heat and allow the liquid to simmer and reduce until it is thick and glossy. Then, return it to the Dutch oven and stir it well into the beef. Serve immediately.

Dora Keogh's

The closest thing to the Irish pub experience outside of the country itself can be had in Toronto at Dora Keogh's. This wood-lined space looks for all the world as though it were born in Ireland, with its classic snug, diminutive stools and copper-topped oval tables. Past the long handsome bar at the rear of the spacious, wide room, is a stone fireplace and adjacent to it, the door to Yer Ma's Kitchen. Here small groups gather to enjoy a traditional dinner inspired by old Ireland favourites, such as baked ham, roast lamb, chicken or turkey with the attendant sides of champ, mashed turnip, cauliflower in cheese sauce and the like. Regular music nights are held on Thursday and Sunday evenings each week and you know it's going to be authentic because Matt Malloy and Paddy Moloney of the Chieftains and Canada's Natalie MacMaster have been guests in the past. This is a wonderful place to relax with mates over a few excellent pints, something we've done often — and will do again and again.

Distiller's Arms Pork Hocks with Carrickfergus Champ

Ted's Choice Bulmers Cider.

Makes: 4 servings

After touring the distillery in the small Ulster town of Bushmills, we had dinner one lovely September evening at the Distiller's Arms, a pretty restaurant with an old-fashioned façade. On entering, we were quite surprised — pleasantly so — to find a modern, contemporary dining room of light-toned wood and exposed brick. The menu featured much in the way of local fish and seafood, but I just had to have the special that night: pork hocks with champ. Was it Miss Piggy who said never to eat anything bigger than you can lift? Well, that was what came to mind when my order was set before me. Because of the girth of the average pock hock, I suggest that two will be sufficient for four servings. If you think you and your dinner company can manage a whole hock each — be my guest — and increase the amounts of the remaining ingredients accordingly. And the best of Irish luck to you.

For the pork hocks:

2 fresh pork hocks

4 cups (1 L) dry cider

4 large carrots, peeled, trimmed, cut into thirds

4 white turnips, scraped, quartered

2 leeks, trimmed, rinsed well, cut into thirds

2 onions, quartered

1 *bouquet garni*: 2 bay leaves, 6 sprigs parsley, 2 celery tops, 2 sprigs thyme, tied in a bundle with kitchen twine

Place the pork hocks in a Dutch oven or similar large, heavy-based pot. Add all the vegetables, tucking them in and around the hocks. Pour the cider and the whiskey over all. Place over high heat and add a little freshly ground pepper (you won't need salt). Bring to the boil, reduce the heat to medium-low and let simmer, loosely covered, for 1 1/2 hours, skimming the foam from time to time.

Carefully remove the vegetables with tongs or a slotted spoon. Continue cooking the pork hocks for another hour or so, until they are tender and cooked through well.

Towards the end of the cooking time, return the vegetables to the pot to heat them through again. Transfer the hocks to a cutting board, remove the skin and excess fat. Cut into portions and place in shallow soup plates with vegetables. Ladle a little of the broth over each serving. Serve with champ.

Place potatoes in a large saucepan, just cover with cold water, add salt and bring to the boil over high heat. Reduce heat to medium-low and cook potatoes until tender, about 20 minutes.

Meanwhile, simmer the green onions in milk until just soft, about 5 minutes. Strain through a small sieve, reserving warmed milk and onions.

Drain poatoes well, cover, and then return to very low heat to thoroughly dry out; shake the pan over the heat a few times. When all the water has evaporated, remove potatoes from the heat and cool slightly. When cool enough to handle, peel the potatoes with a little paring knife.

Mash the potatoes well. Add the milk and green onion mixture and the buttermilk and mash well together. Season to taste. Spoon into a warmed serving bowl. Make a well in the centre of the potatoes and place the butter in it to slowly melt. Serve at table with the pork hocks.

3/4 cup (175 mL) Bushmills Irish Whiskey
sea salt and freshly ground pepper

For the champ:
2 lb. (1 kg) floury potatoes (Yukon Golds are particularly good for this dish), scrubbed, cut into chunks
1/2 tsp. (5 mL) sea salt
4–5 slim green onions, trimmed, chopped
1/2 cup (125 mL) milk
1/2 cup (125 mL) buttermilk
freshly ground (white) pepper to taste
1/4 cup (60 mL) butter

Allen's St. Patrick's Day Lamb Shanks in Guinness

Ted's Choice Guinness or if you hanker for a red with this, choose a Shiraz or Niagara's Henry of Pelham Baco Noir.

Makes 4 servings

If you have an Irish background and live in Toronto and don't know about Allen's, where have you been? Allen's is simply the best place to enjoy a good pint and a good meal. The joint is always jumping but never more so than on St. Patrick's Day when owner John Maxwell reluctantly has to turn away as many people as he admits. This is the sort of hearty fare on the menu on the day — perfect for the still chilly days of March. Serve with any of the good soda bread recipes to be found in Chapter 2 and the Ballymaloe Mustard Mash on page 110 in Chapter 4.

Guinness, Ireland's deep, dark stout, and a little whiskey combine to add a distinctively Celtic flavour to meaty lamb shanks. You might come to think of this as a sort of Irish *osso buco*.

6 lamb shanks

1/2–3/4 cups (125–175 mL) unbleached all-purpose flour

1/4 cup (60 mL) unsalted butter

2–3 tbsp. (30–45 mL) olive oil

2 medium onions, roughly chopped

4 cups (1 L) beef broth

2 330-mL bottles Guinness Draught

1/4 cup (60 mL) Irish whiskey

1 *bouquet garni*: 2 bay leaves, 6 sprigs parsley, 2 celery tops, 2 sprigs thyme, tied in a bundle with kitchen twine

Wipe lamb shanks dry with paper towels. Dredge in flour, shaking off the excess. Reserve the remaining flour.

In a Dutch oven, or similar heavy-based pot, combine the butter and oil over high heat. Do not allow butter to brown. Sear the lamb shanks, two at a time, and when browned on all sides, transfer to a platter and set to one side.

Reduce heat to medium, add a little more butter or oil if necessary, add onions and sauté until softened, about 5 minutes. Scrape up any bits of meat as you cook the onions. Add reserved flour and stir a minute or two until well blended.

Add beef broth, Guinness and whiskey. Stir until well blended and somewhat thickened. Add lamb shanks, any collected juices and *bouquet garni*. Cover and allow to just come to the boil. Lower heat so the mixture is gently simmering. Cook for about an hour. Add the carrots and push them down into the liquid to cook. Cook for a further 30 minutes.

Remove pot from the heat. Using tongs, carefully transfer meat and carrots to the platter. Discard the *bouquet garni*. Strain liquid through a coarse sieve into a large, shallow mixing bowl, pushing the solids through the sieve with the back of a large spoon. Scrape the underside of the sieve into the bowl, too. Place bowl in the refrigerator or freezer just until the fat has risen to the surface and set. Once it has solidified, it can be easily peeled off with a spoon or fingers. Discard.

Spoon the mixture back into the pot. Return it to a gentle boil. Add salt and pepper and the lamb shanks and carrots. Cover and gently heat through. Arrange on a platter and sprinkle with chopped parsley.

6 large carrots, peeled, trimmed, cut into thirds
sea salt and freshly ground pepper
1/4 cup (60 mL) chopped parsley

Valvona & Crolla

Every city should have a shop like this award-winning Italian grocery in Edinburgh. In addition to the cheeses, meats, oils and pastas, the handsome store houses a substantial selection of wines and the café bar features some terrific regional Italian fare. Breakfast, lunch and dinner are served here where the menu features exceptional *panatella* sandwiches, salads, soups and housemade sausages with sides of caramelized shallots and olive oil mash.

East Coast Chowder with Potatoes & Dulse

Ted's Choice Peculiar from Halifax's Granite Brewery.

Makes 4–6 servings

Cape Breton is home to the Glenora Inn & Distillery located between the villages of Inverness and Mabou. We visited Glenora to find out more about Glen Breton, its single malt whisky. After walking through the Mabou Highlands and along the beautiful Ceilidh Trail, we returned to the inn's spacious dining room where we enjoyed a rich, creamy thoroughly Celtic chowder that left little room for anything else. Best served with lots of warm whole wheat bread and butter.

2 ¹/₂ lb. (1.25 kg) clams

2 tbsp. (30 mL) dried dulse
   (or other dried seaweed),
   finely chopped

1 small onion, chopped

1 leek, trimmed, rinsed, white
   part only, chopped

1 small carrot, peeled, chopped

2 sprigs parsley

2 sprigs fresh thyme

2 cups (500 mL) water

1 cup (250 mL) dry white wine

1 onion, finely chopped

6 slices good-quality bacon,
   chopped

2 tbsp. (30 mL) butter

1 cup (250 mL) fish broth
   (or chicken broth)

2 large Yukon Gold potatoes,
   peeled, diced

Wash the clams under cold running water, discarding any that do not close when firmly tapped against a hard surface. Combine the dulse, onion, leek, carrot, parsley and thyme in a large, wide pan. Add the water and bring to the boil over high heat. Reduce heat and let simmer for 10 minutes or so to release the flavours of the ingredients. Now add the wine and return to a boil. Add the cleaned clams, cover and let boil for a minute or two until the clams have opened, shaking the pan frequently. Discard any clams that have not opened. Transfer the clams to a large colander set over a bowl to collect any cooking liquid. Pull the clam meat from their shells and put in the bowl along with the cooked vegetables. Discard shells and herb sprigs.

Wipe the pan clean and add the butter to it to melt over medium heat. Fry the onion and bacon together in the butter until the onion is softened and the bacon just cooked, about 6 minutes. Add the broth, scrape up any bits clinging to the bottom of the pan and bring to a gentle boil. Add potatoes and cook gently for 10–12 minutes until potatoes are tender.

Transfer half of the mixture (liquid and solid ingredients) to a blender or food processor. Blend to a purée. Return the purée to the pan along with the clams, vegetables and cooking liquid. Add the cream and reheat gently to allow everything to simmer until heated through. Season to taste with salt and pepper. Portion into warmed soup plates and sprinkle each serving with parsley and chives. Serve immediately.

1 cup (250 mL) whipping cream
sea salt and freshly ground
    pepper to taste
2 tbsp. (30 mL) chopped parsley
1 tbsp. (15 mL) chopped chives

Springbank

Dubbed the "Campbeltown Single Malt," Springbank remains in the ownership of the founder's descendants, a state of affairs that is sadly unusual for many of Scotland's distilleries. Campbeltown is located on the narrow peninsula made famous by the Paul McCartney song of the same name, "Mull of Kintyre," where "the mist rolls in from the sea," one of the aspects of nature that doubtless influences the aging whisky. Because there is no visitors' area catering to busloads of camera-toting tourists, Springbank has a quiet reputation as the serious whisky drinker's distillery. Look for Springbank 12-year-old aged in a sherry cask; it features a smooth body, an almost walnut hue, an aroma of the sea and a long, lingering finish.

Oxtails in Red Wine with Parsnip Purée

Ted's Choice Tempranillo or Rioja.

Makes 4 servings

A little bit Galician, a little bit Irish and all good, this hefty main course is one of the best things to happen to oxtail, a much-neglected cut of beef, as far as I am concerned. The attendant parsnip purée does much to add an upscale elegant note. Plan to make this terrific dish the day before serving. It only gets better.

For the oxtails:

4 lb. (2 kg) oxtails, cut into 2-inch (5-cm) pieces (ask the butcher to do this for you if they don't come precut)

sea salt and freshly ground pepper to taste

3 tbsp. (45 mL) unbleached all-purpose flour

1/2 cup (125 mL) olive oil

1 medium onion, chopped

2 medium carrots, peeled, trimmed, chopped

2 plum tomatoes, diced

2 leeks, trimmed, rinsed well, chopped

2 cloves garlic, chopped

3 cups (750 mL) Tempranillo or red Rioja

2 cups (500 mL) water

Trim the oxtails of as much fat as possible. In a large bowl, cover oxtail pieces with cold water and leave to soak for a few hours. Drain and rinse under cold running water, and then dry thoroughly with paper towels. Sprinkle the oxtails with salt and pepper. Place flour in a plastic bag, add oxtails and shake until lightly coated with flour, shaking off the excess.

In a Dutch oven or similar heavy pot, heat oil over medium heat. Add the onion, carrots, tomatoes, leeks and garlic and stir to combine all the ingredients well. Cook, stirring, until vegetables begin to soften, about 6 minutes.

Add pieces of oxtail and brown on all sides, turning frequently with tongs. Pour in the wine and the water, increase the heat somewhat, and cook at a gentle boil for about 3 minutes. Reduce heat and let simmer 4–5 hours, checking occasionally to make sure the sauce is not drying out. If so, add more wine.

When oxtails are tender, transfer with a slotted spoon to a large platter, let cool, and then cover with plastic wrap and refrigerate overnight. Strain the sauce through a sieve into a large bowl; discard solids. Cool and cover with plastic wrap to sit in the refrigerator overnight.

When ready to serve, remove and discard any fat that has solidified atop the surface of the sauce. Return sauce to the heat along with the oxtails and let simmer until thoroughly heated through.

Cut out and discard any woody core at the base of the parsnips. Chop parsnips roughly. Combine the butter and oil in a skillet, add parsnips and chopped potato and gently sauté the vegetables until they are just beginning to colour, about 5 minutes or so. Add the broth, season to taste and bring to a boil. Butter a piece of wax paper large enough to cover the vegetables. Place it over the vegetables and let them simmer beneath it for about 15 minutes until the vegetables are soft and the liquid has evaporated.

Remove the wax paper, add the cream and bring everything back to the boil. Simmer for a few minutes, at which point the vegetables should have absorbed almost all of the cream.

Pour everything into a blender or food processor (or use a hand-held blender) and blend until you have achieved a smooth purée. Serve sprinkled with the parsley alongside the oxtails.

For the parsnips:

5 medium parsnips, peeled

3 tbsp. (45 mL) butter

2 tbsp. (30 mL) olive oil

1 large Yukon Gold potato, peeled, roughly chopped

1 1/2 cups (375 mL) chicken broth

sea salt and freshly ground pepper

3/4 cup (175 mL) whipping cream

2 tbsp. (30 mL) finely chopped parsley

Of Dad and St. Patrick

Dad was born in Carrickfergus in Northern Ireland. Although he maintained an ongoing pledge of allegiance to the Queen, I couldn't help but notice as a child that when St. Patrick's Day rolled around each March, he celebrated the day as thoroughly, as heartily — and with as much spirit, so to speak — as anyone from the South.

When he had celebrated a little too fervently, he would dispatch my Nottingham-born mum to make champ, the traditional Irish recipe of potatoes lightly mashed with a handful of chopped green onions and much butter. Often, he would ask for the addition of a soft-boiled egg to be nestled in its centre, for extra fortification — his, not the dish's.

I would sit on his knee and share it with him as he drank the extra strong, sweet tea he called *scalt* and regaled me with the story of how the patron saint, reputed to have brought Christianity to the "pagan Irish," had rid the island of serpents so efficaciously that one wasn't to be seen to this very day. He did it *sevendibly*, Dad would say, using one of his "Irish words," as Mum called them, not to be found in any dictionary.

What Dad didn't tell me was that apparently, in the fourth century, the clever monk had also learned the mysteries of grain distillation while travelling in Egypt. When he returned to Ireland, he brought with him an Arabic *alembic* (still), all the better to produce the spirit that doubtless warmed his heart during those cold, damp Irish winters.

If there were vines in the monasteries of Ireland, perhaps we would celebrate the day with an Irish wine. But barley is what they had and barley is what they used to make the forerunner of today's most popular, distinctively Irish whiskeys, Jameson and Bushmills among them.

The Scottish may dispute the fact that the world's oldest whisky distillery is found in Ireland and that the Irish in fact invented *uisce beatha* ("blessed water" in Gaelic), but my money's on the Irish.

Grace Neill's

Quite a few pubs describe themselves as the oldest bar in Ireland, but not all are slotted that way in the *Guinness Book of Records*. This famous old inn-turned-pub in Northern Ireland's little town of Donaghadee, Co. Down, has been in business since 1611 when it began life as the King's Arms. A former clay-pipe-puffing landlady named Grace Neill took great pleasure in greeting visitors to the inn with a kiss and it is said to be her friendly spirit that haunts the beautiful old building today. The front bar with its two lovely snugs is heavily wooded and beamed with massive old ship timbers, and worn pine doors open at the rear of the bar. Long is the list of famous names that have stayed at the inn or stopped for a pint, among them Peter the Great, poet John Keats and Franz Liszt. Through the rear of the pub is found the newer high-ceilinged, book-lined library bar and the bistro. No ordinary pub grub here where the menu shows the likes of perfectly cooked smoked haddock fillets resting on satiny mashed potatoes and overstuffed pork and leek sausages served in a glossy "brown sauce gravy."

CHAPTER 7

OFF THE HEARTH —
MEAT, FOWL & GAME

Some hae meat, and canna eat,

And some wad eat, that want it,

But we hae meat and we can eat,

And sae the Lord be thankit.

– The Selkirk Grace by Robert Burns

Celtic culinary styles and foods are derived from the most honest of roots and this is never more true than when it comes to pork, lamb, beef, birds and game meats. And while it is more than possible to enjoy hearty meat, fowl and game prepared in classic, traditional ways in all of the Celtic countries — lamb shanks in stout, slow-cooked pork, roasted beef and haunches of venison — a new generation of Celtic cooks is creating some of the world's most exciting contemporary dishes using these and other long-favoured foods.

Kerveller Lamb & Flageolet Beans — Page 170

Guinea Fowl with Savoy Cabbage &
Pommery Mustard Sauce — Page 208

St. Nicolas du Pelem Pork with Mustard & Apples

Welsh Pork Pie with Cheddar & Red Onion Jam

Cider-roasted Leg of Lamb with Butter Beans & Polenta

Carrickfergus Cottage Pie with Cheese Mash

Dunbrody House Loin of Bacon with Irish Mist Glaze on Colcannon Cakes

Loin of Rabbit with Pancetta & Irish Whiskey

Guinea Fowl with Savoy Cabbage & Pommery Mustard Sauce

Corrigan's Roast Chicken with Lentils, Chorizo & Almonds

Partridges with Pears & Oban Single Malt Scotch Whisky

Braised Beef in Welsh Ale with Cheddar Toasts

Roast Rare Breast of Duck with *Puy* Lentils & Red Currant Glaze

Celtic Spiced Beef

Galician Empanada with Berberecho Clams

Gleneagles Chop & Loin of Lamb with Parsnip & Apple Compote

Carpaccio of Scottish Beef with Parmesan Crackling, Walnut Oil & Fine Herbs

St. Nicolas du Pelem Pork
with Mustard & Apples

Ted's Choice Jeanne d'Arc Ambre des Flandres or another malty, golden ale with a dry finish (this is what the French call *bière de garde* — beer for storage, a country-style farmhouse ale intended to be matured in bottle).

Makes 4 servings

The first time we drove into the old town of St. Nicolas du Pelem in Brittany we were excited to see a sign proclaiming that the lovely old town was twinned with one in Ireland — Milltown, Co. Kerry. Surrounded by rolling farmland, studded with ancient mills and stone wells, St. Nicolas du Pelem is a quiet little place and home to a beautiful fifteenth-century church, a few shops and restaurants. I remember the meal we had there one evening that featured local pork and apples served with lengths of sturdy, buttered cabbage-like greens with a flavour reminiscent of collard greens. Add steamed baby potatoes tossed with butter and salt.

1 1/2 lb. (750 g) pork tenderloin, cut into 1/2-inch (1-cm) slices

2 tbsp. (30 mL) olive oil

1 medium onion, peeled, finely chopped

2 tbsp. (30 mL) unbleached all-purpose flour

Place the slices of pork tenderloin in between two sheets of wax paper and flatten slightly using a kitchen mallet or a rolling pin. Add the oil to a frying pan and place over high heat. Fry the pork slices for 2–3 minutes per side, a few at a time, in the hot pan, until browned on both sides; don't overcook. Transfer the meat to a plate and keep warm.

If necessary, add a little more oil to the pan and sauté the onion for a few minutes until softened. Sprinkle the flour over the onions and work in well with a wooden spoon. Now add the chicken broth and blend in well with a whisk to avoid lumps. Whisk in both of the mustards and blend well. Bring this mixture up to a boil, stirring, reduce the heat and add the apple slices. Season with salt and pepper. Add the cream and blend once again.

Slip the meat back into the pan along with any accumulated juices and, using tongs, turn the meat over in the sauce to coat all the pieces well. Let the meat simmer gently in the sauce for about 5 minutes before sprinkling with parsley and serving.

3/4 cup (175 mL) chicken broth, heated
2 tbsp. (30 mL) coarse-grain mustard
2 tbsp. (30 mL) Dijon mustard
2 medium Royal Gala apples, peeled, sliced
sea salt and freshly ground pepper to taste
1/2 cup (125 mL) whipping cream
1/4 cup (60 mL) chopped parsley

The Celtic Manor in Newport, Wales

Terry Matthews is a Welsh-born billionaire who made his fortune in Canada building technology companies. When he returned to Newport, Wales, he decided to revamp the Victorian mansion where he was born in 1943, a place that served as a maternity hospital for many years. Today Celtic Manor Hotel is a splendid five-star, four-hundred-room resort that includes a convention centre and three championship golf courses, winning the prestigious Egon Ronay Award for Best Hotel in Wales for five years running.

The culinary team at the manor have received dozens of awards for their innovative ways with wonderful local Welsh foods and products. Housemade tortellini are filled with Welsh goat's cheese; Welsh salt-marsh lamb is plated with black pudding; local scallops are teamed with Carmarthen ham. A little quail tartlet features roasted quince and salsify with truffle foam. There is a "compilation of Celtic appetizers" on the menu that includes twice-baked *pant ys gawn* (a Welsh cheese) soufflé with toasted hazelnuts, a "mosaic" of organic chicken with baby leeks and saffron potatoes, tian of crab with avocado and yogurt "ice cream" and a satiny broad bean soup with Arbroath smoked haddock. For dessert, "Celtic infusion" melds a trio of Celtic products — Irish Mist and cocoa cappuccino with raspberries, Abergavenny honey ice cream and Scottish shortbread. Wow!

Welsh Pork Pie with Cheddar & Red Onion Jam

Ted's Choice Old Timer from Wadworth Brewery in Devizes, Wiltshire. Kathleen's choice this time — an ale that she first enjoyed at a pub in Bristol called the Phoenix. Failing that, choose a malty ale with full flavour and nicely balanced hops.

Makes 8 servings

Sort of a cross between a classic raised pork pie and a French-Canadian *tourtière*, I remember having a wedge of this delicious savoury one wild rainy afternoon in a pub in Wales just over the border from England. I sat near an open fire watching the rain slash the windowpane and ate as slowly as I could to lengthen the comforting experience. It was served with a sharp-tasting onion condiment that worked perfectly against the richness of the pie's filling. Start by making the onion jam.

For the onion jam:

2 tbsp. (30 mL) butter

2 tbsp. (30 mL) olive oil

1 1/2 lb. (750 g) red onions, thinly sliced

1/2 cup (125 mL) brown sugar

1/3 cup (75 mL) sherry or red wine vinegar

1/2 cup (125 mL) dry red wine

1/4 tsp. (1 mL) ground cloves

1/2 tsp. (2 mL) ground nutmeg

1/2 tsp. (2 mL) ground ginger

In a large skillet or frying pan, melt the butter in the oil over medium heat. Add the onions, stir to coat well with the fat and cook until softened, about 15 minutes, stirring frequently.

Add the sugar, vinegar, wine, cloves, nutmeg and ginger and stir to incorporate all the ingredients. Reduce the heat and cook until thick and jam-like, about another 10 minutes or so. Remove from heat and allow to cool. Pack into a sterilized jar. This will keep refrigerated for about a month.

Combine the flour with the salt in a mixing bowl (or use a food processor). Cut in the shortening with a fork or a pastry blender until the mixture begins to look crumbly. Stir in the ice water, a little at a time, until you can gather the pastry in a ball in your hands. Wrap in plastic and refrigerate for half an hour.

In a large saucepan, combine the pork with the onion, leek, garlic, salt, pepper, sage and cider. Bring to a gentle boil, stirring to blend all the ingredients, then reduce heat to a simmer. Cook for 20 minutes stirring occasionally. Remove from the heat and stir in the cubes of bread. Add the apricots and grated Cheddar and fold into the meat mixture. Season with salt and pepper. Set to one side to cool slightly.

To complete the pie: On a floured board, roll two-thirds of the pastry to fit a 9-inch (23-cm) pie plate. Preheat oven to 400F (200C). Pour the meat mixture into the pastry shell and spread it out evenly. Roll out remaining pastry and use it to cover the top. Pinch the edges of the pastry together and trim. Cut slits in the top to allow steam to escape and brush with a little milk to help it to brown. Bake for 45–55 minutes until the pastry is golden brown. Let cool slightly before serving with red onion jam.

For the pastry:
1 1/2 cups (375 mL) unbleached all-purpose flour
1/2 tsp. (2 mL) sea salt
1/2 cup (125 mL) vegetable shortening, chilled, diced
3–4 tbsp. (45–50 mL) ice water
milk for brushing

For the filling:
1 1/2 lb. (750 g) lean ground pork
1 medium onion, peeled, chopped
1 leek, trimmed, rinsed well, chopped
1 large clove garlic, finely chopped
1 1/2 tsp. (7 mL) sea salt
1 tsp. (5 mL) freshly ground pepper
2 tbsp. (30 mL) chopped fresh sage
1 cup (250 mL) dry cider
1 slice white bread, cubed
sea salt and freshly ground pepper to taste
8 dried apricots, finely chopped
1 cup (250 mL) grated old Cheddar

Cider-roasted Leg of Lamb with Butter Beans & Polenta

Ted's Choice Australian Shiraz or a Cabernet Sauvignon from Coonawarra District.

Makes 6 servings

This method of cooking a leg of lamb at a lower temperature for a relatively long length of time results in a very tender, well-done piece of meat. While it has been the culinary vogue for some time to cook lamb just to medium rare, I often think that lamb really benefits from this longer, slower cooking method. We had slow-cooked lamb often in Brittany, Ireland and Scotland and thoroughly enjoyed it each time.

For the lamb:

5 lb. (2.2 kg) leg of lamb

juice of 1 lemon

2 cloves garlic, thinly sliced

1 branch rosemary, roughly
    chopped

1/4 cup (60 mL) liquid honey

4 cups (1 L) dry cider

Preheat oven to 400F (200C). Pat dry the lamb and place in a roasting pan. Make small, shallow slits throughout the leg. Insert slivers of garlic and a bit of rosemary into each slit. Rub with the lemon juice and honey. Season with salt and freshly ground pepper. Place on the middle rack of the oven and pour all but 1 cup (250 mL) of the cider around the lamb. Roast for 20 minutes, then turn the heat down to 300F (150C) and cook the lamb for another 2 hours and 30 minutes, turning the meat at least twice during this time. Transfer to a warmed serving platter to rest.

For the butter beans:

12 oz. (1 1/2 cups/375 mL) dried
    butter beans, soaked in water
    to cover overnight, drained

Place the soaked beans in a large pot, add about 8 cups (2 L) cold water and bring to a boil over high heat, skimming any foam that rises to the top. Reduce heat to allow the water to gently boil. Add the leeks, rosemary and half of the garlic and the olive oil. Give it all a good stir and simmer for 1 hour, then add another 1 1/4 cups (310 mL) cold water and continue to cook until tender.

Heat the olive oil in a saucepan and sauté the garlic, onion and sage leaves gently for 5 or 6 minutes until softened. Add the boiling water and let the mixture return to the boil. Add the salt. Slowly add the polenta, blending it in with a whisk to prevent lumps forming. Stir with a wooden spoon for a minute or two until it is smooth and thick and pulls away from the sides of the pan. Now, blend in the cream with the whisk and cook, stirring, until it is heated through.

To serve: Remove as much excess fat as you can from the lamb's roasting pan. Place the pan over a low heat and add the remaining cider to deglaze the pan, scraping up any bits clinging to the bottom of the pan. Let this boil briskly for a few minutes, then strain into a little saucepan and keep warm. Slice the lamb. Divide the polenta among 6 warmed plates. Spoon the butter bean mixture on top and around the polenta. Lay slices of lamb over top and serve immediately with the reduced cider mixture.

2 leeks, trimmed, rinsed well, finely chopped

2 branches rosemary

5 cloves garlic, peeled, roughly chopped

1/2 cup (125 mL) olive oil

For the polenta:

1/4 cup (60 mL) olive oil

3 cloves garlic, peeled, roughly chopped

1 medium red onion, peeled, finely chopped

8 sage leaves, roughly chopped

2 cups (500 mL) boiling water

1 tsp. (5 mL) sea salt

1 1/2 cup (375 mL) quick-cooking polenta

1/2 cup (125 mL) whipping cream

Carrickfergus Cottage Pie with Cheese Mash

Ted's Choice St. Ambroise Pale Ale from Quebec, or an Irish red ale.

Makes 4–6 servings

A cottage pie is quite like a shepherd's pie, the difference being the ground meat in the former is beef and in the latter, lamb. I was pleasantly surprised to see this comfort dish — one of my dad's favourite suppers — showcased on the contemporary menu at Deane's, a stylish brasserie in Belfast. The only update was the addition of good, aged Irish Cheddar to the mashed spuds.

2 tbsp. (30 mL) olive oil

1 large onion, chopped

1 large carrot, chopped

2 cloves garlic, finely chopped

1 1/2 lb. (750 g) lean ground beef

2 cups (500 mL) chopped plum tomatoes (fresh or canned)

3 tbsp. (45 mL) tomato paste

2 tsp. (10 mL) Worcestershire sauce

sea salt and freshly ground pepper to taste

1 1/4 cups (310 mL) beef broth

3–4 large floury potatoes, peeled, quartered

3 tbsp. (45 mL) butter

1 cup (250 mL) milk (approx.)

1 cup (250 mL) grated old Cheddar cheese

In a large, heavy skillet over medium heat, warm the oil and sauté the onion, carrot and garlic until softened and lightly coloured. Increase the heat and add the ground beef, breaking it up as it cooks. When lightly browned, add the tomatoes, tomato paste, Worcestershire sauce, salt, pepper and beef broth. Stir everything together to blend well. Bring to the boil, reduce heat and let simmer gently, stirring occasionally, for about an hour, adding a little more hot water if needed. Halfway through the simmering, cover loosely with a lid.

Preheat oven to 400F (200C). Place potatoes in a saucepan, just cover with cold water. Add a little salt to taste and bring to the boil over high heat. Reduce heat and cook until potatoes are tender, about 20 minutes. Drain, return to the heat and dry out thoroughly by shaking the pan over the heat for a few seconds. Mash the potatoes well, adding the butter and milk as you mash. When well mashed, stir in the grated cheese and beat well into the mashed potatoes. Set to one side.

Transfer the beef mixture to a pie dish or similar ovenproof dish. Top with mashed potatoes. Dot with a little butter and bake until heated through, when it is bubbling round the edges and the potatoes are golden brown, about 30 minutes.

Cayenne Restaurant in Belfast

Paul Rankin from Co. Down, Northern Ireland, met his wife, Jeanne, who was born in the US but raised in Winnipeg, Manitoba, while they were both working on a boat in Greece. After travelling the world together, and working within the restaurant industry, they took additional training in London before eventually working in kitchens in North America. Finally, they returned to Ireland and bought a bankrupt Belfast restaurant, renamed it Roscoff and within no time it received its first Michelin star. At the time, Belfast was not exactly rich in outstanding restaurants. But the success of this establishment, and Nick's Warehouse in Belfast's Cathedral Quarter that opened around the same time, spawned a good food and restaurant renaissance in the city. Today, the Rankins own and operate Cayenne, an eclectic, thoroughly contemporary dining space in Belfast where Vietnamese garlic clams, aubergine and cashew pot stickers, crispy duck confit with Thai lemongrass salad, share menu space with peppered duck breasts, Moroccan spiced loin of lamb and the finest Irish salmon and seafood.

Dunbrody House Loin of Bacon with Irish Mist Glaze on Colcannon Cakes

Ted's Choice A dry Rosé from Tavel, Southern Rhone.

Makes 4 servings

Chef Kevin Dundon at Ireland's Dunbrody House urged me to have this for dinner when we were fortunate enough to spend a couple of nights at this magnificent country house hotel. There were so many local foods on the menu, among them the pork for this dish that clearly defines, in the most delicious way, the new Irish cuisine. I have substituted a whole Canadian back bacon for the loin of bacon originally called for in this recipe. While it makes a good stand-in, you could also use a small boneless loin of pork. In the original dish, the chef served the cabbage separately, but I thought it would be nice to make little potato-and-cabbage cakes to go with. Sweet baby carrots, simply steamed and buttered, would be perfect alongside.

For the bacon:

2 lb. (1 kg) whole back bacon

16 whole cloves

1/2 cup (125 mL) liquid honey

1/4 cup (60 mL) Irish Mist

2 cups (500 mL) dry apple cider

Preheat the oven to 425F (220C). Place the bacon in a steamer and steam for about 40 minutes until cooked through. Allow to cool, and then trim the ends of the piece of back bacon and reserve. Now, slice the bacon into four thick slices and stud each slice with four cloves each. Place the bacon slices in a roasting pan and brush with the honey and the Irish Mist. Slip the pan into the oven and roast for about 10–15 minutes until the honey is caramelized.

Remove from the oven, transfer the bacon to a warm serving platter. Keep warm while you prepare the sauce.

Place the roasting pan over a high heat, add the apple cider and bring to the boil, scraping up any bits clinging to the bottom of the pan. Let this mixture cook briskly, reducing it by half. Keep warm.

Melt half the butter in a frying pan, add the chopped bacon and onions and sauté for a few minutes until the bacon is slightly crisped and the onion softened. Scrape the contents of the pan into a bowl along with the mashed potato, cabbage, flour, cream and egg yolk. Mix together well and shape this mixture into four cakes. Add the remaining butter to the pan along with the olive oil and place over medium-high heat. Place the colcannon cakes in the pan and fry until golden brown on both sides about 4 minutes in total.

To serve: Place a colcannon cake on each plate, place a slice of bacon on top of each, pour some sauce over and around the bacon and the cake. Serve immediately.

For the colcannon cakes:

3 tbsp. (30 mL) butter

2 green onions, trimmed, finely chopped

trimmed back bacon ends, chopped (see opposite page)

2 cups (500 mL) mashed potato

1 1/2 cups (375 mL) cooked cabbage, shredded

2 tbsp. (30 mL) unbleached all-purpose flour

1/4 cup (60 mL) whipping cream

1 egg yolk

1 tbsp. (15 mL) olive oil

Shanks Restaurant in Bangor, Northern Ireland

Just outside of Belfast, in Bangor, is the Blackwood Golf Centre where you will find what is surely the ultimate in fine dining in the Belfast area and, in fact, the whole of Northern Ireland. Shanks is owned and operated by Chef Robbie Millar and his wife Shirley. Housed within one of the most modern buildings in Northern Ireland, Shanks' interior was designed by Sir Terence Conran. The surroundings are stylish, tasteful, warm, the service informed, fine-tuned, expert and the food, well, superb, worthy of the Michelin star it received in 1996. Local and homegrown ingredients are the focus of the menu where Millar showcases sumptuous duck breast, lamb loins, wild salmon and local beef with skillful integrity and invention. An appetizer of *fritto misto* featured small, perfectly crisped pieces of lobster, shrimp, squid and tiny artichoke hearts, all so fresh they very nearly squeaked when bitten (see page 148 for a recipe inspired by this dish). Demure quails' eggs and oven-dried cherry tomatoes filled in the blanks, with droplets of brilliant pesto and aïoli contributing to a plate filled with colour, light and intense tastes. If our schedule had permitted, I would have returned every night while we were in Ireland in an effort to try everything on the menu.

Loin of Rabbit with Pancetta & Irish Whiskey

Ted's Choice Tyrconnell Single Malt Irish Malt Whiskey.

Makes 4-6 servings

Farm-raised rabbit is lean, mildly flavoured and tender; however, it does need to be treated with care so it does not dry out. This recipe is inspired by two individual dishes, one of which we enjoyed in a lodge in the Scottish Highlands where it was based on rabbit's large relative — hare. Then, in a stylish dining room in Belfast, I ordered a more contemporary version much like this one. Rabbit tenderloin comes from the saddle. A good butcher will be able to obtain these for you. Serve with really well-made mashed spuds and brilliant green spinach.

6 juniper berries

2 whole cloves

1/2 tsp. (2 mL) dried thyme

1/2 tsp. (2 mL) paprika

1/2 tsp. (2 mL) whole black
   peppercorns

1/2 tsp. (2 mL) coarse salt

1 1/2 lb. (750 g) boneless rabbit
   tenderloin

12 slices pancetta

1/3 cup (75 mL) Irish whiskey

2 tbsp. (30 mL) olive oil

2 tbsp. (30 mL) butter

1 cup (250 mL) chicken broth

3/4 cup (175 mL) whipping cream

1/4 cup (60 mL) chopped parsley

Place the juniper berries, cloves, thyme, paprika, peppercorns and salt in a spice grinder (or use a mortar and pestle) and process to a powder.

Slice the rabbit loin into 12 segments. Sprinkle each with some of the spice mixture on both sides. Then use a little of the whiskey to drizzle over each. Wrap each piece in pancetta and secure with a toothpick.

Combine the oil and butter in a heavy-based frying pan set over high heat. When the butter has melted, fry the pieces of rabbit until it is beginning to colour, turning once, for about 3 minutes per side. Do this in batches if necessary. When all the meat has been cooked, return it to the pan, add the remaining whiskey and quickly set it alight. When the flame has died down, transfer the meat to a warmed platter and return the pan to the heat. Add the broth and bring it to a boil, scraping up any bits clinging to the bottom. Reduce the heat to medium and add the cream and let cook until thickened and glossy. Pour over the rabbit, sprinkle with parsley and serve immediately.

MacNean's Bistro, County Cavan, Ireland

Grassy and lush, Ireland's County Cavan is quiet, dotted with lakes and endless hiking trails. At the very top of the county, sitting on the border of Northern Ireland is the tiny village of Blacklion, home of MacNean's House & Bistro. Food lovers from both sides of the border regularly make the journey to this little town to dine at this multi-award-winning restaurant. Twentysomething chef Neven Maguire, blue-eyed and fresh-faced, runs the show along with his parents and siblings. With his strong focus on local, organic foods and stylish presentations, Maguire is the very definition of the new Irish chef, warm, unpretentious, talented and extraordinarily busy with a successful television career also to his credit. Ireland's *Food & Wine Magazine* recently dubbed MacNean's the Best Ulster Restaurant, high praise indeed considering the North has some of the best chefs in the whole of Ireland. Bests include spring rolls filled with confit of local duck combined with red cabbage and Asian spices, lasagna of wild salmon, young lamb in herbs with couscous ratatouille and fresh hake — a wonderful fish from Ireland's west coast Canadians rarely see — served with local scallops.

Guinea Fowl with Savoy Cabbage & Pommery Mustard Sauce

Ted's Choice Rosebank Single Malt Whisky, a Lowland malt, or an Irish like Redbreast.

Makes 4 servings

Halo, the chic restaurant of the visually arresting Morrison Hotel, is set in Dublin overlooking the River Liffey. One of the designers responsible for its inimitable style is Ireland's John Rocha who, among many other achievements, is renowned for his work with Waterford crystal. The food in Halo is as artful as the almost theatrical surroundings — dramatic, bold and quite unlike any other restaurant in Dublin. One of the menu stand-outs on the evening we dined there was seared salmon raviolo placed on a tangle of spinach and Jerusalem artichoke, topped with a butter-saffron emulsion and draped with lengths of chive, while five tiny mussels dotted the edges of this magnificent plate. Edible art. Here is a dish that is an approximation of another of Halo's outstanding presentations.

Guinea fowl has more flavour than a domestic chicken, but take care when cooking it because it has a tendency towards dryness — hence the butter in the ingredient list. I should also tell you that I'm stretching things a bit — literally — to say that one guinea fowl will serve four. You can double the recipe to provide half a guinea fowl per person. Alternatively, provide a substantial first course and the recipe as given will certainly be sufficient.

For the guinea fowl:

1 plump guinea fowl

3 tbsp. (45 mL) butter

1 tbsp. (15 mL) melted butter

2 tsp. (10 mL) fresh marjoram leaves

3 tbsp. olive oil

sea salt and freshly ground pepper to taste

Preheat oven to 400F (200C). Combine the 3 tablespoons (45 mL) of butter with the marjoram and season to taste. Blend this mixture together and insert it under the skin of the breasts. Use the melted butter to brush over the entire surface of the bird and season with a little more salt and pepper. Place a roasting pan on medium-high heat and add the olive oil. When hot, add the guinea fowl on one side and fry for a few minutes until it is just beginning to turn golden brown. Turn the bird over and repeat on the other side. Place the bird breast-side up and transfer the pan to the oven. Roast the bird for about 40 minutes, basting frequently. Remove from the oven, transfer to a warm serving platter and keep warm by loosely covering with foil.

Place the roasting pan on medium heat, drain off a little of the accumulated fat. Return pan to the heat, add the wine and as it comes to the boil, scrape up any bits clinging to the bottom of the pan. Let it reduce by half, then add the chicken broth and let reduce by one-third. Now, add the cream and let it cook until mixture thickens and is glossy. As it cooks, blend the butter with the flour and then blend this well into the simmering liquid to thicken and cook for a few minutes. Pour through a fine sieve and then whisk the mustard and parsley into the sauce. Keep warm.

For the sauce:
1/3 cup (75 mL) dry white wine
2 cups (500 mL) chicken broth
1/2 cup (125 mL) whipping cream
1 tbsp. (15 mL) butter
1 tbsp. (15 mL) unbleached
   all-purpose flour
1 tbsp. (15 mL) Pommery
   (or Dijon) mustard
1 tbsp. (15 mL) chopped parsley

Place cabbage leaves in a saucepan and just cover with boiling water. Add salt and cook cabbage until tender, about 10–12 minutes. Drain, add butter and bacon and freshly ground pepper and toss together.

To serve: Cut guinea fowl into four portions. Place a portion of cabbage mixture on a plate and top with one portion of guinea fowl. Pour the sauce over the guinea fowl and around the cabbage. Serve immediately.

For the cabbage:
6 Savoy cabbage leaves, cut into
   3-inch (7.5-cm) strips
sea salt to taste
1 tbsp. (15 mL) butter
3 strips double-smoked bacon,
   cut into 1-inch (2.5-cm) pieces,
   cooked
freshly ground pepper to taste

Corrigan's Roast Chicken with Lentils, Chorizo & Almonds

Ted's Choice Crus Beaujolais, like a Morgon or Moulin-à-Vent.

Makes 4 servings

Richard Corrigan is an Irish chef who set up shop in London's Soho. On a business trip to London, where I lived and worked long ago, I decided to make a reservation for dinner. I was enthralled with every aspect of that evening, with the black and white photos of writer Brendan Behan on the wall, with the astonishing flavours of my first course of crab with fresh artichokes and my main course of a hefty loin of Gloucester Olde Spot, a special breed of pig, teamed with light-as-air potato dumplings. I succumbed to a beautifully designed cheese course that included Cashel Blue and sharp Irish Cheddar and even found room for a sweet little round of baked apple cake with raisin syrup and calvados crème fraîche. Even the memory of that meal makes me happy.

The following recipe is a simple one from the chef who describes it as not particularly "cheffy" but in line with the sorts of dishes prepared at Lindsay House in that it is based on four or five honest ingredients that rely on their individual quality to make the whole great. Look for *puy* lentils at specialty food shops.

For the chicken:

4 lb. roasting chicken (preferably organic, free-range)

3 tbsp. (45 mL) extra virgin olive oil

sea salt and freshly ground pepper to taste

Preheat oven to 400F (200C). Place the chicken on a clean work surface and, with good kitchen shears, cut along each side of the backbone, removing it (keep it for making stock). Now, using the heel of your hand (or a kitchen mallet or rolling pin), push down hard on the breastbone to break it and flatten out the bird.

Transfer the chicken to a roasting pan, rub all over with the olive oil and season with salt and pepper. Make sure the chicken is breast-side down and place in the oven for 20 minutes, baste with the juices and turn skin-side up. Continue to cook for another 35–40 minutes, or until the chicken is golden brown and crispy and juices run clear when tested.

In a large saucepan, combine the lentils with the broth (use just enough to cover), bacon, carrot, leek, celery, garlic, bay leaf, thyme and tarragon. Bring to a boil over high heat, reduce heat to medium and continue to cook until lentils are soft and the stock has all but evaporated, about 20–30 minutes. Halve the slices of chorizo and add to the lentils. Add the butter, allow to melt and then swirl it into the lentils. Season to taste, and then add the almonds. Keep warm.

To serve: Remove chicken from the oven and allow to rest for 10 minutes or so before carving into four sections. Use a large spoon (not slotted) to divide the lentil mixture among four plates and top with the pieces of chicken. Serve immediately.

For the lentils:

2 cups (500 mL) green *puy* lentils

2 cups (500 mL) chicken broth

1/2 cup (125 mL) smoked bacon, chopped

1 large carrot, peeled, chopped

1 small leek, trimmed, rinsed, chopped

1 stalk celery, trimmed, chopped

1 clove garlic, sliced

1 bay leaf

2 sprigs fresh thyme

10 leaves fresh tarragon

1/2 lb. (250 g) chorizo, sliced

1/4 cup (60 mL) cold butter, diced

sea salt and freshly ground pepper to taste

3/4 cup (175 mL) whole blanched almonds, toasted

Partridges with Pears & Oban Single Malt Scotch Whisky

Ted's Choice Oban Double-Matured Single Malt, Western Highlands.

Makes 4 servings

Whether in the form of venison, mountain hare, wild geese or small birds, the procuring and preparing of game has long been indigenous with the larder of the Scottish Highlands because it was a staple of the early clanspeople's diets. That tradition continues today and is showcased in places like the beautiful Glenfeochan Estate, a Victorian shooting lodge at the head of Loch Feochan, five miles south of Oban in Argyll. You can fish for salmon and sea trout here on the River Nell or look forward to an evening meal of venison, grouse or partridge provided by the estate's stalker and gamekeeper.

Partridge or grouse may be used in the following modern recipe that allows for one bird per serving. Failing either of those birds, you could substitute very small, young chickens (what the French call *petit poussin*) or the very available Cornish game hen but you may have to adjust the cooking time accordingly. Serve with crushed or mashed potato and a few buttered Brussels sprouts. If you can't obtain fine-ground oatmeal, use regular oatmeal and grind in a clean spice grinder or use a sharp chef's knife to chop it finely.

For the partridge:

4 partridges

1/3 cup (75 mL) butter

1 medium onion, finely chopped

1/4 lb. (125 g) lean ground pork

1/4 lb. (125 g) lean ground beef

2 tbsp. (30 mL) fine oatmeal

3 ripe pears, peeled, cored, chopped

1/4 cup (60 mL) Oban Double-Matured Single Malt Whisky

Preheat the oven to 400F (200C). Pat the partridges dry with a clean tea towel and make sure to remove any stray feathers. Set to one side while you prepare their stuffing.

Melt the butter in a skillet set over medium-high heat. Add the onion and fry until softened, about 5 minutes. Add the pork and beef, breaking the meat up with a wooden spoon as it cooks, and gently brown the meat. Add the oatmeal and the chopped pear and cook until the fruit is softened, another 5 minutes or so. Add the whisky, cover with a lid, reduce the heat and let simmer for about 20 minutes until the pears are completely soft. Season with salt and pepper and remove from the heat. Let cool and then add the egg and blend it in well. Use a spoon to stuff the birds with this mixture then tie the drumsticks together with a bit of kitchen twine. (Any remaining stuffing may be roasted in a separate pan alongside the birds in the oven.)

Drizzle a little olive oil in the base of a roasting pan large enough to hold all the birds without crowding and transfer the birds to it. Rub the birds all over with the butter and sprinkle with the thyme. Roast in the oven for about 10 minutes, then reduce the heat to 350F (175C) and continue to cook for about 40–45 minutes, basting frequently (add a little more butter if necessary), until a drumstick is quite loose and comes away easily from the body when tested. Remove from oven, transfer the birds to a cutting board, loosely cover with foil and let rest while you prepare the sauce.

Place the roasting pan over high heat. Add the whisky and use it to scrape up any bits clinging to the bottom of the pan. Bring it to the boil for a minute or two, and then remove from the heat. Melt the butter in a skillet over high heat, add the pears, sugar and nutmeg and stir to coat the fruit. Reduce heat and cook until pears are just tender but still have their shape. Return the roasting pan to the heat and scrape the pear mixture into it. Add the crème fraîche or sour cream and give it all a good stir. Let it come to a gentle boil and cook for a minute or two until thickened and hot.

sea salt and freshly ground
  pepper to taste
1 egg, beaten
2 tbsp. (30 mL) olive oil
4 tbsp. (60 mL) butter
2 tsp. (10 mL) dried thyme

For the sauce:
3 tbsp. (45 mL) Oban Double-
  Matured Single Malt Whisky
2 tbsp. (30 mL) butter
2 ripe, firm pears, peeled, sliced
1 tsp. (5 mL) sugar
1/4 tsp. (1 mL) ground nutmeg
2/3 cup (150 mL) crème fraîche
  or sour cream

To serve: Scoop out the stuffing from each partridge. Quarter the birds and place on individual plates along with a portion of stuffing. Spoon the sauce over and around each serving, making sure each portion receives slices of pear. Serve immediately.

Glenfeochan Estate, Argyll

Located about five miles south of Oban, this Victorian shooting lodge has a magnificent setting courtesy of the coastal scenery of Argyll — all sea lochs, islands and softly rounded mountains — and the lovely position it enjoys, complete with green parkland and pasture. In the sixth century, an Irish tribe known as the Scotti formed the state of Dalriada in this region and for hundreds of years following, this area was home to much feuding with battles conducted by romantic heroes such as Robert the Bruce.

As Scottish sporting estates go, this is one of the most beautiful, serving some of the finest food in the country. Because of their proximity to the River Nell, salmon and sea trout, and other seafood — such as their steamed mussels and oysters in a creamy saffron-tinged broth — are often showcased on their menu. Dishes that illustrate the historic link between Scotland and France are also included in their outstanding game dishes, like venison and wild mushrooms in claret served beneath a golden brown crust of puff pastry.

Smoked foods, fish, meat and game, are a long tradition in the area, born out of necessity to preserve foods that would otherwise spoil. That tradition continues at lodges such as Glenfeochan with a smokehouse still in use. What they don't smoke themselves they obtain from a nearby smoked-fish specialist, Inverawe Smokehouse. As well as the standard smoked haddock, herring and cold-smoked salmon, they offer the unique and intensely flavoured smoked cod's roe and trout caviar. Quite the memorable experience when coupled with a dram or two of a regional single malt such as Oban or Tobermory.

The Macallan

Perched romantically on a hill overlooking the pastoral village of Craigellachie, this Speyside distillery produces one of the world's top-selling malts. Originally a farm distillery established in the eighteenth century, Macallan has a reputation for particularly rich single malts (due in part to the use of especially small stills), and a devotion to aging in sherry casks. Over the years the distillery has acquired manzanilla, fino and amontillado sherry casks from sherry producers in Jerez, Spain. However, for the past 30 years or so it buys Spanish oak and has its own barrels coopered in Spain, then loans them to a number of sherry producers for a couple of years before importing them to Scotland for their use. Another contributing factor to the Macallan signature style is the barley used by the distillery. Of the 5,000 tons of Golden Promise barley grown in Scotland, Macallan buys about 4,500 tons. We spied a bottle of The Macallan Select Reserve 1948 at The Whisky Shop in Edinburgh tagged at around £2,000 and decided it was a bit of a deal, considering that a 1960 Macallan auctioned at Christie's recently fetched a record £13,200.

Braised Beef in Welsh Ale with Cheddar Toasts

Ted's Choice Brains Welsh Ale or St. Peter's Brewery (Suffolk) Winter Ale, a deep, strong ruby-red ale.

Makes 6 servings

The Welsh are justifiably proud of their beef, their full-flavoured ale and their very good family of local cheeses. This recipe features all of these ingredients in a slow-cooked combination of thinly sliced braising beef and vegetables. Choose a pot roast of beef for this preparation and ask the butcher to slice it for you beforehand. Think of this as a Welsh pot roast and serve with a mixture of mashed potato and turnip. Since it may be difficult to obtain Brains Welsh Ale, use any strong, dark ale in its place.

1/4 cup (60 mL) unbleached
   all-purpose flour
2 tsp. (10 mL) dry mustard
2 lb. (1 kg) braising beef, cut
   into thin slices
3 tbsp. (45 mL) olive oil
2 medium onions, peeled, thinly
   sliced
4 cloves garlic, crushed
2 large carrots, peeled, cut into
   2-inch (5-cm) sticks
2 cups (500 mL) strong ale
1 1/4 cups (310 mL) beef broth
1 bay leaf
1 tbsp. (15 mL) brown sugar
sea salt and freshly ground
   pepper to taste

Preheat the oven to 300F (150C). Combine the mustard and flour together in a shallow bowl. Dip the slices of meat in this mixture, shaking off the excess and transferring the coated meat to a plate as you work. Heat a tablespoon of the oil in a frying pan set over medium-high heat. Cook the onions and garlic until softened, about 6 minutes. Add the carrots (and a little more oil if needed), and cook for another 5 minutes. Scrape the contents of the pan into a casserole or other ovenproof dish with a lid. Add the remaining oil to the pan, place it over the heat and sear the slices of meat on both sides to brown before laying over the vegetables. Pour the ale into the pan and bring it to a boil, scraping up any bits clinging to the bottom of the pan as you work. Let it boil for a minute, then add the broth, bay leaf, sugar and salt and pepper to taste. Pour this mixture over the meat and vegetables and cook in the slow oven for 2 1/2–3 hours until the meat is very tender. Remove the casserole from the oven and let sit for a few minutes while you make the accompanying toasts.

Preheat the oven broiler. Lay the slices of bread on a baking sheet and toast the bread on one side. Remove from the oven, sprinkle with the cheese and slip back beneath the broiler to toast the cheese. When it is melted and bubbling, remove the toasts from the oven. Serve the beef and vegetables in shallow bowls with two cheese toasts placed on top of each serving.

For the toasts:
12 slices baguette
1 cup (250 mL) grated old
   Cheddar cheese

Maclachlan's Brew Bar in Glasgow

Homemade organic beer is the specialty of this brewpub located in Glasgow's city centre, which also includes a number of other reputable Scottish ales. For sheer Celtic glory, the dramatic and huge standing stone set in the doorway is hard to beat. There are Pictish carvings and designs, stone floors, candlelight and live Celtic music. The menu features classic Scottish specialties, including very good haggis and clapshot (a mixture of potato and turnip).

The Ubiquitous Chip, Glasgow

The Chip, as this restaurant is known by savvy Glaswegians, is a bit of a legend within the city and beyond. After 30 years of featuring modern Scottish cuisine, it still enjoys the reputation as one of the town's best dining spots where celebs, locals and tourists alike regularly flock. Within the space itself are a number of room choices — dine in the cobbled, covered courtyard with its large fishpond and lush greenery. There is a main dining room and up the stairs is a brasserie and bar. The wine list is one of the best and most comprehensive in Scotland and the frequently changing menu — always sans chips — features the likes of savoury venison haggis, Darjeeling tea-smoked Orkney organic salmon and a fine assortment of Scottish cheeses and sweets. A must-visit-at-least-once spot.

Roast Rare Breast of Duck with Puy Lentils & Red Currant Glaze

Ted's Choice A Pinot Noir from New Zealand.

Makes 4 servings

At the Coach House Restaurant in Lochaber, in Scotland's West Highlands, they feature duck breasts treated to a fruity red currant and blood orange reduction. In Glasgow's award-winning Papingo Restaurant, chef David Clunas pairs the same meat with *puy* lentils. Farther west, in Newport, Wales, at the stunning Celtic Manor Resort, executive chef Peter Fuchs likes to team salt-marsh lamb with slow-cooked lentils to which he has added smoked garlic cloves, shallots and fresh herbs in a rich lamb stock. This recipe takes a bit of inspiration from all of these sources and results in one great main course.

For the duck and lentils:

2 tbsp. (30 mL) olive oil

2 red onions, peeled, diced

3/4 cup (175 mL) *puy* lentils

2 cups (500 mL) chicken broth

1 carrot, peeled, diced

sea salt and freshly ground
   pepper to taste

4 duck breasts, 8 oz./250 g each

12 large shallots, peeled

1 tbsp. (15 mL) sugar

Heat the oil in a saucepan placed over medium-high heat. Add the onions and cook until softened and beginning to colour, about 10 minutes. Add lentils and stir well into the onions, cooking gently for a couple of minutes. Add the chicken broth, bring to a boil, then reduce heat and simmer for 12 minutes. Add diced carrot and continue to cook until lentils are tender, about another 12–15 minutes until all the liquid has been absorbed. Season to taste with salt and pepper. Set to one side and keep warm.

Place the duck breasts, skin-side down, in a fairly hot skillet placed over medium heat. Leave them undisturbed for about 15 minutes until their skin is crispy and much of the fat has been rendered. Use a metal spatula to turn the breasts over and continue to cook on the other side just for about 5 minutes (the duck breasts will be rare as recommended for this recipe). Transfer to a warmed serving platter and keep warm. Add the whole shallots to the duck fat in the skillet and sauté until they are beginning to colour, then add the sugar, toss to coat the shallots and continue to cook until they are relatively tender and golden brown, another 10 minutes or so. Transfer the shallots to the serving platter with the duck and keep warm.

Pour the port into the skillet and bring to a boil. Scrape up any bits clinging to the bottom, and then add the beef broth and the red currant jelly. Stir to dissolve the jelly and bring back to the boil, cooking the mixture until it is quite reduced and thick, about 15 minutes or so. Add the vinegar and let it come back to the boil. Season with a little salt and pepper to taste.

To serve: Place a portion of the lentils in the centre of each plate. Slice the duck and lay the slices over the lentils. Put four shallots on each plate and drizzle the glaze over the duck and around the edges of the lentils. Serve immediately.

For the glaze:
1/2 cup (125 mL) port
1 cup (250 mL) rich beef broth
1/4 cup (60 mL) red currant jelly
1/4 cup (60 mL) sherry vinegar

CELTIC SPICED BEEF

Ted's Choice Kilkenny Irish Cream Ale.

Makes 6 servings

We arrived at Ballymaloe House in County Cork on a Sunday afternoon – lucky us. Here, in place of the usual menu, the tradition on Sundays is for a magnificent presentation of roasted meats – beef, turkey, ham, lamb – to be offered along with huge bowls of floury mashed potatoes, tomato and cucumber salads, vegetables, chutneys, all accompanied by the kitchen's beautiful breads. This old-fashioned beef preparation is the sort of thing one would see on that table and it's no wonder it continues to be as popular as it is. Traditionally, this was made in Ireland at Christmas time and used a boned rib of beef rolled and tied by the butcher. However, you will get good results with a brisket of beef or even a large flank steak and each of the latter will be a little more economical, too. Make this well ahead as it needs a long chilling time before enjoying (although you can also serve it hot). Perfect for a summer table beneath the trees. Demerara is raw sugar, pale brown in colour and with a coarse texture. Most supermarkets now carry more than the conventional white and brown sugar. If not, a good food shop should have it, or use regular brown sugar. Serve the beef with pots of sharp mustard and warm potatoes tossed with fresh thyme and good olive oil.

For the spice mixture:

1/4 cup (60 mL) Demerara (raw) sugar

2 tbsp. (30 mL) sea salt

2 tbsp. (30 mL) coarsely ground black pepper

1 tbsp. (15 mL) ground juniper berries

1 tbsp. (15 mL) ground allspice

1 tsp. (5 mL) ground cloves

1 tsp. (5 mL) ground nutmeg

1/4 tsp. (1 mL) ground cayenne

In a bowl, combine all the ingredients for the spice mixture and blend well. Place the beef on a cutting board and rub the spice mixture into the entire piece of beef, making sure to get the spices well into the meat. Continue this application for several minutes until the meat is completely coated with the spices. Place the meat in a shallow earthenware, ceramic or glass dish, cover with plastic wrap or a pot lid and refrigerate for at least 24 hours, but 36 hours is preferable. The longer it sits in the spice mixture, the more flavourful it will be. During this time, turn the meat occasionally.

After this time, remove the beef from the dish. Roll the meat up and tie neatly with kitchen twine in two or three places. Place all the vegetables and the parsley in the bottom of a large, heavy-based Dutch oven or similar heavy pot. Barely cover the meat with cold water, place the pot over medium heat and simmer the beef gently, covered, for 2–3 hours or until very tender. Remove the beef from the pot and transfer to a platter or baking sheet. Let it cool somewhat, and then cover with a sheet of wax paper. Lay a board on top of the beef and weigh it down with bricks or heavy cans. Chill the meat for 12 hours before slicing across the grain and serving.

For the beef:

3 lb. (1.5 kg) beef brisket or flank steak
1 onion, peeled, chopped
2 carrots, peeled, chopped
1 white turnip, peeled, chopped
1 stalk celery, trimmed, chopped
3-4 sprigs parsley

Scotch Irish Brewing Company

This Ottawa-based brewery specializes in what they call "beers for grownups" and if you have ever had the chance to taste their family of beers — ale, pale ale and porter — you'll know why they describe them this way. Their Session Ale is a dry hop bitter with a barely perceptible sweetness, while their Black Irish Plain Porter mimics the style of dry Irish plain porters that were the vogue in Dublin in the 1920s — the original workingman's pint. Scotch Irish Brewing's Black Irish Plain Porter is brewed from pale ale with crystal and chocolate malts malted in England from Canadian two-row barley. It is a very deep brown with faint red highlights. Full-bodied with a dry finish characteristic of Irish porters and stouts. A great food brew.

Galician Empanada with Berberecho Clams

Ted's Choice Spanish Cava.

Makes 6 servings

I have a wonderful friend in Teresa Barrenechea, a Basque-born chef who now calls New York City home. Her famed restaurant, Marichu, enjoys the reputation as the most authentic Spanish restaurant in North America. No surprise then that I turned to Teresa for the definitive recipe for classic empanada, the huge bread pie for which Galicia is known. And here, I will let Teresa take over: "Empanadas are bread pies stuffed with shellfish, fish or meats, and are some of the special national dishes of Galicia. The crusts and fillings vary from place to place, and every Galician family, restaurant and tavern claim to have that 'secret formula' that makes the best empanada. Obviously, I haven't been able to taste all the empanadas there are in Galicia, but from the many I have tasted, this one from my friend Menchu Briz is by far the best. *Berberecho* is a shellfish similar to Manila clams, also known as *vongole* and sometimes I use these instead."

For the dough (makes sufficient for one 15-inch/38-cm pie or two 10-inch pies):

1 tsp. (5 mL) active dry yeast

2 eggs

1 tsp. (5 mL) sugar

2 tsp. (10 mL) sea salt

1 cup (250 mL) milk, heated to lukewarm

3 1/2 cups (875 mL) unbleached all-purpose flour

Sprinkle the yeast over a little warm water to which you have added a bit of sugar. Stir and let sit for a few minutes. While it is proofing, combine the two eggs, sugar and salt in a large mixing bowl and mix well. Add the milk and whisk into the egg mixture along with the yeast and half of the flour. Mix well with a spatula or wooden spoon. Turn out of the bowl and add the rest of the flour to the mixture, working it in well with your hands. Knead the dough for about 10 minutes until it is smooth and has lost its stickiness. Cover with a damp tea towel and let rise at room temperature for 1 1/2 hours or until doubled in bulk.

Heat the oil in a skillet over high heat and sauté the onion, peppers and garlic for a few minutes. Reduce the heat to medium, season with a little salt and cook for about 30 minutes, or until the vegetables are softened. Remove the skillet from the heat and let the vegetables cool completely. *Note:* The filling should always be cold and not too liquid when spreading it onto the dough, otherwise it will leak through and make the dough soggy.

Preheat the oven to 450F (230C). Divide the raised dough in half. If you are making only one small pie, keep one-half refrigerated or freeze for another time. Knead it lightly and cut into two pieces, one slightly bigger than the other.

On a floured surface, roll the dough halves into very thin flat rounds large enough to cover a 10-inch (25-cm) pie dish. Place the slightly larger round on the bottom and sides of the dish. With a fork, prick the dough.

Make sure the vegetables are not warmer than room temperature. Then use a slotted spoon to transfer the cooled vegetables from the skillet to the pie shell, spreading them evenly over the dough. Spread the clams among the vegetables and, if using, drizzle with tomato sauce.

Place the remaining dough on top of the empanada and, with your fingertips, pinch the edges of the dough together. Trim any excess dough. Prick the surface of the empanada with a fork in a few places and brush with the beaten egg. Bake in the oven for 30 minutes or until the empanada is nicely browned. Remove from the oven and let cool slightly. Use a metal spatula to loosen the pie around the edges, and then slip out onto a wire rack to cool to room temperature. Cut into wedges and serve.

For the filling:
1/2 cup (125 mL) olive oil
1 onion, chopped
1 green bell pepper, seeded, chopped
1 red bell pepper, seeded, chopped
2 cloves garlic, minced
sea salt to taste
1 lb. (500 g) *vongole* or Manila clams, steamed and shelled
2 tbsp. (30 mL) tomato sauce (optional)
1 egg, beaten

Gleneagles Chop & Loin of Lamb with Parsnip & Apple Compote

Ted's Choice A good burgundy such as Gevrey-Chambertin.

Makes 4 servings

A member of the prestigious Leading Hotels of the World group, the Gleneagles Hotel in Perthshire is a golfer's paradise. As usual, I was far more interested in the cuisine of the two restaurants, Strathearn and Dormy, of which I had heard very good things. The quality of the local Scottish lamb and beef — truly some of the best in the world — is outstanding. No surprise, then, that the chefs, so inspired, produce dishes like the following one. This was served with pan-fried potatoes, thin green beans tossed with shallots and borlotti beans. It is equally outstanding with creamy mashed potatoes and fresh peas with pearl onions.

For the compote:

1 large parsnip, peeled, diced

1 large apple, peeled, cored, diced

1 tbsp. (15 mL) butter

1 large shallot, peeled, diced

Bring a small saucepan of water to the boil, add a little salt and blanch the diced parsnip for 10 minutes. Heat the butter in a heavy-based frying pan over medium-high heat. Sauté the shallot for a few minutes until softened and translucent. Drain the parsnips and add them to the pan along with the diced apple. Cook slowly over a low heat until the vegetables and fruit start to break down, about 15 minutes or so. Remove from the heat and keep warm.

For the lamb:

2 tbsp. (30 mL) olive oil

1 lb. (500 g) loin of lamb, trimmed, but with a little fat

4 lamb chops, trimmed of excess fat

Preheat oven to 400F (200C). Heat the vegetable oil in a heavy-based frying pan and sear the loin all over, turning it with tongs to ensure this. Once it has been seared, transfer the lamb to a little roasting pan and slip it into the oven to continue cooking for another 6 minutes, longer if you prefer it medium or well done. Return the frying pan to the heat (add a little more oil if necessary) and when the pan is hot, fry the lamb chops for 3 minutes per side, longer if you prefer them medium or well done. Remove the chops from the frying pan and keep warm. Remove the lamb loin from the oven and keep warm. Tip out the excess fat from the frying pan and place over medium-high heat. Add the red wine and, as it comes to a boil, scrape up any bits clinging to the bottom of the pan. Add the vinegar and broth and let it return to a boil. Let it boil gently for a few minutes until reduced and thickened to a saucelike consistency. Add a little salt and pepper to taste and pour the sauce through a sieve, discarding any solids. Return the sauce to the pan to keep warm.

To serve: Place a quarter of the compote in the centre of each plate and lay a lamb chop on one half of the compote. Slice the loin into 12 slices and place 3 overlapping slices on the other half of the compote. Spoon the sauce around and serve immediately with the suggested sides.

1/4 cup (60 mL) dry red wine

3 tbsp. (45 mL) balsamic vinegar

2 cups (500 mL) lamb or beef broth

sea salt and freshly ground pepper to taste

Carpaccio of Scottish Beef with Parmesan Crackling, Walnut Oil & Fine Herbs

Ted's Choice Chianti.

Makes 4 servings

Can you think of a better place to order the luxury of beef carpaccio than in Scotland where prime-quality beef reigns supreme? This recipe is from Howie's Restaurants — there are four in Edinburgh, one in Dundee and one in Aberdeen. Owner David Howie Scott says it isn't a chain because each restaurant develops its own menu and style, which allows the individual chefs the freedom to establish his or her own reputation. The restaurant serves this with a mixture of fresh whole herb leaves — basil and chervil sprigs — and a little endive and baby red Swiss chard leaves. But you could also use a mesclun-style salad mix if you wish. If you do, include a few whole herb leaves, too. Choose top-quality beef tenderloin from the best butcher you know.

For the marinade:

2 tbsp. (30 mL) each, chopped thyme, chopped rosemary, chopped sage, chopped bay leaf

2 tbsp. (30 mL) each, peppercorns, coriander seeds, sea salt, whole cloves, dried mushrooms

1 cup (250 mL) sherry

1 cup (250 mL) extra virgin olive oil

Combine all the seasonings in a bowl and mix together thoroughly. Use this mixture to coat the beef completely. Place the beef in a dish and cover with the sherry and oil. Cover with plastic wrap and refrigerate overnight.

Carpaccio of Scottish Beef with Parmesan Crackling,
Walnut Oil & Fine Herbs — Page 226

Jenna's Lemon Tart with Chantilly Cream — Page 236

Classic Scottish Shortbread — Page 254

Irish Whiskey Brownies with Sticky Toffee &
Thick Cream — Page 258

Remove the beef from the marinade and pat dry. Discard marinade. Season the beef with the salt and pepper. Place a heavy-based frying pan on high heat and when hot, sear the beef on all sides until golden brown. Remove from the pan and let cool slightly.

Lay out a double thickness of plastic wrap large enough to place beef in the middle and leave 6 inches (15 cm) all around. Combine all the fresh herbs and transfer to the plastic wrap. Roll the beef in the fresh herb mixture making sure to cover it well. Roll the beef up into a tight parcel and tie the ends of the plastic wrap to resemble a Christmas cracker.

Place the beef in the freezer until partly frozen — this will enable you to slice it as thinly as possible with a sharp knife — and then transfer to the refrigerator.

Preheat oven to 500F (260C). Place the cheese in four circular mounds, about 3 inches (7.5 cm) across, on a non-stick oven mat or baking sheet. Place in the oven for 3–4 minutes or until the cheese starts to become golden around the edges. Remove from the oven and carefully drape each one over a rolling pin allowing it to set.

To serve: Unroll the beef and slice it very thinly into 16 slices. Lay 4 slices of beef around a plate to cover the bottom. Place some of the greens in one of the Parmesan cracklings and place in the centre of the beef. Drizzle everything with walnut oil, season with salt and pepper.

For the beef:

1 ¹/₃ lb. (600 g) tenderloin of beef

¹/₃ cup (75 mL) each, chopped parsley, chopped chervil and chopped chives

sea salt and freshly ground pepper to taste

For the parmesan crackling:

1 cup (250 mL) approx. freshly grated Parmigiano-Reggiano cheese

4 cups (1 L) assorted baby greens and fresh whole herbs

walnut oil for drizzling

sea salt and freshly ground pepper to taste

CHAPTER 8

CAKES & ALE — SWEETS & DRINKS

When God had made the oak trees, And the beeches and the pines, And the flowers and the grasses, And the tendrils of the vines, He saw that there was wanting a something in His plan,
And He made the little apples, The little cider apples; The sharp, sour, cider apples, To prove His love for man.

– Anon

Tea cakes and sweet buns filled with thick cream, gingery puddings with sticky sauces, crepes with seasonal fruit, scones studded with raisins, short-crusted pies, tarts and shortbread, in all its glorious forms — it seems there is no shortage of "a little sweetie with your tea" in the Celtic home. And today, some of the most splendid, contemporary desserts owe more than a little allegiance to the foodstuffs of another time.

Chef Robbie Millar at Northern Ireland's Shanks restaurant features a gratin of local raspberries and apricots with a housemade almond milk ice cream. Hazelnut shortbread is used to add a bit of textural crispness to a subtle warm rhubarb "soup" with crystallized ginger ice cream.

At Rhodes & Co. in Edinburgh, a dessert called pancake "fettuccine" is an inventive combination of thin crepes, sliced into thin strips to resemble pasta strands, then treated to a Grand Marnier "suzette" sauce and classic crème anglaise. Chocolate mousses and puddings are enlivened with quality single malt whiskies, humble rice pudding is given a crème brûlée crown and teamed with a cinnamon-infused shortbread, and ingredients as ancient as oatmeal, apples and wild honey are partnered in new and exciting ways to create five-star desserts.

In Santiago de Compostela in Galicia, Chef Toni Vicente composes a rich cinnamon biscuit sided with wild thyme ice cream, a unique leek and chocolate drizzle, perfectly accented with a shard of caramelized sugar wafer.

Perhaps the best example of sweets that are infused with the past yet thoroughly new are those created by superstar chef Gordon Ramsay. Scottish raspberries are hung in suspended animation within a lemongrass jelly and topped with double cream. Mascarpone and dense Scottish cream cheese are blended with sugar and vanilla and shaped into the traditional French dessert *coeur à la crème* and sided with paper-thin hazelnut shortbreads dipped in dark chocolate, the whole garnished with a strand of white currants.

Just as with first and main courses, there is a new finesse afoot here that leaves a light-as-air trace on the dessert plates of today's Celtic cook — making the most of yesterday's classic ingredients finely spun with an *au courant* culinary sensibility.

Crêperie La Forge *Crêpes Belle Hélène*

Jenna's Lemon Tart with Chantilly Cream

Cape Breton Cranachan

Macallan *Mousse au Chocolat*

Caledonian Ice Cream

Banana *Tartlette Tatin* with Caramel & Cream

All Saints' Potato Apple Griddle Cake from Armagh

Beech Hill Chocolate St. Emilion with Crème Anglaise & Lavender Ice Cream

Brittany Butter Cake

A Quartet of Shortbreads

    Classic Scottish Shortbread

    Jessie's Dundee Shortbread

    Ramsay's Breton Shortbread

    Cape Breton Oatmeal Shortbread

Irish Whiskey Brownies with Sticky Toffee & Thick Cream

Brittany Oat Cream

Vanilla Custard with Bramble Berries & Oatmeal Shortcakes

Tarta de Santiago

The Little Irish Whiskey Cake

Ballencrieff Castle Bride's Cake

Spiced Scottish Ale

Pure Gallus Whisky Sour

Braveheart Hot Toddy

Bushmills Inn Classic Irish Coffee

Single Malt Whisky 101

All whiskies are made from just three ingredients: water, barley and yeast. Malt whiskies are based on malted barley, that is, barley that has been steeped, germinated and finally, kilned. A single malt whisky is the product of a single distillery. Blended whiskies, like J & B, Johnnie Walker, Chivas Regal and the like, can be based on a variety of malt and grain whiskies from different distilleries, blended together. Johnnie Walker Black Label, a 12-year-old deluxe blend, for instance, is composed of more than 40 malt and grain whiskies, a high proportion of which, by the way, are Islay malts. Blended whisky styles may be smooth, fruity, oaky, full-bodied, malty or smoky, depending on the profile of the predominant whisky.

As one familiarizes oneself with the different whisky regions, the distinctive characteristics of each are learned. There are Highland, Lowland, Campbeltown, Speyside, Islands and Islay single malts; and to give the uninitiated some idea of the differences, it is said that Highlanders use Lowland whiskies to brush their teeth! Speyside malts are generally sweet, fruity and flowery and are thought to be quite complex and elegant. Malts from the Islands can be quite peaty, but not to the extent of Islay malts, which are renowned for that feature. Generally speaking, Islay single malts are not for the faint of heart; they are famous for a complex, refined smokiness and the strong influence of peat in two forms, first in the island's soft, peaty water and secondly when used in the kilning of the malt.

Ted's Infallible Whisky-tasting Tips

Tasting single malt whisky is not unlike tasting fine wine. Here are the six essential tasting tips:

1. The Prep Choose a glass that is narrower at the top than the bottom. Hold it by the stem so that your hand doesn't warm the whisky. Pour a small measure (a dram) into the glass. Don't add water — yet. (With some whiskies, the addition of water isn't recommended at all.) And certainly, no ice. Adding ice to good whisky is like adding it to hot soup.

2. Colour Hold the glass to the light to determine how the spirit was matured. A golden hue means a sherry oak cask was used, while a paler whisky suggests a bourbon cask.

3. Body Hold the glass at an angle and swirl it quickly once so that the inside walls of the glass are coated. Now, hold it upright and watch as the whisky flows down the inside of the glass. "Long legs" means it slowly slides down the glass, indicating a richer, fuller-bodied spirit, higher in alcohol.

4. Nosing Your first impression is your best. (Unlike wine, single malt vapours may anaesthetize your nose if you inhale them repeatedly.) Take note of the characteristics, which can run the gamut from sweet and floral to mineral (slate) to smoky and peaty. If the characteristics aren't readily apparent, add a very small amount of still spring water. This helps the whisky to relax and open up and, as the Scottish say "release the serpents from within." At this point it is wise to point out the folly of adding water to anyone's whisky other than your own: in Scotland they maintain that "watering another man's whisky is like kissing another man's wife."

5. Taste Take a good mouthful and swallow. Note whether it's creamy, smooth, warm, astringent or soft. Take another sip. This time swirl it around in your mouth, so that it covers your entire tongue. Sweetness will be noted on the tip of your tongue, saltiness on the sides, bitterness at the back.

6. Conclusion Recall your first impressions. Overall, is it a balanced whisky? Did your mouth confirm what your eyes saw and your nose smelled? For example, if it looked full-bodied in colour and had long legs, but was thin and disappointing in the mouth, it's not balanced. Finally, does the aftertaste linger in your mouth after swallowing? Is it pleasant and does it have medium or longer length or is it short and crisp? Repeat the experience (often) and enjoy!

Crêperie La Forge Crêpes Belle Hélène

Ted's Choice If you can find it, Perry (pear cider) would be great here.

Makes 4 servings

With their classic filling of poached pear, vanilla ice cream, dark chocolate sauce and chantilly cream, no wonder Ted would barely share these dessert crepes with me when he ordered them at a lovely little restaurant in Brittany. The basic crepe recipe here makes about 16 (6-inch/15-cm) crepes, certainly more than you will need. However, once they are cool, you can wrap them in plastic wrap and pack in self-sealing plastic bags. Either refrigerate for up to three days or freeze them. You'll find many delicious uses for them.

For the crepes:

2 large eggs

1 cup (250 mL) milk

1/3 cup (75 mL) water

1 cup (250 mL) unbleached
   all-purpose flour

2 tbsp. (30 mL) sugar

1 tsp. (5 mL) pure vanilla extract

2 tbsp. (30 mL) melted butter

additional melted butter for the
   pan

Combine the eggs, milk, water, flour, sugar, vanilla and melted butter in a blender or food processor. Blend just for a few seconds, scrape down the sides of the container, then blend again briefly until smooth. Cover and refrigerate the mixture for about 2 hours (or overnight).

Before using, give the batter a little stir. Place a 6-inch (15-cm) non-stick pan over medium-high heat until hot. Brush a little melted butter over the surface and pour about 3 tablespoons (45 mL) of the batter into the pan. Swirl the batter around the pan until the entire surface is coated. Cook the batter for about 1 minute, at which point it should be relatively dry on the surface and just tinged brown around the edges. Use a metal spatula to loosen the crepe around the edges, then, using your fingers or the spatula, flip it over to cook the other side very briefly, about 12–15 seconds. Transfer the crepe to a clean tea towel to cool as you make the remaining crepes. Brush a little melted butter over the surface of the pan and repeat the procedure until all the batter has been used. Combine the water, sugar and lemon zest in a large skillet over high heat. Bring to a boil, stirring to completely dissolve the sugar. Reduce heat and add the pears. Cover and let the pears cook gently for 5–8 minutes or until they are tender when tested with the tip of a paring knife.

Drain the pears and discard the liquid. Cool then chill the pears until ready to serve.

For the pears:
1/2 cup (125 mL) water
1/2 cup (125 mL) sugar
3-inch (7.5-cm) piece lemon zest
4 pears, pared, halved and cored

Place the chocolate pieces in a bowl. Heat the cream in a saucepan placed over medium heat until gently boiling. Add the butter and sugar and stir to dissolve. Pour the hot cream over the chocolate in the bowl. Let sit for 2 minutes then stir to melt the chocolate. Keep stirring until the mixture is smooth and saucelike.

For the chocolate sauce:
8 oz. (250 g) dark chocolate, chopped
1 1/2 cups (375 mL) cream
1 tbsp. (15 mL) butter
2 tbsp. (30 mL) sugar

To serve: Place each crepe on a dessert plate. Place two pear halves and one scoop of ice cream on each crepe, drizzle with a little chocolate sauce, fold the crepe over and add a dollop of whipped cream and another drizzle of chocolate sauce. Serve immediately.

vanilla ice cream
whipped cream

Jenna's Lemon Tart with Chantilly Cream

Ted's Choice Jenna's choice here — nothing but a good strong cup of Irish tea,
like Barry's Classic.

Makes 8–10 servings

Jenna is my beautiful auburn-haired daughter, possessed of more than a little of her Irish grandfather's spirit and love of life. Ted calls her our Queen of Tarts because she has such a wonderful way with pastry, cakes, biscuits and cookies, a natural talent inherited, no doubt, from her beloved grandmother Kathleen, my mum. Of all the things Jenna bakes, I think this is my favourite — an intensely flavoured lemon tart without equal. It takes a bit of time, but this is the best one I have ever tasted. It's so good that a professional chef dining at our house once asked her for the recipe. I was reminded of this tart in Ireland when we dined at Dunbrody House in Co. Wexford. Chef Kevin Dundon serves one like it in his beautiful dining room and drizzles each slice with a dark sauce of cassis. I like this easy, food processor–made method for the pâté sucrée, but you may use your own if you prefer. This recipe makes enough for one 9-inch (23-cm) tart. You will need a tart pan with a removable bottom for this recipe.

For the pastry shell:

4 tbsp. (60 mL) unsalted butter,
    softened
1/2 cup (125 mL) icing sugar,
    sifted
2 large egg yolks
1 cup + 2 tbsp. (280 mL)
unbleached all-purpose flour,
    sifted
pinch of sea salt
unsalted butter, for the tart pan

Place the butter in the bowl of a food processor and pulse a couple of times until it is light and smooth. Add the sugar and process again until well blended. Add the egg yolks and process again until blended. Now, add 1 cup (250 mL) of flour and the salt and process again, using the pulse button, just until the flour is incorporated. At this point, if the dough will be quite sticky, add the remaining flour and pulse again, but not to the point where the mixture forms a ball.

Tear off a sheet of wax paper, and use a rubber spatula to scrape out the dough mixture onto the sheet. Flour your hands lightly and gently shape the dough into a ball and then a flattish circle. Wrap the dough and refrigerate for a minimum of 1 hour (or overnight).

Butter the bottom and sides of the tart pan and set to one side. Tear off a large sheet of wax paper and lay it on a work surface. Place the chilled dough on the wax paper, cover with another sheet of wax paper and roll out the dough to make a circle a little larger than the tart pan. Carefully pull back the top sheet of wax paper. Pick up the edges of the remaining wax paper and drape the pastry over the rolling pin and transfer to the tart pan. Very gently press the dough into the tart pan, letting the excess hang over the edge. (This will be trimmed after baking.) Prick the base of the tart shell and refrigerate for an hour.

Preheat oven to 375F (190C). Place the tart pan on a baking sheet and transfer to the centre of a hot oven for 5 minutes. After this time, remove from the oven and use a small, sharp knife to trim off the excess pastry. Slide it back into the oven and bake for another 15–20 minutes until it is golden brown. Remove from the oven and let cool completely before filling.

Use a stainless steel or glass double boiler or fashion one by placing a medium-sized saucepan over a larger one filled with boiling water set over high heat. In the top of the double boiler, or the medium-sized saucepan, combine the lemon juice and sugar and stir to dissolve the sugar. Add the butter, piece by piece, whisking well after each addition and making sure each piece is completely melted and incorporated before adding the next. Add the lemon zest and bring this mixture to a boil,

For the lemon filling:

2/3 cup (150 mL) freshly squeezed lemon juice

1 cup + 2 tbsp. (280 mL) sugar

8 tbsp. (120 mL) unsalted, chilled butter, cut into pieces

finely grated zest of 1 lemon

2 large eggs, at room temperature

3 large egg yolks, at room temperature

1/4 tsp. (1 mL) sea salt

whisking all the while. Cook until the mixture thickens, about 6 minutes or so. Blend in the eggs and the egg yolks, one at a time, with the whisk, beating well after each one. Reduce heat and whisk constantly until the mixture is thick and smooth, about 10–15 minutes. Use a rubber spatula to scrape the filling into a bowl, cover with wax paper or plastic wrap pressing down on it so that it comes in contact with the filling and set to one side (not refrigerated) for about 1 hour or until it is cooled. (It is important that the filling not be hot or very warm when you use it to fill the pastry shell.)

unsweetened whipped cream
icing sugar

To complete the tart: Make sure both the filling and the pastry shell are cool, then pour the filling into the shell, smoothing it out as you do so. Cover with a sheet of plastic wrap and refrigerate for a few hours until the filling is completely set. Remove from the refrigerator a half an hour before serving. Slice and serve with a dollop of whipped cream and a dusting of icing sugar.

Cape Breton Cranachan

Ted's Choice Glenfarclas 15-year-old Single Malt Whisky.

Makes 4 servings

This simple but delicious dessert takes its inspiration from the oat-eating tradition beloved by Celts. To make it truly memorable, drizzle with a little good single malt Scotch just before serving. To toast oatmeal, spread it out on a baking sheet and place in a moderate oven until golden brown, about 10–15 minutes, checking it now and then to make sure it is not browning too quickly or too much. When raspberries or blackberries are plentiful, they work wonderfully well here.

Whip the cream until fairly stiff peaks form. Gently fold in the icing sugar, vanilla and oatmeal. Spoon mixture into four individual serving dishes and top with fresh berries. Drizzle with whisky if using. Serve immediately.

1 cup (250 mL) whipping cream

1/4 cup (60 mL) icing sugar

1/2 tsp. (2 mL) pure vanilla extract

1/2 cup (125 mL) oatmeal, toasted

1 cup (250 mL) fresh strawberries, hulled, halved

Macallan Mousse au Chocolat

Ted's Choice Macallan 12-year-old Single Highland Malt Scotch Whisky.

Makes 6 servings

Chef Donald Angus Munro of Loop Restaurant in Glasgow, took his grandmother's recipe for chocolate pudding and jazzed it up with Macallan whisky. So, I thought, well why not do the same for good old chocolate mousse — it works, as they say, a treat. Make sure the cocoa content of the chocolate you use is at least 50% — the higher the better. You will need those pretty little white ceramic ramekins for this recipe. Serve each with a plop of whipped cream and a chocolate curl.

1/3 cup (75 mL) Macallan Highland Single Malt Scotch Whisky

1/2 cup (125 mL) sugar, divided

3 eggs, at room temperature, separated

6 oz. (185 g) fine quality, bittersweet dark chocolate

1/2 cup (125 mL) whipping cream

In a small bowl, whisk together the whisky, half of the sugar and the egg yolks until well blended. Place the chocolate in a medium-sized, heavy-based saucepan and place over very low heat, stirring continuously to melt the chocolate. (You can also use your microwave to melt the chocolate.) When melted, add the whisky mixture, whisking it well into the melted chocolate. Remove from the heat and set to one side.

In a medium-sized bowl, whip the egg whites until soft peaks form, then add the remaining sugar and beat until they are stiff. Set to one side. In another bowl, whip the cream until stiff.

Now, carefully fold both the chocolate mixture and the whipped cream to the egg whites until fully incorporated. Pour mixture into the individual ramekins, smooth the surface and refrigerate for 3 hours or until well set. Serve as described above.

Irish Chocolate

Who would have thought that luxurious chocolate would emanate from the west coast of Ireland?

Unlikely it may be, but in the tiny town of Ballinskelligs in County Kerry, an ancient place where Celtic monks formed settlements during the Dark Ages, Amanda and Michael MacGabhann operate the Skelligs Chocolate Company. Each of the finely crafted chocolates is packed in hand-painted boxes before being tied by a length of ribbon and fastened by hand with wax, seal and label. As the names suggest, the Bucks Fizz truffles are filled with Champagne and orange juice, and the Porter truffles hold Beamish stout. The fabulous Chequers truffles (eight dark chocolates filled with Irish whiskey cream and eight white chocolates filled with cream truffle and coffee) are set in a square wooden box made to look like a draughts (checker) board. This is a bespoke operation with all the chocolates being made to order for customers, including one of New York's finest department stores, Bergdorf Goodman.

Caledonian Ice Cream

Ted's Choice Glenmorangie Sherry Wood Finish Single Highland Malt Scotch Whisky.

Makes 4–6 servings

In one of my previous cookbooks — *The Global Grill* — there is an old-fashioned recipe that I found in England for Brown Bread Ice Cream. It is based on cream and fine brown bread-crumbs that are toasted and caramelized with brown sugar. At a great restaurant in Glasgow called The Ubiquitous Chip (famous for the fact that they *don't* serve chips!), I had a similar ice cream but it was somehow better, nuttier. Then, while drifting through the lovely little book called *Good Things* by renowned English food writer Jane Grigson, I read that if you substitute toasted oatmeal in place of the breadcrumbs you will have what the Scottish call Caledonian ice cream. By the way, Caledonia is the ancient and romantic name for Scotland. It is said to stem from a corruption of the word *celyddon*, a Celtic word meaning "a dweller in the woods and forests." The word *Celt*, from the same source, means the same thing.

So, here you are then. If you have saved a large plastic ice cream container with lid, you could use it here.

½ cup (125 mL) old-fashioned
  rolled oats

½ cup (125 mL) packed light
  brown sugar

1 tbsp. (15 mL) butter

2 cups (500 mL) whipping cream

2 tbsp. (30 mL) blended whisky

1 large egg white

Preheat oven to 400F (200C). In a small bowl, combine the oats with the sugar and toss together until well blended. Lightly butter a baking sheet and spread the oat mixture over the surface. Bake in the oven, stirring occasionally, for 6–8 minutes or until sugar caramelizes and oats begin to colour. Remove from the oven and let cool, and then break up into small bits.

Whip the cream in a chilled bowl until soft peaks form. Stir in the caramelized oats and whisky. Pour the mixture into a plastic container with a lid. Freeze for a few hours until the mixture has begun to set around the edges and the centre is mushy.

Whisk the egg white until just stiff. Remove semi-frozen ice cream from the freezer. Beat lightly with an electric mixer or hand-held blender (do this right in the container) for a few minutes. Fold in the egg white with a spoon. Replace lid; return ice cream to the freezer until completely frozen.

Companions of the Quaich

If you live in Ontario and you're a fan of single malt whiskies — I mean, *great* single malts — or would like to be, you should attend one of the dinners put on by the International Order of Companions of the Quaich, Canada's Premier Malt Whisky Appreciation Society — "a league of ladies and gentlemen who enjoy the finest things in life," as Ed Patrick, originator of the club, describes it. Each month, whisky-loving fans gather to enjoy three distinctive and completely un-run-of-the-mill single malts along with a three-course dinner and the thoroughly entertaining repartee of Mr. Patrick, all for a very modest fee. Besides Toronto, there are a number of chapters across the province. Check out the website for full details about joining: www.thequaich.com.

Banana Tartlette Tatin
with Caramel & Cream

Ted's Choice Royal Brackla 10-year-old Highland Single Malt Scotch Whisky.

Makes 4 servings

There are a number of Howie's Restaurants in Scotland — in Edinburgh, Aberdeen and Dundee. This is my version of one of their most beloved desserts: a warm tart of bananas and sticky caramel. Logically enough, in Scotland it is teamed with a lovely plop of clotted cream, something we in North America are not really privy to, and what a pity that is. We'll have to make do with very good vanilla ice cream or whipped cream as an accompaniment. Use individual tartlette pans (about 4 inches/10 cm in diameter). Frozen puff pastry is available in supermarkets and is a great boon to the busy. Just thaw one of the packages, roll out and use your tartlette pan to determine the size of the round of dough you need.

1 cup (125 mL) packed light brown sugar

finely grated zest and juice of 1 small lemon

1/3 cup (75 mL) blended whisky

1/4 cup (60 mL) unsalted butter

5 medium-sized, firm bananas, peeled

1 cup (250 mL) pecans, lightly toasted, chopped

4 rounds of ready-made puff pastry

Preheat oven to 400F (200C). Tear off a sheet of parchment paper large enough to cover a baking sheet. Spray the interior of each pan with a little non-stick cooking spray. Arrange the tartlette pans on the baking sheet and set to one side.

Combine the brown sugar, lemon zest and juice and whisky in a medium-sized, heavy-based saucepan and set over low heat. Stir constantly until the sugar melts and completely dissolves. Increase the heat to medium and bring the mixture to a boil, then reduce the heat to a simmer and let simmer for about 30 seconds. Now, whisk in the butter, bit by bit, whisk well after each addition, with the pan still on the heat. After the last bit of butter has been added, whisk for another 30 seconds and remove the saucepan from the heat.

Slice the bananas about ¹/₂-inch (1.2-cm) thick. Return the caramel sauce to the heat and carefully add the banana slices. Use a wooden spoon to gently move the slices around in the sauce to coat them well. Then, use tongs to carefully transfer the slices of coated banana to the tartlette pans, arranging them to cover the bottom of each pan. Distribute the pecans among the four pans and then pour more of the caramel sauce over the bananas and nuts in each pan (you may not use it all; if you have any left over, use it to drizzle over the cream when serving).

Cover each with the round of puff pastry, tucking it in around the edges to enclose the filling.

Place the tray in the oven for 15 minutes or until the pastry is puffed and golden brown. Carefully remove from the oven, let sit for a minute or two then place a dessert plate upside down over each one and invert the tartlettes out onto the plate, being careful of the hot caramel.

Place a dollop of loosely whipped cream or a scoop of good vanilla ice cream on each one and serve, drizzled with more caramel sauce if using.

All Saints' Potato Apple Griddle Cake from Armagh

Ted's Choice Connemara Single Malt Irish Whiskey.

Makes 4–6 servings

Apples have long been a revered fruit in Celtic mythology. Paradise was called Avalon — the Isle of Apples — a place where there was no rain, no sorrow, no illness and where the fruit of life grew in abundance. More than one traditional apple dessert comes from Ireland, especially in the northern county of Armagh, an area dubbed "the orchard of Ireland," that has been known for more than 200 years for the quality of her apples. This one is actually more a cross between potato bread and a sweet pancake, cooked as it is on a hot griddle. Make this in celebration of All Saints' Day, October 31, a significant date in the ancient Celtic calendar as it marks New Year's Eve, with the new Celtic year starting on November 1. This is *Samhain*, when from dusk to dawn, the spirits of the dead walk the earth and are more than willing to join in with celebrations involving friends and family. And that includes food and drink, so place a candle in the window to guide them home. Fill a glass or two with ale, make an extra cake to go with it and leave them outside for those otherworldly members to enjoy. This is an especially good choice for this evening as apples and potatoes are two of this festival's most sacred foods.

1/4 cup (50 mL) chilled butter (approx.)

1 cup (250 mL) all-purpose flour (approx.)

1/2 tsp (2 mL) salt

1/2 tsp (2 mL) baking powder

3 cups (750 mL) dry mashed potatoes

2 large apples, peeled, cored (Spys are a good choice)

Combine the butter and flour in a mixing bowl. Work the butter into the flour as for making pastry. When crumbly, add salt and baking powder and mix in well. Now, add mashed potatoes and use your hands to incorporate all ingredients together, forming a dough. Turn out onto a lightly floured surface and knead lightly for a few minutes, working in a bit more flour if dough is sticky. Divide dough into two balls. Then roll each one out to about a 1/2-inch (1-cm) thickness. Cover with a clean tea towel. Slice the apples thinly directly over a bowl. Add the cinnamon, sugar and cloves and toss to coat. Uncover the dough and layer apple slices on one of the circles. Dot with the butter and then cover with the other dough circle, pinching the edges to seal in the filling. Heat a griddle or cast iron pan over medium-high heat and add a little butter, brushing it over the surface as it melts. Carefully transfer the cake to the griddle, reduce heat to low and slowly fry potato cake until golden speckled brown on both sides, about 15–20 minutes in total. Serve hot with a wee bit of thick cream, if desired, and cups of hot, strong tea.

1 tsp (5 mL) ground cinnamon
1 tbsp (15 mL) sugar, or to taste
1/4 tsp (1 mL) ground cloves
2 tbsp (25 mL) butter

Cider Head

Years ago, I lived just outside Bristol, England, and worked at the *Bristol Evening Post*, the daily newspaper. As a newcomer, I was introduced to the Queen's Head, the pub nearest to the offices and the watering hole for all who worked there. Ken and Enid were the owners and a more West Country set of folk you couldn't hope to meet. I had heard a great deal about the local cider — scrumpy — the real thing, made by farmers in the area and delivered to the pub in big wooden casks. The Queen's Head was home to more than a few faithful "cider heads" as Ken called them. Glassy-eyed and dull-witted they sat, starring at nothing, alone with their pint as was their custom, always in the bar area, never the red velvet–seated lounge. "No cider in the lounge," was the rule. Why, I wondered. "Incontinence," came Ken's terse reply. That should have been my first clue.

On my inaugural visit to the Queen's Head, I asked Ken for a pint of their famed cider. "Not yet," he said sternly, arms crossed over his barrel chest. Eyeing my frame, he explained, "not till o'ive seen yer drink other things." Not fully comprehending that he needed to assess my drinking capabilities before the ultimate test, I ordered a pint of 6-X, a very good ale from Wadworth Brewery in Devizes, not far from Bristol. On my next visit, thinking I had passed muster, I tried again to order a pint of scrumpy and received the same cursory response. This went on for weeks, with me ordering gin and tonics, sherry, lagers, ales, you name it, in a valiant effort to prove to Ken and Enid that this Canadian girl had what it took to partake of the cider barrel. Every Friday, I wondered, will today be the day I'm allowed to cross the threshold and drink from the golden cup? Finally, one evening, I was served my first glass of hard cider. It was slightly opaque, with a few fizzy bubbles careening to the top of the glass. It had a lovely, fresh, essence of apple fragrance and seemed completely, utterly harmless. Just as I was about to take my first long-anticipated sip, Ken took it back. What now, I thought? "Always 'av it wi' a bit of lemon. It'll help tomorrow," he said, floating a thin slice of lemon on the cider's surface. Under Ken's watchful eye, I raised the glass and took a long drink. How I reacted was important. I felt as though I were drinking for Canada. Just a little cooler than room temperature, the cider was fresh, sprightly, bright, rejuvenating and incredibly easy to drink, like a wonderfully fresh, fruity tonic. It tasted as though it was good for you, for Pete's sake, and it cost 25p (about 50 cents). Everything I had been told about the drink was true. My eyes shone, my cheeks bloomed like a wild Irish rose, I was never more amusing, intelligent, charming, happy. Living life to the fullest meant ordering another pint of cider and then, I think, more. And though I swear I may have levitated at one point, I did not fall down. It's difficult to completely describe how I felt the next morning (or, for that matter, how I made it home) except to say that my head felt as though it was firmly caught between the great stones of an ancient cider press. Suddenly the term *sauced* took on a whole new meaning. I was hung to the core.

And just for future reference, Ken was dead wrong about that slice of lemon.

Beech Hill Chocolate St. Emilion with Crème Anglaise & Lavender Ice Cream

Ted's Choice Glengarioch 15-year-old Highland Single Malt Scotch Whisky.

Makes 8–10 servings

When we visited Derry, we stayed just outside the ancient walled city in the beautiful, stately Beech Hill Country Hotel. At that time, the kitchen boasted two chefs from France. Head pastry chef Yannick Fausse is originally from Ardennes and spent time in London, in Digby, Nova Scotia, and also in the Muskokas before heading back to Ireland. This is a version of the dessert I enjoyed at Beech Hill: a dense, intense chocolate *paté*, studded with bits of *amaretti* and served with a luxurious pale custard and a scoop of this most unusual, delicately flavoured ice cream. If you have an ice cream maker, use it to make the fragrant lavender ice cream. If not, just follow the directions outlined for making the ice cream without one. Choose young, fresh shoots of lavender, picked just before the flowers open (unsprayed, of course). Alternatively, use 4 tablespoons (60 mL) dried lavender flowers.

Line a 8x4-inch (1.5-L) loaf pan with plastic wrap. Melt the chocolate by placing it in a saucepan placed inside a larger one filled with boiling water (be very careful not to allow any water to splash into the chocolate). (Alternatively, melt the chocolate in the microwave.) When it has completely melted, stir in the Amaretto. Remove from the heat and allow to cool completely.

In the bowl of an electric mixer (or by hand), cream together the butter and sugar until light and fluffy. In another bowl, beat egg whites with a little salt until soft peaks form. Reserve.

For the chocolate paté:

12 oz. (375 g) fine-quality bittersweet chocolate, finely chopped

1/4 cup (60 mL) Amaretto

1/2 cup (125 mL) butter, softened

2 tbsp. (30 mL) sugar

2 eggs, separated

1/4 tsp. (1 mL) sea salt

12 *amaretti* biscuits, broken into small pieces

Add the egg yolks, one at a time, to the butter mixture, beating well after each addition. Stir in the chocolate mixture, and then gently fold in the egg whites until they all but disappear. Gently fold in the chopped biscuits, incorporating them well.

Spoon the mixture into the loaf pan, spreading the top smooth and evenly with a spatula. Cover with plastic wrap and refrigerate overnight.

For the crème anglaise:

1 vanilla bean

3 cups (750 mL) whole milk

7 large egg yolks

3/4 cup (175 mL) super-fine sugar

Use the tip of a sharp knife to slit the vanilla bean in half lengthwise. Place in a heavy-based saucepan and pour the milk over it. Place over medium-high heat and bring to a boil. Remove from the heat and let cool.

Place the egg yolks in a mixing bowl and whisk in 1/2 cup (125 mL) of the sugar (the remaining sugar is used for the berries). Whisk together well until the sugar has dissolved and the mixture is beginning to thicken.

Take the vanilla bean from the milk and transfer to paper towels to dry before saving for another use. Pour the milk into the egg mixture gradually, whisking as you do so. Return the mixture to the saucepan and place over medium-low heat. Now, stir constantly for about 12–18 minutes, or until the mixture has thickened and resembles thick, heavy cream. It should be thick enough to coat the back of a silver spoon. Pour the custard through a sieve into a large bowl. Let cool at room temperature then refrigerate to chill thoroughly.

Chop the lavender with a sharp chef's knife (if it is easier, use kitchen shears). Place in a saucepan with the cream and the lemon zest. Heat until almost boiling, stir in the sugar and stir until dissolved. Cool, then cover and refrigerate overnight to let the lavender fully infuse the cream.

The next day, warm the cream again over medium heat, then pour through a sieve onto the egg yolks, whisking the mixture thoroughly as you pour. Return this mixture to the saucepan and place over low heat and cook gently until the mixture coats the back of a spoon; do not allow to boil.

Strain once more and leave to cool. Pour into a chilled metal tray to cool.

Freeze the mixture until frozen around the edges (not in the centre). Beat the mixture with a hand-held blender or in a food processor until smooth. Freeze again and repeat this procedure three more times before freezing solid.

To serve: Remove the chocolate paté from the refrigerator about an hour before serving. Loosen the loaf by running a small sharp knife around the edges.

Using the plastic wrap for handles, lift the loaf out of the pan and invert it onto a serving platter. Cut into thin slices with a sharp knife, wiped clean after each slice. Pour some of the crème anglaise onto a dessert plate. Lay a slice of the chocolate paté in the centre of the pool, add a small scoop of the lavender ice cream atop the paté. Add a small sprig of fresh lavender and serve.

For the ice cream:

8 stems English lavender
   (if using lavender in full flower,
   use just 4–6 stems)
   3–4 inches/8 cm in length,
   washed and dried
2 1/2 cups (625 mL) whipping
   cream
zest from 1 small lemon
2/3 cup (150 mL) sugar
4 egg yolks, lightly beaten

Brittany Butter Cake

Makes 8 servings

This substantial and serious butter cake is called *kouign amann* in Brittany. We bought one in the outdoor market at Quimper, not really knowing what it was. However, we found we couldn't stop eating it at every meal — which was just as well since it was a big cake. In truth, it's sort of a bread-dough-cum-butter-pastry that has been made forever in Brittany relying on the farm-fresh butter to make it great. I think this is rather like a sweet version of Aberdeen Butteries on page 44.

5 tsp. (2 envelopes) active dry yeast

1 tsp. (5 mL) sea salt

2 cups (500 mL) unbleached all-purpose flour

1 cup (250 mL) warm water (approx.)

1 cup (250 mL) butter, chilled

1 1/4 cups (310 mL) sugar

Place about 1/3 cup (75 mL) warm water in a large, warmed mixing bowl. Add a pinch of sugar and then the packets of yeast. Stir together then leave for about 10 minutes in a warm place.

Add the salt and about half of the flour to the yeast mixture, stirring together well (you could also mix the dough in an electric mixer with the dough hook attachment). Add some of the warm water and the remaining flour and mix together well. Add remaining water and continue to mix until a dough forms. Work it into a ball and turn out onto a lightly floured surface and knead the dough gently for 10 minutes or until the dough is smooth. Wipe clean and dry the mixing bowl. Lightly butter the bowl and place the dough in it, cover with a clean tea towel and leave to rise in a warm place for about 1 hour.

Preheat oven to 450F (230C). Butter a 9-inch (23-cm) pie dish with butter and dust with a bit of flour. Punch the dough down and transfer to a lightly floured work surface. Dice the butter. Roll out the dough into a large rectangle (about 12x18 inches/30x46 cm). Scatter all but about 3 tablespoons (45 mL) of the butter in the middle of the rectangle and one-third of the sugar. Fold the sides of the dough in towards the centre over the filling of butter and sugar, then sprinkle with more sugar and roll over to seal. Turn the dough so that the shorter side is facing you and fold into thirds, up from the bottom, down from the top. Transfer dough to the refrigerator to chill for 15 minutes.

Now, sprinkle the work surface with a little sugar and roll out the dough again. Sprinkle with another one-third of the sugar and repeat the folding as above. Again, let rest in the refrigerator for 15 minutes.

Repeat the rolling and sugaring, using most of the remaining sugar, rolling the dough out into a squarish shape a little bigger than the pie pan. Transfer dough to the pan. Melt remaining butter and drizzle over the surface of the dough. Sprinkle with the last bit of sugar and bake 35–40 minutes until golden brown and puffed. Serve warm.

A Quartet of Shortbreads

Classic Scottish Shortbread

Ted's Choice Craigellachie Speyside Single Malt Scotch Whisky — for all the shortbreads.

Makes about 30 pieces

You may think — as I do — that this is the best there is — especially since it makes many. These store well if kept in an airtight container.

2 cups (500 mL) unsalted butter,
   at room temperature
1 cup (250 mL) super-fine sugar
3 cups (750 mL) unbleached
   all-purpose flour
1 cup (250 mL) rice flour
1 tsp. (5 mL) sea salt

Preheat oven to 300F (150C). Tear off two pieces of parchment paper and use to line two baking sheets. In the bowl of an electric mixer (or by hand) cream the butter and sugar until well combined. Sift the two flours and salt together on a sheet of wax paper and add gradually to the butter mixture. Work the last bit of flour in with your hands to form a pliable dough.

Divide the dough in half and roll out each half to about a 1/2-inch (1-cm) thickness. Use a 2-inch (5-cm) biscuit cutter to cut out rounds of dough. Prick each one with a fork in a few places and transfer to the baking sheets.

Bake for about 25 minutes or until cream-coloured, not golden brown. Cool for a couple of minutes on the sheets before transferring with a metal spatula to a cooling rack. Dust with sugar if desired.

Jesse's Dundee Shortbread

Now, this is a different sort of shortbread given to me by a British-born friend who lived in Dundee for many years before coming to Canada. As she says, "You don't get this sort of shortbread from a factory. The fine semolina gives it a lovely crunch that other shortbreads don't have and it has the most buttery flavour of any I have tasted." Use an 8-inch fluted tart pan, with a removable base that is about 1 1/4-inches (3-cm) deep. Look for fine semolina in Italian or specialty food shops.

Preheat oven to 300F (150C). In the bowl of an electric mixer (or by hand), beat the butter to soften it, adding the sugar gradually to incorporate the two ingredients. Now add the flour and the semolina and blend the ingredients together thoroughly, working everything together with your hands towards the end of the mixing time.

Transfer the dough to a lightly floured surface and roll it out with quick gentle strokes of the rolling pin until it is the right size to fit in the tart pan. Transfer it to the tart pan and lightly press the dough evenly into the pan, right up the fluted edges. Prick all over with a fork (to prevent buckling when it is in the oven) and transfer to the centre shelf of the oven to bake for about 1 hour or until it is pale golden and firm to the touch.

Remove from the oven and, before it cools, use a metal spatula to mark out 12 wedges on the surface.

Let it cool in the pan. Cut into wedges when completely cold.

1 cup (250 mL) butter, at room temperature

1/3 cup (75 mL) super-fine sugar

1 cup (250 mL) unbleached all-purpose flour, sifted

1/3 cup (75 mL) fine semolina flour

RAMSAY'S BRETON SHORTBREAD

Makes about 20 pieces

Gordon Ramsay is a Scottish-born chef who makes more than one style of shortbread in his famed London restaurant. He describes this ultra-rich version as *pâte brêton* – Breton-style shortbread, to which he sometimes adds toasted cumin seeds. Shortbread lovers (like Ted) think these are amazing.

2 large egg yolks

1/4 cup (60 mL) super-fine sugar

1/4 cup (60 mL) unsalted butter, softened

2/3 cup (150mL) unbleached all-purpose flour

3/4 tsp. (4 mL) baking powder

Combine the egg yolks and the sugar in the bowl of an electric mixer (or mix by hand) and beat until thick and creamy. As the mixer is beating, gradually add the butter and blend together well.

Sift the flour and the baking powder together over the bowl and mix together well. Turn the dough out onto a lightly floured surface and knead lightly until smooth.

Wrap in plastic wrap and chill in the refrigerator for about an hour.

Return the dough to a lightly floured surface and pat the dough out until it is about 1/8-inch (.3-cm) thick. (You can also cover the top of the dough with wax paper and use a rolling pin if it is easier.) Use a 2-inch (5-cm) biscuit cutter and cut out the dough into as many rounds as you can. Use a metal spatula to transfer the rounds to a non-stick baking sheet. When all of the dough has been cut out, transfer the sheet to the refrigerator for 15–20 minutes to chill. While they are resting, preheat the oven to 300F (150C).

Bake for 12–15 minutes until the shortbreads are just golden at the edges. Remove from the oven and let cool on the baking sheet for a minute or two before transferring to a cooling rack.

CAPE BRETON OATMEAL SHORTBREAD

Makes about 30 pieces

These are nutty-tasting shortbreads that I particularly like with sharp Canadian Cheddar, although they are just as good with butter and jam and served with tea.

Preheat oven to 350F (175C). Combine the butter and sugar in the bowl of an electric mixer (or mix by hand) and cream together well. Add the vanilla and blend well. Add the flour, baking powder and oats and continue to mix until all the ingredients are well incorporated. Turn the dough out onto a lightly floured surface and knead slightly until soft and relatively smooth.

Roll out to a 1/4-inch (6-mm) thickness and cut into rounds or squares.

Bake in the oven for 20–25 minutes until pale golden brown. Let cool slightly before transferring to a rack.

1 1/4 cups (310 mL) butter, softened

1 cup (250 mL) lightly packed light brown sugar

1/2 tsp. (2 mL) pure vanilla extract

1 1/2 cups (375 mL) unbleached all-purpose flour

1 tsp. (5 mL) baking powder

1 1/2 cups (375 mL) rolled oats

İrish Whiskey Brownies
with Sticky Toffee & Thick Cream

Ted's Choice Redbreast Irish Whiskey.

Serves 6–8

These are really over the top, inspired by two desserts I fell in love with while in Ireland and then again in Scotland – rich brownie squares made with Irish whiskey and, of course, the very popular sticky toffee pudding that is now so beloved even a large supermarket chain has their own private label version. Anyway, this preparation is what happens when the best of these two desserts meet and fall in love. The recipe for the sticky toffee sauce makes quite a bit, but there are many uses for it. Try it with warmed bananas and ice cream.

For the brownies:

1/3 cup (75 mL) Irish whiskey

1/4 cup (60 mL) semi-sweet
   chocolate chips

1/3 cup +1 tbsp. (90 mL) butter,
   softened

1 cup (250 mL) sugar

2 large eggs

1 1/2 cups (375 mL) unbleached
   all-purpose flour

1/2 cup (125 mL) unsweetened
   cocoa

1 tsp. (5 mL) baking powder

1/2 tsp. (2 mL) sea salt

Lightly butter a 9-inch (23 cm) square pan. Preheat oven to 350F (180C). Place the whiskey in a small saucepan and bring to a boil over high heat. Remove from the heat as soon as it has come to a boil and add the chocolate chips, stirring to melt them completely.

In the bowl of an electric mixer (or by hand), cream together the sugar and butter until smooth. Add the eggs and continue to blend ingredients together well. Sift together the flour, cocoa, baking powder and salt and add gradually to the egg mixture. Add the whiskey and chocolate mixture and beat at low speed just until combined.

Scrape the batter into the prepared pan and smooth over the surface. Bake for exactly 25 minutes. Cool in the pan.

Combine all the ingredients in a medium-sized saucepan and bring to a boil over medium heat, stirring all the while, until thick. Reduce heat to a simmer and cook, stirring frequently, for 6–7 minutes or until the mixture has reduced and is quite thick. Keep warm; set to one side.

To serve: Place a brownie on a dessert plate, drizzle with the warm sticky toffee sauce, top with whipped cream or ice cream and drizzle again with the sauce. Serve immediately.

For the sticky toffee sauce:
4 cups (1 L) whipping cream
2 cups (500 mL) packed dark brown sugar
1/2 cup (125 mL) butter

whipped cream or ice cream

Brittany Oat Cream

Ted's Choice Cardhu 10-year-old Highland Single Malt Scotch Whisky.

Makes 6 servings

As in Ireland, Wales and Scotland, the milk, cream and butter in Brittany is rich and flavourful, due no doubt, to the wonderfully lush grazing land on which the dairy herds roam. For this traditional recipe — that is a cross between a custard and a crème brûlée — you should use good-quality cream and the freshest eggs you can obtain. Simple and sublime.

1 cup (250 mL) old-fashioned
  rolled oats
4 cups (1 L) whipping cream
6 tbsp. (90 mL) granulated sugar
6 large egg yolks
1/2 cup (125 mL) light brown
  sugar

Preheat oven to 425F (220C). Scatter the oats onto a baking sheet and toast them in the oven for about 5–6 minutes until they are deeply toasted. Watch them carefully to make sure they are not burning. Once they are toasted and a deep golden brown, remove from the oven and pour into a medium-sized mixing bowl. Heat the cream in a saucepan over medium-high heat. Once it begins to bubble slightly around the edges, pour the cream over the oats and let this mixture stand for 3 hours at room temperature. Then, set a sieve over a large measuring cup and pour the mixture through it. Set to one side. (Reserve the soaked oats for another use in muffins or breads.)

Preheat oven to 350F (180C). Whisk the sugar and egg yolks together in a mixing bowl until sugar is dissolved and the mixture is smooth. Pour the reserved cream mixture through a sieve into the bowl containing the sugar and egg yolk mixture and blend well.

Pour this mixture into a shallow oven dish and transfer to the oven for 1 hour. When the cream is set, albeit with a bit of a wobble, remove from the oven. Chill thoroughly.

Before serving, preheat broiler to high. Make a bed of cracked ice on a baking sheet. Cover the surface of the oat cream with brown sugar and set the dish on the baking sheet. Sprinkle the sugar over the surface and place beneath the broiler until the sugar is brown and melted. Serve immediately or chill again and serve cold.

Vanilla Custard with Bramble Berries & Oatmeal Shortcakes

Ted's Choice Glenkinchie 10-year-old Lowland Single Malt Scotch Whisky.

Makes 6 servings

The Irish, Scottish and Welsh (and the English) call blackberries bramble berries, a fruit that, when in season, should be used for this lovely old-fashioned dessert. Ripe raspberries or small, ripe strawberries, left whole, are also wonderful with this simple custard. Now, this is an authentic custard, or crème anglaise as the French call it, so don't stint on the egg yolks. A specialty food shop will carry the vanilla beans. When you have finished with the vanilla bean, don't throw it away. Dry it thoroughly and plant it in a small canister of sugar to lend it flavour. Make the accompanying oatmeal shortcakes first. If you like, you can also serve this with rounds of good, homemade shortbread. Choose from one of the shortbread recipes on pages 254–57.

For the oatmeal shortcakes:

1 cup + 1 tbsp. (265 mL) old-fashioned rolled oats

1 cup (250 mL) unbleached all-purpose flour

1/4 cup (60 mL) sugar

1/2 tsp. (2 mL) sea salt

1 tbsp. (15 mL) baking powder

1/3 cup (75 mL) unsalted butter, cold, diced

1/3 cup (75 mL) milk, cold

1/3 cup (75 mL) whipping cream, cold

cream and sugar, as needed, for brushing

Preheat oven to 400F (200C). Tear off a sheet of parchment paper and use it to line a baking sheet. Combine the oats, flour, sugar, salt and baking powder in a large mixing bowl and use a whisk to blend together well. Add the butter and cut into the dry ingredients as you would when making pastry, until the mixture is crumbly. Combine the milk and cream together in a measuring cup and pour all at once into the mixture; mix together with a fork or your hands just until you have achieved a rather sticky, wet dough.

Lightly flour your hands and turn the dough out onto a lightly floured surface. Pat it into an 8-inch (20-cm) wide circle, about 1-inch (2.5-cm) thick. Dip a 3-inch (7.5-cm) round cutter in a little flour, shaking off the excess and use it to cut out as many shortcakes as you can from this first rolling. Transfer them to the baking sheet as you work. Repeat with the remaining scraps of dough until you have made 6 shortcakes. Place the tray in the refrigerator for about 10 minutes. Then, brush each shortcake with cream and sprinkle with a little sugar. Bake for 18–20 minutes or until golden brown. Transfer to a rack to cool while you make the custard.

Use the tip of a sharp knife to slit the vanilla bean in half lengthwise. Place in a heavy-based saucepan and pour the milk over it. Place over medium-high heat and bring to a boil. Remove from the heat and let cool.

Place the egg yolks in a mixing bowl and whisk in 1/2 cup (125 mL) of the sugar (the remaining sugar is used for the berries). Whisk together well until the sugar has dissolved and the mixture is beginning to thicken.

Take the vanilla bean from the milk and transfer to paper towels to dry before saving for another use. Pour the milk into the egg mixture gradually, whisking as you do so. Return the mixture to the saucepan and place over medium-low heat. Now, stir constantly for about 12–18 minutes, or until the mixture has thickened and resembles thick, heavy cream. It should be thick enough to coat the back of a silver spoon. Pour the custard through a sieve into a large bowl. Let cool at room temperature and then refrigerate to chill thoroughly.

While the custard is chilling, sprinkle the berries with the remaining sugar and a spoonful of water. Mix gently then let the berries sit at room temperature for about an hour; give it a stir now and then.

For the custard:
1 vanilla bean
3 cups (750 mL) whole milk
7 large egg yolks
3/4 cup (175 mL) super-fine sugar
4 cups (1 L) fresh blackberries

To serve: Remove the custard from the refrigerator and use a ladle to portion out the custard into 6 individual serving dishes. Split the shortcakes in half and place the bottom half in the centre of each pool of custard. Spoon a generous portion of berries over the shortcake half, ladle out more custard over them, then place the other half of shortcake on top, but not completely covering the berries. Add a few more berries to the pool of custard itself. Repeat with remaining shortcakes, berries and custard and serve.

Aberlour

Speyside is Scottish whisky heartland and whiskies from this region — of which Aberlour (Gaelic for "mouth of the babbling brook") is a prime example — are famous for their sweet, fragrant qualities. Floral and fruity, they have much finesse and have long been thought of as the most elegant, sophisticated and complex of all the malts. Aberlour Distillery was founded in 1826 on the site of a holy well. Although it was rebuilt after a fire in 1898, it was thoroughly modernized in the mid-1970s by Pernod Ricard. Unsurprising then that it is one of France's most popular whisky brands. Aberlour collaborated with famed Austrian glassmaker Georg Riedel in the creation of a single malt whisky glass. Cream toffee notes make the 10-year-old Aberlour a great choice to accompany custards and other sweets.

Tarta de Santiago

Ted's Choice *Oloroso* Sherry.

Makes 8 servings

Santiago is the Spanish name for St. James, the apostle who was said to have travelled to Spain to preach the gospel. Legend has it that after he was martyred in Jerusalem, his body then manifested itself in Galicia in a field that, over time, developed into the city of Santiago de Compostela. The city and cathedral of Santiago de Compostela continue to enjoy a reputation as the destination for the most famous mass pilgrimage in medieval times as millions of the faithful made the journey — many on foot — to the shrine of Santiago. One of the specialties of Galicia is the sponge cake known as *tarta de Santiago* and you will see it throughout the province in bakeries and restaurants with its sugar-dusted design of the distinctive cross of Santiago on the surface. The first time I enjoyed this sweet I was sitting outside a little café, not far from the cathedral, listening to a young woman play a beautiful piece of music — on the bagpipes.

4 eggs, separated

3/4 cup (175 mL) sugar

2 1/4 cups (560 mL) ground almonds

1/4 cup (60 mL) sugar

icing sugar for dusting

 Lightly butter a 9-inch (23-cm) cake pan. Preheat the oven to 375F (190C).

Combine the egg yolks in the bowl of an electric mixer (or mix by hand) and as they are beating, gradually add the 3/4 cup (175 mL) sugar. When well blended, add the ground almonds and continue to blend well. In another bowl, whisk the egg whites until foamy, then gradually add the remaining sugar and continue to beat until egg whites are stiff. Carefully fold the egg whites into the egg yolk mixture, in stages. Then, pour everything into the prepared cake pan and bake for about 35–40 minutes. Remove from the oven and let cool in the pan for a few minutes before dusting with icing sugar.

THE LITTLE IRISH WHISKEY CAKE

Ted's Choice Bushmills Malt 16-year-old Single Malt (matured in three woods).

Makes 6-8 servings

Lovers of Irish whiskey flock to Bushmills to tour the distillery, stay overnight at the nearby inn or take a meal in the inn's restaurant. One day, after visiting the distillery and strolling through the town of Bushmills, we stopped for tea and something sweet at a little tearoom not far from the distillery. I spied a lovely golden cake in the glass case and when I asked what it was, the bright-eyed lady behind the counter said, "Oh, that's our little Irish whiskey cake. It's lovely with butter and tea." How right she was. Start preparation for this cake the night before to allow the whiskey to work its magic on the raisins.

zest of 1 lemon

1 cup (250 mL) golden raisins

1/4 cup + 2 tbsp. (90 mL) Bushmills Irish Whiskey

1/2 cup + 1 tbsp. (140 mL) butter, softened

2/3 cup (150 mL) super-fine sugar

2 large eggs, separated

1 cup (250 mL) self-rising flour

2 tbsp. (30 mL) sugar

Lightly butter a 7-inch (18-cm) square cake pan. Line the base with parchment paper or wax paper. Preheat the oven to 350F (175C).

Place the lemon zest and the raisins in a small bowl and cover with 1/4 cup (60 mL) of whiskey. Cover with plastic wrap and leave to macerate overnight.

Place the butter in the bowl of an electric mixer (or mix by hand). Beat the butter until creamy. Add the sugar and continue beating until the mixture is light and creamy.

Add the egg yolks and beat them into the mixture one at a time. Remove the lemon zest from the raisin and whiskey mixture. Chop some of the zest very finely, about 1 tablespoon/15 mL, and add to the egg and sugar mixture along with the raisins and whiskey. Gently stir into the mixture.

In another bowl, whisk the egg whites until stiff. Fold them into the egg and sugar mixture alternately with the flour. Don't overmix.

Transfer the batter to the prepared pan and smooth the surface. Sprinkle with the sugar and bake in the oven for about 20–25 minutes or until it springs back gently when touched and a tester emerges clean. Remove from the oven and let sit for about 10 minutes, and then turn out onto a cake rack set over a plate so that the cake is upside down. Use a skewer to make about 6 or 8 little holes in the cake's base (don't go all the way through) and pour the remaining bit of whiskey into the holes. Let sit for another 15 minutes, then invert and let cool completely before cutting into thick fingers and serving.

Jameson Heritage Centre

When we stayed at Ballymaloe House, we paid a visit to the nearby town of Midleton and the Jameson Heritage Centre, part of the Irish Distillers group. While Bushmills is the oldest distillery in Ireland, Midleton is the largest. It is actually a series of distilleries, each one responsible for a different brand of Irish whiskey, including Jameson and Tullamore Dew. The world's largest pot still is here (30,000 gallons) and there is a beautiful water wheel in working order.

Ballencrieff Castle Bride's Cake

Ted's Choice Dalwhinnie 15-year-old Single Highland Malt Scotch Whisky.

Makes about 12 servings

This perfect little cake was made by the owners of Ballencrieff Castle, Peter Gillies and his wife Lin Dalgleish, for Ted and me on our wedding day, and what a lovely surprise it was. It was iced with almond paste and then white royal icing, its circumference tied with a bit of tartan ribbon and a sprig of heather. Following the ceremony we had slices of this traditional cake along with a dram or two (or three?) of Dalwhinnie, the soft malt from Inverness in the Central Highlands. This cake improves with age if it is kept well wrapped and treated to additional whisky now and then . . . much like ourselves, really.

For the cake:

1 cup (250 mL) butter

1 cup (250 mL) super-fine sugar

4 eggs, beaten

1 tbsp. (15 mL) marmalade

zest of 1 lemon, finely grated

1/3 cup (75 mL) Dalwhinnie

1 1/4 cups (310 mL) unbleached
  all-purpose flour

1 tsp. (5 mL) mixed spice

1/4 tsp. (1 mL) ground nutmeg

1/2 tsp. (2 mL) baking soda
  (dissolved in a little water)

1 tbsp. (15 mL) treacle or
  molasses

1 cup (250 mL) sultana raisins

1/2 cup (125 mL) currants

1 cup (250 mL) raisins

Preheat the oven to 325F (160C). Prepare an 8-inch (20-cm) round cake pan by lightly buttering the base and sides, then lining with parchment paper or wax paper.

In the bowl of an electric mixer (or by hand), cream together the butter and sugar until creamy, and then add the beaten eggs, a little at a time, beating well after each addition.

Add the marmalade, lemon zest, whisky and mix thoroughly. Now, add the flour and spices with baking soda and molasses and blend the dry ingredients thoroughly into the egg mixture. Fold in the dry fruit and mix again thoroughly. The mixture should be of a soft, dropping consistency.

Pour the batter into the prepared cake pan then rap the pan down sharply on the counter. Dip your hand in water and pat it over the surface of the cake (this will ensure that the cake top is smooth when baked).

Transfer to the oven to bake for an hour. Then, reduce the heat to 300F (150C) and continue to bake for 3–3 1/2 hours after which time a tester placed in the centre should emerge clean. If it doesn't, continue to bake for another half an hour. Then, take it from the oven and pour a little more whisky over the top, if you wish, and allow the cake to cool in the pan overnight. The next day, remove the cake from the pan.

A Sweet Island Fling

When you are passionately in love, you wed. When you are passionately in love with a McIntosh, you wed in Scotland. And when you are both passionate about the distinctive single malt whisky from the Hebridean islands, you honeymoon in Islay. That was our dream and this is how it became a reality.

Before I fell in love with the man who taught me to love Islay's single malts, the only other term of reference I had for Islay (pronounced *EYE-la*) was through the lyrics of a song written by the 1960s Scottish folkie Donovan: *". . . how high the gull flies o'er Islay . . ."* The name Islay held sweet mystery with such a romantic, poetic quality, I felt it had to have been fabricated from the poet's imagination. But it wasn't. As ethereal as it is, Islay is real. It is one of the larger of many scattered Southern Inner Hebridean islands — Jura, Colonsay, Seil, Luing, Lismore, Iona, Tiree and Coll. Most languish above the Mull (or tip) of Kintyre, made famous by the Paul McCartney song.

There are more than one hundred distilleries in operation in Scotland today. Little Islay (only about a tenth the size of Prince Edward Island with a population just over 3,500) is home to a magnificent seven. Collectively they produce about 20 million litres of single malt scotch whisky a year. They are Ardbeg, Bowmore, Bunnahabhain, Bruichladdich, Caol Ila, Lagavulin and Laphroaig. An eighth, Port Ellen, at the western end of the island, is closed as a distillery; however, the handsome buildings remain and it still supplies all-important malt to a number of operating distilleries. The combination of the sea, the peat, the barley malt and the briny Atlantic air produces a family of singularly distinctively smoky, peaty single malt whiskies, unlike any made anywhere else. The Kintyre Peninsula is also home to Campbeltown and the whisky-making tradition of Springbank Distillery, while the nearby Isle of Jura is home to another respected distillery of the same name.

Had I known years ago what I know now about Scotland's fine whisky heritage, I would have recognized all of the above place-names as synonymous with *uisge beatha* (ooshkuy beh huh), the water of life, as the Gaelic word for whisky describes it.

In the vernacular of the millennium, who knew that one day I would not only have a passion for Islay malts, but that I would marry a Celtic-blue-eyed man of Scottish heritage and that we would honeymoon on this special little island.

While we longed to visit Islay, we had first to fulfill another fantasy: marrying in a Scottish castle. In the pre-Internet days, I suppose we would have enlisted the help of one of those exclusive travel companies to source and secure a venue for our nuptials. Instead, it became our habit to sit of an evening, single malt of choice at the ready, perusing the Web as we discovered a seemingly endless network of sites linked to Scotland. Not only did we find a castle, we found sites outlining everything from Celtic rings, pipers and wedding vows, to kilts, salmon fishing, whisky and B&Bs. One can even track the myriad details and legalities that need to be addressed and put into place when a Canadian decides to wed in Scotland.

Originally we had envisioned travelling the length and breadth of the country, marrying in one place and travelling well up into the Highlands and perhaps beyond to the northern isles, and finally ending in Islay. But with limited time to spend away from home (and with a budget that fell a little shy of Madonna's, whose $2 million-and-counting wedding in Scotland took place in the Highlands at Skibo Castle) it seemed prudent to choose to narrow our search and our sites, literally. The area that ushers in the Highlands proper, just east of Edinburgh, seemed perfect. After a few evenings' worth — and malts' — worth of Web research, we discovered Ballencrieff Castle, about half an hour east of Edinburgh in East Lothian, near the pretty little holiday town of North Berwick. Castles in Scotland are almost as common as maple trees in Ontario, dotting the land in one form or another, in complete or partial ruin, demi-derelict or divinely restored.

Not only is Ballencrieff Castle authentically restored, it is also unique in that it is only one of three castles that are private residences offering wedding packages. Most of the others are not private homes but hotels, which may not matter at all in the grand scheme of things. However, the beauty of Ballencrieff is that weddings here are a private affair; the castle will be home only to you and your guests (from 2 to 40) during your stay, a factor that makes everything even more special and not something one can expect from a hotel.

As we drove up the winding approach to the castle, a Dudley Moore–sized man emerged from one of the castle's many low doorways, followed by his chunky chocolate Lab, Angus. "Welcome to Ballencrieff," he called out with a wave and a huge smile. "Come up and meet the good reverend, he's waiting to talk to you about your vows," he said behind his hand with mock seriousness. We had chosen to wed on the first of May, a significant date in the Celtic calendar. In addition to the set ceremony we wanted to include our own vows that were rather, well, let's say hippie-Celtic in style and philosophy. The kilt-clad Reverend Brown, however, had other ideas. After the formalities and pleasantries were exchanged, he drew himself up to his full ministerial self, thumbs thrust into the waistband of his kilt, and intoned: "The ceremony that I will be conducting has been used for over five hundred years here in Scotland and as it's been *gud* enough for all those years, I *canna* see any reason to change it *noo*." We dutifully drank our tea, and discreetly nudged each other now and then while listening to the preview of the ceremony. At a pivotal point in the text he paused, "You'll notice there's nothing in there about OBEY," he said to me with a wink, stressing the last word emphatically. Grateful for small mercies we decided that in its own proven way, the text was rather like the words we had chosen, albeit more traditional. He seemed relieved, and we were happy as clams just to be there.

Ballencrieff was built in 1586 and over the last eight years has been magnificently restored by the current owners, Peter Gillies and his wife Lin Dalgleish. To say the castle was better than anticipated may sound odd considering we had viewed its turreted splendour and our four-postered bedchamber before even leaving home. Yet it was. No detail in terms of authenticity, beauty, quality and fine taste is overlooked at Ballencrieff. Exquisite bed and bath linens, antique furnishings, toiletries, flowers, china and silverware, all contribute to a regal and memorable stay.

Via numerous emails, it was the magnanimous Peter who helped us with every detail of the wedding — minister, flowers, Champagne (and malt!), photographer and piper. He had informed us well ahead of time that we would need to collect our marriage licence the day before our wedding from the local registrar's office in North Berwick. So we decided to spend our first night in that town at a particularly pretty B&B. The following day, we had little more to do than relax, browse the local shops and have lunch. We had a couple of local pints and a substantial lunch of salmon fishcakes, tatties, 'neeps and mince (potatoes, turnips and ground beef in a savoury gravy — delish!) at a sweet little pub before heading for the castle to prepare for our ceremony.

We Wed

It is close to 3 p.m. as I sink back into my deep lavender-scented foam bath, gazing out the window, past the gardens and the farmland to the softly rounded Lammermuir Hills, which were immortalized first by Sir Walter Scott and then by Donizetti in the opera *Lucia di Lammermoor*. Lost in a loving reverie, I am realizing my dream. My betrothed is sequestered in another of the castle's bedchambers (this is the way you talk when you're in a castle), but before leaving me to attend to my toilette (where *are* those handmaidens when you need them?) he has poured me a dram of Ardbeg, one of the slightly smoky, peat-sweet whiskies from Islay. The very air is redolent with romance and happiness.

Following our ceremony, complete with bagpiper, we are presented with a perfect little traditional Scottish bridal cake before our dinner. This evening Peter had booked the reservation for the two of us at the Waterside Bistro, a nearby restaurant. Decked out in our finery and looking every inch the newlywed couple, we received a little soft round of applause, winks, grins and congratulations as we arrived.

Thinking that everything that went before meant a hard act to follow, Peter outdid himself at breakfast the next morning. Papaya halves and other fresh fruit were teamed with terrific Scottish yogurt and muesli. Porridge was offered and – simply because of space limitations – politely declined. Then it was on to local pork sausages (*really* local, as we were to learn that the rare breed Gloucester Old Spot pigs we had photographed earlier were raised for Peter by the farmer next door), rich black pudding, tattie scones (Scottish potato bread), thick-cut bacon, sumptuous kippers, fried spuds, tomatoes and haggis. Now, here is a don't-knock-until-tried food if ever there was one. I've always believed haggis just suffered from the lack of a good PR person. You may know it consists of offal (organ meats) combined with oatmeal and seasonings and cooked within a sheep's stomach, all of which does sound pretty horrible. But, if you've never tried it, think of it as a large, rich, savoury sausage and you're off to the races. Similarly stuffed, we began our journey toward Islay.

After an overnight stop to experience Stirling and its immensely impressive castle, we headed for Tarbert, a tiny little port at the top of the Kintyre Peninsula.

The winding, scenic drive from Stirling led us past the famed Loch Lomond and up into Rob Roy country, into the narrow glen known as The Trossachs, between Loch Katrine and Loch Achray, through some of the most glorious countryside. This sea-fringed West Highland area is known as Mid Argyll and it is rich in history and beauty with lush green valleys and typically attractive villages like Inveraray, overlooked by its elegant castle, still the seat of the once powerful Dukes of Argyll. Loch Fyne is here, famous for splendid salmon, all manner of smoked fish, kippers and the freshest oysters — just the ticket for newlyweds.

Once in Tarbert, we walked by the sea before settling in to try a few Islay malts and an especially good dinner at the Columba Hotel. We helped "wet the baby's heed," joining in a communal toast to a brand new baby boy who slumbered peacefully as a young couple enjoyed an evening out with the grandparents. The hotel is named for St. Columba who arrived near the Mull of Kintyre from Ireland in AD 574 bringing Christianity to Scotland. Its pub and dining room overlook the scenic approach to Tarbert Harbour with views of the surrounding hills.

As we ate local lamb and fresh salmon, we watched the early spring sun take hours to finally set. A lavender-coloured light bathed the softly rounded green hills, glinted off the prow of the fishing boats returning with their catch and was caught in the faces of tow-headed boys playing soccer in the town streets.

Back at our bed and breakfast, we learned from the owner that we should book a space on the ferry that would take us the next morning to Islay. The car ferry docks at the nearby Kennacraig terminal just outside Tarbert. In addition to Islay, ferries also depart here for other tiny islands in the area including Oban, Gigha and Colonsay and there are numerous tour packages available. After about two hours, we passed through the Sound of Islay spying the Paps of Jura. These conical mountains reach almost 800 metres in height and are visible from many Islay viewpoints. Like Islay, the island is famous for its own single malt, Jura, and for many species of birds and wildlife. As well, author George Orwell stayed there while he wrote *1984*.

There are two distilleries at Port Askaig, Caol Ila (cull-EELA) and Bunnahabhain (bonna-HAV-en). Caol Ila boasts a magnificent setting in a sheltered cove overlooking the Isle of Jura and is just a half mile or so walk north of here. There are guided tours and tastings throughout the year by appointment. Bunnahabhain is open from March to October for guided tours and tastings. The short, pretty drive to the village of Bowmore, the capital, is done on the island's typically narrow roads. The very air is redolent of the malting art in Bowmore, with the whitewashed buildings of the Bowmore Distillery dominating the town's shoreline as they have done since 1779, making the distillery the oldest on Islay. Water with a crystal clarity from the nearby Laggan River, and the peat upon which the island seems almost solely based, give Bowmore malts their unique pedigree. A great place to taste the largest selection of Islay single malts is at the nearby Lochside Hotel. The four hundred or more malts available include the 29-year-old Black Bowmore, tagged at £150 per 35 millilitres! During the months of January, March, September and November, the hotel offers Malt Whisky Weekends that include everything from tours and tastings to peat cutting.

We head up the town's main road, passing the famous Round Church that sits at the top. Legend has it the church was built in the round so that there would be no corners in which the devil could reside.

We head towards the southeast coast of Islay where three active distilleries are placed. Laphroaig (la-Froyg) means "the beautiful hollow by the broad bay" in Gaelic. Located just outside Port Ellen, the distillery is open year round. However, as we were to discover, visits need to be arranged in advance, and the same is true of Lagavulin (lagga-VOO-lin) and Ardbeg,

As a Canadian with Celtic roots in Ireland, I am of the conviction that the Irish introduced Scotland to the wonders of distillation. After all, it is Northern Ireland where Bushmills, the world's oldest whisky distillery, resides. This makes perfect sense when one stands in Port Ellen, at the edge of Islay's most westerly tip. On a clear day, lights can be seen outlining the coast of Northern Ireland, a mere 17 miles (27.2 km) away.

That night, over a pint and a dram or two, I mentioned this to an Ileach (an Islay islander) who said, "Och aye, the Irish have long used that vantage point to peer through binoculars and learn how we make our whisky."

Our only regret was that we visited the island a little too early to take part in the annual Islay Whisky and Music Festival held in May/June each year. This is a very special time to be on the island because each single malt distillery is involved in tours, events and much traditional Celtic music, dance and food. A return visit is definitely in order.

Give an Irishman lager for a month and he's a dead man. An Irishman is lined with copper, and the beer corrodes it. But whiskey polishes the copper and is the saving of him.
– Mark Twain

Spiced Scottish Ale

Makes 4 servings

Here's the perfect antidote to winter weary souls. For full soothing effect serve to the one you love in front of a roaring fire with a batch of warm sausage rolls, sharp Cheddar and good chutney.

4 eggs

5 cups of a premium-quality ale, such as Scotch Irish Brewing's Session Ale

1/4 cup (60 mL) liquid honey

2 tbsp. (30 mL) butter

1/4 tsp. (1 mL) each, ground nutmeg, ground cinnamon, ground cloves

Whisk the eggs in a mixing bowl with 1/2 cup (125 mL) of the ale until frothy. Heat remaining ale in a saucepan over medium-high heat until hot, being careful not to let it come to a boil. Whisk the egg/ale mixture into the hot ale in a slow stream, whisking constantly.

When all the ale has been incorporated, turn heat to low and add the honey, butter and spices, stirring well. Heat through. Do not allow the mixture to boil. Pour into mugs and serve at once.

Hilden Brewery, Lisburn, County Antrim

Ireland's oldest independent brewery, Hilden Brewery, recently celebrated its twentieth anniversary. The brewery is situated outside of Belfast and currently produces a porter called Molly Malone, and two ales, Hilden Ale and Scullion's Irish Ale. The Tap Room Bar and Restaurant is reputed to be the only establishment in Ireland serving draught "real ale" exclusively. A great place to stop for a very good lunch or an evening meal — and a great pint.

Pure Gallus Whisky Sour

Makes 1 serving

"Pure gallus" is a Glaswegian expression that, loosely translated, means simply "the best" and that sums up how I feel about a really good whisky sour. Now, some say it isn't a real whisky sour unless it is made with bourbon but I like the quality that a light malt such as Glengoyne 10-Year-Old Highland Single Malt lends to this popular cocktail. Make sure to use only fresh lemon juice. And, again, make these one at a time. You'll need a cocktail shaker or a jar with a good lid and a little strainer.

Pour the lemon juice through a little strainer into the cocktail shaker and add the sugar. Stir thoroughly to dissolve. Add the whisky, egg white and Angostura bitters and 4 or 5 ice cubes and shake vigorously. Pour into a glass (without the ice cubes) and serve.

juice of 1 lemon

1/4 cup (60 mL) Glengoyne 10-Year-Old Single Highland Malt Scotch Whisky

2 tsp. (10 mL) super-fine granulated sugar

1 medium egg white

few drops Angostura bitters

Braveheart Hot Toddy

Makes 1 serving

When the British microbiologist Sir Alexander Fleming was asked for a cure for the common cold, he replied, "A good gulp of hot whisky at bedtime. It's not very scientific, but it works." Herewith: the real thing. Make as many as you like, but make them one at a time.

¹/₃ cup (75 mL) boiling water

2 sugar cubes

¹/₃ cup (75 mL) Aberfeldy 15-year-old Highland Single Malt Scotch Whisky

Fill a heat-proof tumbler or other glass with hot water to heat. When it is warmed, discard the hot water and add the sugar cubes to the glass. Pour boiling water over them to cover. Stir with a spoon (preferably silver) and as sugar dissolves add a portion of the whisky. Add a little more boiling water, and then top with more whisky, continuing to stir. Sip slowly. Repeat the exercise if the situation warrants.

Good For What Ails Us

We can thank the spirited Robbie Burns and his winter birthday for giving us something to celebrate during the depths of winter. Most celebrants toast the dead poet with a dram or two of single malt whisky served neat and unheated (after all, good malt whisky packs the power to warm on its own), but there is no denying the restorative powers of a hot whisky toddy, made simply of single malt whisky, sugar and hot water.

Single malt lovers will probably consider it heresy to tamper with their tipple, but adding hot water to inferior whisky is said to produce unpleasant fumes that take away from the experience. John Maxwell, owner of Allen's, the lovely and popular Toronto bar that sells more than two hundred different whiskies, is a firm believer in using the good stuff. "Just as you shouldn't cook with low-quality wine, using the least expensive whisky in a hot toddy is a foolish savings," he says. "I'd probably opt for a Speyside, like the 10-year-old Aberlour, to make a fine hot toddy."

Maxwell concedes, however, that a good-quality blended whisky also works well in a hot toddy. He recommends Haig, if you can find it, or Famous Grouse. But the whisky doesn't have to be Scottish. "In Ireland, hot whisky is very commonly drunk with a bit of hot water and lemon or orange studded with cloves, and honey or sugar sometimes added. I would recommend Jameson's whisky for this because it seems to have an oakiness that stands up well to the dilution."

A variation on the classic toddy was enjoyed each year at Hogmanay, the Scottish new year. The mixture of ale, eggs, sugar and whisky was seasoned with nutmeg, gently heated and served by the pint out of huge copper vessels known as toddy kettles carried through the streets and offered to passers-by. Refusing a cup of it was not an option.

The term *toddy*, by the way, is thought to be a corruption of a Hindi word, *taudi*, which refers to a fermented date-palm sap used to make *arrack*, a rough, raw spirit whose name, fittingly enough, derives from the Arabic meaning "sweat." Toddy parlours in Singapore specialized in drinks made with this spirit. It fermented so quickly and forcefully that it had to be consumed the day it was made or destroyed, presumably lest it do the same to the drinker.

Bushmills Inn Classic Irish Coffee

Makes 1 serving

You may think, as I did, that Irish coffee is a bit of a tired old thing. Then I enjoyed one after dinner at the Bushmills Inn and have since completely changed my mind. Hot whiskey-flavoured coffee sipped through thick, cold Irish cream is something I'm not likely to forget. Don't whip the cream until stiff; stop whipping when it reaches a loose but still pourable consistency. What I call ploppy-floppy cream.

2 tsp. (10 mL) light brown sugar
1/4 cup (60 mL) Bushmills Irish
    Whiskey
strong black coffee, as needed
softly whipped cream, as needed

Warm a medium-sized wineglass with hot water. Pour out the water and place the sugar and whiskey in the glass. Place a teaspoon in the glass and pour the hot coffee over the sugar and whiskey, stirring well to dissolve the sugar.

Pour the loosely whipped cream over the back of the spoon over the surface of the coffee. Do not stir — it should rest on top of the coffee. Serve and enjoy immediately.

ÍNDEX

Acknowledgements

First and foremost, our warmest thanks to John Maxwell for sharing his passion and enthusiasm for Celtia and for his unwavering belief in the project from the very beginning through to the end.

Thank you to Kim McArthur for saying "yes!" and thanks to all at McArthur & Company for their hard work and diligence.

To designer Tania Craan, whose talents have made our book as beautiful as we imagined.

To editor Pamela Erlichman, sincere thanks.

Very appreciative thanks to photographer Chris Freeland and food stylist Rosemarie Superville for "getting it" once again.

A very special thank you to Alison Metcalfe and Tourism Ireland for all the generous support for this book and for providing the Irish experience of a lifetime. We simply could not have done it without your knowledge and assistance.

Thank you to José Luis Atristain and the Spanish Trade Commission for the opportunity to experience the magnificence of Galicia, for research materials and artwork. Much appreciated.

To Peter Gillies and Lin Dalgleish at Ballencrieff Castle in Scotland, many thanks for making our wedding so wonderfully special – and for the wedding cake recipe!

Thank you to Jason Nykor of Pernod Ricard.

Warmest thanks to Myrtle Allen of Ballymaloe House and to her daughter-in-law, Darina Allen of the Ballymaloe Cookery School, for their time and generosity.

Thanks to Beech Hill Country House Hotel in Derry, to Bushmills Inn, to the Glenora Distillery and Inn in Cape Breton, and to Catherine and Kevin Dundon of Dunbrody House in County Wexford, Ireland.

To François Baillargeon, a thank you for your willing help in translating.

Thanks to Moira Caton of Fife, Scotland, for providing her winning porridge recipe.

To Fadò Restaurant and Halo Restaurant in Dublin, a heartfelt thank you and thanks, too, to chefs Paul Rankin of Cayenne Restaurant in Belfast, Michael Deane of Deane's in Belfast and Robbie Millar of Shanks Restaurant, Bangor.

To my friend, the best Spanish chef in the U.S., Teresa Barrenechea for her willing help in clarifying Galician cuisine for us.

Finally, but most importantly, we would like to offer our most heartfelt thanks to a special group of friends who are always there when needed – Win and Arnold McIntosh, David and Marian Kingsmill, Denise Schon, Kathy Muldoon, Peter Rickwood, Ted Reader, Chris McDonald and Raeann and Henry Fisker – we could not have done it without you.